DICTIONARY
OF
CRIMINAL JUSTICE
TERMS

Including
Definitions and Terms
National Crime Classification
and NCIC Uniform Offense Classifications

GOULD PUBLICATIONS, INC.
1333 North US Highway 17-92
Longwood, FL 32750-3724

Published by
GOULD PUBLICATIONS, INC.
1333 North US Highway 17-92
Longwood, FL 32750-3724
(407) 695-9500

ISBN 0-87526-276-7

**Every attempt has been made to ensure the accuracy
and the completeness of the law contained herein. No
express or implied guarantees or warranties are made.**
**Since laws change very often and vary from jurisdiction
to jurisdiction, it is very important to check the timelines
and applicability of the laws contained herein.**

Preface

This **Dictionary of Criminal Justice Terms** contains a large portion of the work published by the United States Department of Justice in their book "Dictionary of Criminal Justice Data Terminology." In addition, new terminology with definitions and annotations have been added by the publisher.

A companion volume, **Dictionary of Bilingual Criminal Justice Terms,** presents terminology and defintions in both Spanish and English. This publication also contains flow charts on the nature of offenses and arrest to conviction procedures. Contact the publisher for inquiries.

Comments from users of this book and ways to improve it to facilitate its use would be appreciated by the publisher.

Contents

Organization and explanatory notes

The arrangement of the dictionary material is in part oriented toward words and phrases as in a standard dictionary and in part oriented toward subject matter, as in an encyclopedia. This compromise format is necessitated by the need to present classificatory terminology in sections large enough to clearly delineate hierarchical relationships and contrasts, yet at the same time provide space for full discussion of individual data items.

Alphabetized text

All of the definitional material in this Dictionary is presented in the alphabetized text.

Alphabetical sequence

All terms that are or should be part of the basic criminal justice statistical vocabulary and terms needed to explain the meaning or function of statistical terms are presented in alphabetical sequence, irrespective of punctuation and spaces.

Where a term is defined within the annotation for another term it is nevertheless listed in the alphabetical sequence, with a "see" reference to the term heading the entry in which it is defined.

Entries

The basic organizational unit of the alphabetized text is, as in standard dictionaries, the entry. An entry contains, at minimum:

term   *(main entry term)*
definition(s)

Additional, optional contents of entries include:

defining features
annotation:
information about usages
explanation of recommendations
other terms and definitions (subentry terms)
cross references to other entries
outlines of model data structures

Main entry terms

The main entry term is the large type, boldfaced term by which a given entry is alphabetized.

Subentry terms

These are terms which have been placed with their definitions within the body of entries, in order to indicate class-subclass relationships and contrasts of meaning among groups of related terms. As mentioned above, each subentry has also been listed in the alphabetical sequence and referred to the entry where it is defined.

Term qualifications

When a term must be qualified to indicate the context in which it is being defined, a qualifier is added in parentheses, e.g. "abscond (corrections)."

When a term has a particular statistical program usage the program is indicated by the initials by which it is commonly known, e.g. "UCR" for "Uniform Crime Reporting."

Recommended terminology and informational entries

Where a term plus definition establishes a basic categorical distinction for nationally comparable data, the phrase "recommended statistical terminology," in italics, precedes the statistical definition. Special program usages are also noted in italics. Other particular usages are usually indicated in the first words of the definition.

Where there is no italicized phrase between the term and definition, no recommendation is being made for that terminology. However, in some instances, recommendations may be found in the annotation.

Definitions

Every entry term is followed by one or more definitions, setting forth one or more established and/or recommended usages. When the common usage is different from the (usually narrower) statistical usage, the common is placed first, in order to ensure recognition of such differences. Multiple definitions are marked with roman numerals for convenient reference.

Defining features

Where necessary, the critical aspects of a statistical definition are set forth in list form in order to emphasize and clarify precise categorical distinctions.

Cross references within entries

Many terms appear boldfaced within annotations, without accompanying definitions. All of these terms are defined elsewhere in the Dictionary, and can be found listed in the alphabetical sequence of entries. These cross references should be followed up. In order to fully understand the meaning of a term or to see the need for a particular recommendation, it is often necessary to consider the term in relation to other terminology and/or consider its status and function as a member of a set of terms naming basic categorical distinctions or labelling parts of a given classification structure.

Appendices

The appendices present material supplementing and aiding access to the information in the alphabetized text.

Appendix A lists the recommended and/or established statistical terms covered in this edition of the Dictionary (other than offenses). These statistical terms are grouped by subject area to provide readers with an overview of the basic Dictionary content.

Appendix B contains a list of the recommended and tentatively recommended post-arrest offense data categories defined in the alphabetized text, and a discussion of problems in crime classification.

Appendix C reproduces the Uniform Crime Reports (UCR) offense category lists. The UCR categories are defined in the text.

Appendix D contains the National Crime Information Center's Uniform Offense Classifications (UOC) code structure outline.

Appendix E presents a term list outline of recommended statistical case categories and manner of disposition categories from the model court caseload statistical system developed by the National Court Statistics Project.

abandon (abandonment)   To intentionally forsake, renounce
all claim of ownership.

The act of abandonment is the voluntary relinquishment of all rights, claims, possession or title to one's property.

To have an abandonment one must have had the "intention" to abandon plus the "act by which said intention is effectuated."

abet   see parties to offenses

abduct (abduction)   see kidnapping

abortion   The intentional unlawful act of miscarriage or premature discharge of a "viable" foetus by the female herself or by another person.

annotation

The United States Supreme Court found in *Roe v. Wade* (1973) that a constitutional right of privacy exists for a woman to control the use of her own body to carry a child.

A three part formula governing anti-abortion laws was created:
> First trimester - the woman and her physician may choose the procedure to terminate pregnancy.
> Second trimester - state can regulate procedure for abortion.
> Third trimester - state can both regulate and/or forbid abortions except when necessary to save the life of the mother.

Recently, the United States Supreme Court in *Webster v. Reproductive Health Services,* 109 S.Ct. 3040 (1989) ruled that individual states have the constitutional right to regulate abortions in their respective jurisdictions. In *Webster,* the State of Missouri's "interest in protecting potential human life should come into existence only at the point of viability, and that there should therefore be a rigid line allowing state regulation after viability but prohibiting it before viability." While the Court did not "revisit" *Roe* and left that case "undisturbed," it (the Court) stated that "we would modify and narrow *Roe* and succeeding cases."

abscond (corrections)   *recommended statistical terminology*   To depart without authorization from a geographical area or jurisdiction, in violation of the conditions of probation or parole.

annotation

To abscond from probation or parole supervision is a violation of individually specified conditions of probation or parole, not a violation of a statute, and is thus not a crime. Such behavior, however, may cause a current probation or parole status to be revoked. The term is frequently used in statistics describing correctional population movement to designate a type of reason for probation revocation or parole revocation. See **probation supervisory population movement, parole agency caseload entries and removals, paroling authority decisions** and **prison/parole population movement.**

"Absconding" in correctional usage is distinct from **abscond (court)** and **escape** (see entries), which are violations of law.

abscond (court)   To intentionally absent or conceal oneself unlawfully in order to avoid a legal process.

annotation

When a defendant absconds, the case is taken off the court calendar and is usually not counted as court caseload.

The time period of a defendant's unlawful absence is discounted in measurements of time elapsed between filing and court disposition of cases for the purposes of determining court efficiency or meeting speedy trial requirements.

Fleeing to avoid prosecution or the execution of a sentence can result in prosecution for **contempt of court** under state law.

Flight across a state or national border to avoid prosecution is a federal crime. See **wanted person.**

accessory after the fact   see **parties to offenses**

accessory before the fact   see **parties to offenses**

accomplice   see **parties to offenses**

acquittal   *recommended statistical terminology*   The judgment of a court, based on the verdict of a jury or a judicial officer, that the defendant is not guilty of the offense(s) for which he or she has been tried.

annotation

This is a type of **defendant disposition** (see entry) which, when the acquittal is on all charges in the case, terminates criminal justice jurisdiction over the defendant. In statistics describing judicial activity it is a final court disposition.

It should be noted that a not guilty verdict rendered by a jury is equivalent to a judgment of acquittal because a jury verdict of not guilty compels the court to acquit the defendant. This equivalence does not exist in the case of guilty verdicts. A judge can, when appropriate grounds exist, disregard a jury finding of guilty and pronounce a judgment of acquittal.

Statistical presentations of the results of adjudication should therefore use "guilty" or "not guilty" to indicate the verdict (the result of the **trial** phase of the judicial process), and "acquittal" or "conviction" to indicate the judgment. See **verdict** and **judgment.**

Since acquittals can be arrived at by routes significantly different with respect to impact on defendants and prosecutorial and court workload, statistical presentations generally distinguish between acquittals:

by jury   jury trial resulting in a not guilty verdict

by court   nonjury trial or acquittal pronounced by court notwithstanding jury verdict

active supervision   see **supervised probation**

adjudication   The process by which a court arrives at a decision regarding a case; also, the resultant decision.

annotation

"To adjudicate" means to settle by the exercise of judicial authority, to determine something finally. In criminal justice usage, "adjudication" is often used with the specific meaning of final decision, that is, judgment of acquittal or judgment of conviction. **Judgment** (see entry) is the preferred usage for purposes of statistical data presentations, to avoid confusions which might otherwise arise.

The word, "adjudicated," and various phrases employing it are used with special meanings in the correctional vocabulary:

pre-adjudicated   The status of an adult defendant or a juvenile who is subject to court proceedings that have not reached judgment or dismissal. See **adjudication withheld** and **defendant dispositions** for recommended criminal justice data terminology for pre-judgment dispositions of such persons.

adjudicated or **post-adjudicated**   The status of a convicted adult, or of a juvenile who has been adjudged (judicially determined to be) a juvenile offender. Such persons can be compelled to accept supervision or be committed to confinement, hence these terms and the equivalent terms, "post-placement" or "commitment" or "post-commitment" are often used to characterize correctional programs, facilities or groups of clients.

adjudication withheld   *recommended statistical terminology*   In criminal justice usage, a court decision at any point after filing of a criminal complaint, to continue court jurisdiction but stop short of pronouncing judgment.

annotation

The usual purpose in stopping criminal proceedings short of judgment is avoidance of the undesirable effects of conviction, which effects can include both unnecessary harm to the offender and unnecessary expense or harm to the public interest. "Withholding adjudication," as defined here, places the subject in a status where the court retains jurisdiction but will not re-open proceedings unless the person violates a condition of behavior.

"Adjudication withheld" is an important category of defendant dispositions. The term is here defined for statistical use to account for those cases which receive what is sometimes effectively a sentencing disposition but one occurring without conviction. In court caseload data, this category is recognized, but is often combined for presentation in a single category with convictions.

In defendant flow data and statistics concerning the general budgetary impact of court decisions, "adjudication withheld" dispositions should be subdivided by the accompanying status change or program placement: (1) referral to probation or other criminal justice agency, (2) referral to a non-criminal justice agency, and (3) no referral.

See **defendant dispositions**. See also **diversion**.

adjudicatory hearing   *recommended statistical terminology*   In juvenile justice usage, the fact-finding process wherein the juvenile court determines whether or not there is sufficient evidence to sustain the allegations in a petition.

annotation

An adjudicatory hearing occurs after a **juvenile petition** (see entry) has been filed and after a **detention hearing**, if one is necessary. If the petition is not sustained, no further formal court action is taken. If it is sustained, the next step is a **disposition hearing** to determine the most appropriate treatment or care for the juvenile. These last two stages of judicial activity concerning juveniles are often combined in a single hearing, referred to as a "bifurcated hearing," meaning a process that encompasses both adjudication of the case and disposition of the person.

For statistical purposes, the adjudicatory hearing ends when a finding is entered, that is, a **juvenile court judgment** is made.

An adjudicatory hearing concerning an alleged **delinquent** is analogous to a trial in criminal proceedings since both proceedings determine matters of fact concerning alleged acts in violation of criminal law. Modern opinion is that an adjudication of "delinquent" should require proof "beyond a reasonable doubt." An adjudication of "status offender" should require that the "preponderance of evidence" support the allegation(s). See **levels of proof.**

Transfer hearings and **disposition hearings** are not adjudicatory hearings. See those entries.

administrative judge   A judicial officer who supervises administrative functions and performs administrative tasks for a given court, sometimes in addition to performing regular judicial functions.

annotation

Typical duties of administrative judges are assigning cases to other judicial officers within a court; setting court policy on procedure; and performing other tasks of an administrative nature, such as those concerned with personnel and budgets.

Those courts which have a **court administrator** generally do not also require an administrative judge.

See **judicial officer** for recommendation.

admission (corrections)   In correctional usage, the entry of an offender into the legal jurisdiction of a corrections agency and/or physical custody of a correctional facility.

annotation

This term and others such as "initial admissions," "first admissions," "new admissions," and "readmissions" are used as category names in correctional statistics with some consistency but enough variation to cause problems in interpretation. "Admissions" or "first admissions," for example, may represent all persons admitted to **physical custody** or only those for whom the agency is acquiring **jurisdiction** (see **custody**). "Readmissions" may describe only those returned to continue service on a sentence or may also, for example, include those returning to custody pending a decision on their legal status.

See **prison/parole population movement** for a detailed model data structure and recommended statistical terminology.

adult   *recommended statistical terminology*   In criminal justice usage, a person who is within the original jurisdiction of a criminal, rather than a juvenile, court because his or her age at the time of an alleged criminal act was above a statutorily specified limit.

annotation

The assumption of jurisdiction by a criminal or juvenile court is based on the age at the time of occurrence of the alleged offense or offenses, and not the age at time of arrest or initiation of court proceedings. See **juvenile**.

A juvenile court may waive jurisdiction and transfer a juvenile to a criminal court for prosecution as an adult. However, the available sentencing dispositions may exclude commitment to adult prisons (see **youthful offender**). Cases transferred from juvenile courts should be identified as such in criminal case **filing** and **defendant disposition** data.

UCR classifies anyone 18 years of age or older as an adult.

adultery   Generally, unlawful sexual intercourse between a married person and a person other than that person's spouse.

annotation

Statutory definitions of the offense called "adultery" vary. Sometimes only a married participant has committed an offense. In some jurisdictions, this type of behavior is not criminal.

In UCR, adultery is included in **sex offenses UCR 17.** See **sex offenses** for general recommendation. Adultery is classified as "other nonviolent sex offense."

ADW   see **assault**

aftercare   *syn*   **juvenile parole**   In juvenile justice usage, the status or program membership of a juvenile who has been committed to a treatment or confinement facility, conditionally released from the facility, and placed in a supervisory and/or treatment program.

annotation

In a few states "aftercare" or "parole" status does not exist for juveniles. Post-release supervision cases are assigned to probation caseloads.

aggravated assault   see **assault**

aggravated assault   UCR 4a-d   *Uniform Crime Reports usage*   Unlawful intentional causing of serious bodily injury with or without a deadly weapon, or unlawful intentional attempting or threatening of serious bodily injury or death with a deadly or dangerous weapon.

annotation

This category is also recommended for use in post-arrest statistics. See **assault** for defining features and general recommendation.

Aggravated assault is a UCR Crime Index offense. The annual publication, *Crime in the United States*, presents data both on reported occurrences of aggravated assault offenses and on arrests relating to such offenses. See **Crime Index.**

In UCR data reporting, aggravated assault is subdivided as follows:
  4.a. firearm
  4.b. knife or cutting instrument
  4.c. other dangerous weapon
  4.d. hands, fists, feet, etc.—aggravated injury

Examples of aggravated injury are broken bones, loss of teeth, internal injuries, injuries requiring stitches, and loss of consciousness. Police agencies customarily count as an aggravated assault any assault causing an injury that requires medical treatment beyond first aid.

Attempted murder and assault to commit murder are classified in UCR as aggravated assault. Assault for the purpose of unlawful taking of property is classified as **robbery UCR 3.** Assault to commit rape is classified as **forcible rape UCR 2.**

UCR classifies as aggravated assault the "commonly titled offenses of assault with intent to kill or murder; poisoning; assault with a dangerous or deadly weapon; maiming, mayhem, and assault with intent to maim or commit mayhem; assault with explosives; and all attempts to commit the foregoing offenses."

Assault where no dangerous or deadly weapon is used and no serious injury is inflicted is classified as "other assaults—simple, not aggravated" in UCR terminology. See **simple assault UCR 9** for their conventions concerning non-aggravated assaults.

aggravating circumstances   Circumstances relating to the commission of a crime which cause its gravity to be greater than that of the average instance of the given type of offense.

annotation

Examples of aggravating circumstances are the causing of serious bodily injury, the use of a deadly or dangerous weapon, or the accidental or intentional commission of one crime in the course of committing another crime, or as a means to commit another crime.

Aggravating circumstances may be formally or informally considered by a judge or paroling authority in deciding the sentence for a convicted person within the penalty range provided by statute for a given offense.

The behavior and circumstances which constitute an "aggravated" form of an offense are also often explicitly defined in penal statutes and provided with a more severe penalty range than that of the basic offense. One way this is expressed is through the structure common to most penal codes establishing different degrees within a given type of offense, with different penalties attached. Another way is through the provision of separate code sections defining "aggravated" offenses, for example, "aggravated robbery" vs. "robbery." In some codes both structures appear. See also **mandatory sentence.**

Mitigating circumstances are the opposite of aggravating circumstances: Circumstances surrounding the commission of a crime which do not in law justify or excuse the act, but which in fairness may be considered as reducing the blameworthiness of the defendant.

Mitigating circumstances may be taken into account when setting bail, deciding what crime the defendant will be charged with in court, or in determining a penalty. Examples of mitigating factors are extreme youth or old age, lack of a prior record, willingness to pay restitution, voluntary confession, and provocation.

The expressions "aggravated sentence" and "mitigated sentence" are used in some jurisdictions to indicate that a given penalty is greater or less than the norm for the offense.

aggregate maximum release date   see **expiration of sentence**

aider or abettor   see **parties to offenses**

AKA   see **alias**

alias   Any name used for an official purpose that is different from a person's legal name.

annotation

An alias is a false name that has been substituted for a correct legal name on such documents as a driver's license or a check, or a false name established for the purpose of such substitution. Nicknames and monikers not used on official documents are not aliases.

Criminal records often list aliases but do not usually list nicknames or monikers. In criminal history records, false names may be designated by "AKA," an abbreviation for "also known as."

alleged delinquent   see **delinquency**

alleged offender   see **offender**

alleged status offender   see **delinquency**

all other offenses   UCR 26   In Uniform Crime Reports terminology, the name of the UCR residual category used to record and report arrests made for offenses other than those included in UCR offense categories 1 through 25 and 27 through 29.

annotation

This "all other" category in UCR excludes arrests for minor traffic violations.

The *Uniform Crime Reporting Handbook* provides, as examples of offenses included in this category, the following list:

Admitting minors to improper places
Abduction and compelling to marry
Abortion (death of an expectant mother resulting from abortion is a homicide, offense class 1.a.)
Bigamy and polygamy
Blackmail and extortion
Bribery
Combination in restraint of trade; trusts, monopolies
Contempt of court
Criminal anarchism
Criminal syndicalism
Discrimination; unfair competition
Kidnaping
Marriage within prohibited degrees
Offenses contributing to juvenile delinquency (except as provided for in offenses 1 to 28 inclusive) such as employment of children in immoral vocations or practices, admitting minors to improper places, etc.
Perjury and subornation of perjury
Possession, repair, manufacture, etc., of burglar's tools
Public nuisances
Riot and rout
Trespass
Unlawfully bringing weapons into prisons or hospitals
Unlawfully bringing drugs or liquor into State prisons, hospitals, etc.; furnishing to convicts
Unlawful disinterment of the dead and violation of sepulture
Unlawful use, possession, etc., of explosives
Violations of State regulatory laws and municipal ordinances (this does not include those offenses or regulations which belong in the above classes)
Violation of quarantine
All offenses not otherwise classified
All attempts to commit any of the above

amnesty   see **clemency**

anticipatory offense   see **inchoate offense**

appeal   Generally, the request that a court with appellate jurisdiction review the judgment, decision, or order of a lower court and set it aside (reverse it) or modify it; also, the judicial proceedings or steps in judicial proceedings resulting from such a request.

annotation

In general usage the term "appeal" has no fixed meaning. It is variously defined in statutes respecting appellate procedure. "Appeal" can stand for a type of case, a type of proceeding, or all the post-trial proceedings relating to a given case. For recommended statistical terminology in this area of court activity see **appeal case, request to appeal case, sentence review,** and **appellate court case.**

The rules governing circumstances in which an appeal is permitted, and in which a hearing is guaranteed, are complex and differ somewhat from state to state. They vary according to the type of case (e.g., criminal vs. civil), whether the appeal is by the defendant or by the plaintiff or prosecution, and the specific grounds for appeal.

Initiation of the appeal process is usually permitted only after completion of trial proceedings, and is a request for reexamination and alteration of the final judgment of the trial court. A few states also allow appeals during the course of trial court proceedings in certain circumstances. See **interlocutory appeal.**

appeal case   *recommended statistical terminology*   A case filed in a court having incidental or general appellate jurisdiction, to initiate review of a judgment or decision of a trial court, an administrative agency or an intermediate appellate court.

annotation

This and other recommended terminology for court caseload statistics reflect the usages of the model court caseload statistical system developed by the National Court Statistics Project under Bureau of Justice Statistics sponsorship. A term list outline of the complete model classification scheme for general caseload inventory and for case and defendant manner of disposition is presented in Appendix E of this volume.

Where appeal caseload data are presented separately by individual court, a natural distinction will be made between appeal cases before trial courts having incidental appellate jurisdiction and those before appellate courts. It is recommended that separate counts of appeal cases by level of court be maintained in more generalized data presentations as well.

Statistical presentations should also distinguish between appeal cases which are "of right," and those which are discretionary reviews:

appeal of right   An appeal which the court having appellate jurisdiction must hear and decide on its merits, at the request of an appellant. In criminal cases, defense appeals of trial court final judgments are most frequently appeals of right; that is, a defendant's right to appeal from a conviction is generally guaranteed by law.

discretionary review   An appeal which the court having appellate jurisdiction may agree or decline to hear, at its own discretion. Procedurally, in these cases, a party wishing to appeal must first make a request to the court for permission to make the appeal, stating the reasons for doing so. The court can grant or deny the request.

For statistical purposes, only those discretionary review cases in which the court has decided to hear and decide an appeal on its merits should be counted as "appeal cases." Cases submitted for an initial determination by the court of whether an appeal will be heard, should be counted separately as **request to appeal cases** (see entry).

Both appeals of right and discretionary reviews are elective, in that the parties to the original action can choose whether or not to make an appeal. A few states also provide for **automatic appeal** in certain situations, typically where the death sentence has been pronounced on a defendant in a criminal case. Such appeals are initiated as a matter of course, without action of either party, and the appellate court must hear and decide the appeal. For statistical purposes, automatic appeals should be treated as appeals of right, unless separately counted.

appeal of right   see **appeal case**

appeal proceedings   The set of orderly steps by which a court considers the issues and makes a determination in a case before it on appeal.

annotation

The major steps in appeal proceedings are as follows:

1. The appeal is initiated by the filing of a formal document in the court having appellate jurisdiction.
2. A record of the original proceedings in the trial court (the court reporter's transcript) is obtained by the appellate court.
3. Briefs are filed in court by the opposing parties (appellant and respondent).
4. If there are to be oral arguments, a hearing is scheduled and the arguments heard.
5. Following completion of arguments or submission on briefs, the court deliberates, reviewing the record of the earlier proceedings and considering the allegations and arguments of the parties, and announces its decision in the case. This decision may be embodied in an **opinion** which also gives the reasons for the decision.

The various steps in appeal proceedings have a statistical function in defining categories for measuring the age of pending caseload in appellate courts. The following items, from the *State Court Model Annual Report* (see bibliography, under National Center for State Courts), are recommended as basic categorical distinctions for such caseload measures:

- Awaiting court reporter's transcript
- Awaiting appellant's brief
- Awaiting respondent's brief
- Ready for oral argument or submission
- Under advisement

appearance (court)   The act of coming into a court and submitting to the authority of that court.

appellant   The person who contests the correctness of a court order, judgment, or other decision and who seeks review and relief in a court having appellate jurisdiction, or the person in whose behalf this is done.

annotation

The **appeal** (see entry) process may begin by petitioning for leave to appeal. At this point there is no **respondent**, that is, the court does not conduct an adversary proceeding to determine whether or not to hear the appeal. Later, as an appeal case is being processed, when briefs must be submitted and arguments presented, the party who answers the claims and allegations of the appellant is the respondent (also called "the appellee").

In appeal proceedings relating to criminal cases, the appellant is usually a defendant who has been convicted, and consequently the respondent is "the people" (of a state or of the United States), represented by the prosecution.

appellate case disposition   *recommended statistical terminology*   The final determination made in an appeal case, request to appeal case or application for postconviction relief or sentence review by a court having appellate jurisdiction.

annotation

When an appeal is permitted only by leave of the court (see **request to appeal case**) the first determination is, of course, whether the court will conduct an appeal proceeding, that is, review the arguments and material submitted by the appellant. The disposition at this point may be described as request to appeal **granted** or **denied**.

In appeals of judgments in criminal proceedings, the court decisions regarding **appeal cases** (see entry) are: the appeal is **dismissed**, or the trial court judgment is **reversed** (set aside), **affirmed**, or **modified**, or the case is **remanded** (sent back) to the trial court for entry of a proper judgment, for further proceedings, or for a new trial. A given criminal appeal case disposition may be a combination of these alternatives, for example, reversed and remanded.

When a convicted person has applied for **sentence review** or **postconviction remedy** (see entries), the case disposition may be described as petition granted, denied, or dismissed.

The court's decision may be delivered by an order stating only the decision itself, or by one of the several types of **opinion** (see entry).

A model court caseload statistical system has recently been developed by the National Court Statistics Project, under Bureau of Justice Statistics sponsorship. The model provides an extensive classification scheme recommended for statistical presentation of appellate case disposition data. The categories in the scheme characterize the manner in which completed appellate court cases were disposed of:

Manner of disposition, appellate court case

Opinion
    Affirmed
    Modified
    Reversed
    Reversed and remanded
    Remanded
    Granted/denied

Memorandum decision
    Affirmed
    Modified
    Reversed
    Reversed and remanded
    Remanded
    Granted/denied

Order
    Affirmed
    Modified
    Reversed
    Reversed and remanded
    Remanded
    Granted/denied

Dismissed/withdrawn/settled

Transferred

Other manner of disposition

A term list outline of the complete model classification scheme for general caseload inventory and for case and defendant manner of disposition is presented in Appendix E of this volume.

appellate court   see **court**

appellate court case   *recommended statistical terminology*   A case which has been filed in an intermediate appellate court or court of last resort, including appeal cases, requests to appeal, original proceedings cases, and sentence review cases.

annotation

This and other recommended terminology for appellate court caseload statistics reflect the usages of the model court caseload statistical system developed by the National Court Statistics Project. In that model, "appellate court case" is the major classification category for appellate court caseload. It includes four major subcategories:

> **request to appeal case**
> **sentence review** only case
> **appeal case**
> original proceeding case

A term list outline of the complete model classification scheme for general caseload inventory and for case and defendant manner of disposition is presented in Appendix E of this volume.

appellate judge   A judge in a court of appellate jurisdiction, who primarily hears appellate cases, and also conducts disciplinary or impeachment proceedings.

annotation

See **judicial officer** for recommendation.

appellate jurisdiction   see **jurisdiction**

armed robbery   see **robbery**

arraignment   I.   Strictly, the hearing before a court having jurisdiction in a criminal case, in which the identity of the defendant is established, the defendant is informed of the charge(s) and of his or her rights, and the defendant is required to enter a plea.   II.   In some usages, any appearance in court prior to trial in criminal proceedings.

annotation

Since the usage of "arraignment" varies, it is recommended that the entering of the initial plea (see **plea**) be the event reported to indicate that the arraignment process has been completed. One reason that usage varies is that the individual actions comprising a formal arraignment occur at other appearances of the defendant in the course of court proceedings after arrest, and the distinctive event of the entering of a plea can itself occur whenever the court chooses to accept a plea to a charge.

Besides the pleas of guilty or not guilty, many states and the federal court permit pleas of nolo contendere and some accept pleas of **not guilty by reason of insanity** or former jeopardy.

In misdemeanor cases where the offense is minor (a "petty offense"), all actions comprising adjudication are often taken on the first and only occasion on which the defendant appears before the court; in more serious misdemeanor cases the arraignment may be the subject of a separate hearing.

In felony cases the arraignment occurs after proceedings are begun in the **trial court** (see **court**) by filing of an **information** or **indictment**. In jurisdictions where probable cause is determined in a lower court and trial takes place in a higher court, there may be a **preliminary arraignment** in the lower court.

arrest   *recommended statistical terminology*   Taking an adult or juvenile into physical custody by authority of law, for the purpose of charging the person with a criminal offense or a delinquent act or status offense, terminating with the recording of a specific offense.

defining features

taking into custody by placing under control by actual or potential physical restraint of person's movement

by authority of law

specific offense(s) recorded by law enforcement agency in relation to identified adult or juvenile, by booking or other official registration at a law enforcement or detention facility

annotation

This definition differs from the legal definition of the term, which does not require that the action be completed by actual specification of the offense in writing.

Since the recording of the identity of the person and the charge typically occurs as the person is officially received in a detention area or facility, and this is called "booking," the recommended definition may be read as equating arrests to bookings. However, procedures in different jurisdictions and cases vary, and arrests can result in registration at a police station without official entry into a detention area or facility (see **booking**).

This definition of "arrest" also distinguishes the event from those called **citation (appear), summons,** or **field interrogation** or the like (see entries). The issuance of a citation or summons is less costly in fiscal and human terms than the transport of the subject to a police station for registration of the arrest.

The **UCR** unit of count, "arrests," includes all arrests as defined above, and in addition all citations: all instances where a person is "cited, or summoned by police for criminal acts," or is taken into custody on grounds of "suspicion" and no offense is recorded. UCR arrest totals include juveniles. See **arrests (UCR)** and **delinquency**.

Interagency and state level data systems conventionally treat arrest together with most serious offense charged as an indivisible unit of count.

In some states, statutes require that certain classes of offenders be fingerprinted at the time an arrest is registered.

A "citizen's arrest" is the taking of a person into physical custody, by a witness to a crime other than a law enforcement officer, for the purpose of delivering him to the physical custody of a law enforcement officer or agency.

arrestee dispositions　The class of law enforcement or prosecutorial actions which terminate or provisionally suspend proceedings against an arrested person before a charge(s) has been filed in court.

annotation

This suggested data structure complements **defendant dispositions**, which is designed to describe post-filing dispositions.

The major system exits at this stage, permanent or provisional, are:

- **police release**　arrestee released after booking because of law enforcement agency decision not to request complaint
- **complaint rejected**　prosecutor declines to prosecute case on grounds such as insufficient evidence, lack of witnesses, or interests of justice
- **prosecution withheld**　prosecutor suspends proceedings conditional upon behavior of arrestee
  - **with referral to probation or other criminal justice agency**
  - **with referral to noncriminal justice agency**
  - **with no referral**

See also **prosecutorial screening decision.**

arrest register　The document containing a chronological record of all arrests made by members of a given law enforcement agency, containing at a minimum the identity of the arrestee, the charges at time of arrest, and the date and time of arrest.

annotation

This kind of record is also called an "arrest register book" and "initial entry record." In some agencies the information is entered directly into an electronic processing system. These records and **arrest reports** are key sources of statistical information. A "police blotter" is used in some jurisdictions to record arrests and other information about police activity. All these types of records, being chronological accounts of government activity, are usually open to public inspection.

Jail registers or jail books are records of "bookings," that is, admissions of persons into detention facilities. In some jurisdictions these may be the chief or only source of information about completed arrests. See **arrest** and **booking.**

arrest report　The document prepared by the arresting officer describing an arrested person and the events and circumstances leading to the arrest.

annotation

Arrest reports are the basic source of information for a variety of other records and functions, depending on the procedures in a given jurisdiction. Information in an arrest report may be the basis for the complaint filed by the prosecutor. Some crimes, such as drug law violations, may never be the subject of offense reports and statistical information on their occurrence can therefore be obtained only from arrest reports.

arrests (UCR)　In Uniform Crime Reports terminology, all separate instances where a person is taken into physical custody or notified or cited by a law enforcement officer or agency, except those relating to minor traffic violations.

annotation

In UCR, arrests are classified according to type of offense (see **Part I offenses** and **Part II offenses**).

The national UCR annual publication *Crime in the United States* contains data on arrests broken down by offense and geographical area, and by the age, sex, and race of persons arrested.

This UCR unit of count is also called "persons arrested" or "arrestees."

This dictionary's recommended statistical definition is less broad. See **arrest**.

arrest warrant   *recommended statistical terminology*   A document issued by a judicial officer which directs a law enforcement officer to arrest an identified person who has been accused of a specific offense.

annotation

In order for a judicial officer to issue an arrest warrant, he must have had presented to him either a sworn complaint or evidence that **probable cause** (see entry) exists. The person to be arrested must be identified by name and/or other unique characteristics, and the crime described.

When a warrant for arrest does not identify a person by name, it is sometimes called a "john doe warrant" or a "no name warrant."

See also **bench warrant** and **search warrant**.

arson   *tentatively recommended national category for prosecution, courts and corrections statistics*   The intentional damaging or destruction or attempted damaging or destruction, by means of fire or explosion of the property of another without the consent of the owner, or of one's own property or that of another with intent to defraud.

defining features of tentatively recommended national category

intentional damaging or destruction by means of fire or explosion

of the property of another without his or her consent, or of any property with intent to defraud

or

attempting the above act(s)

annotation

The above definition repeats the substance of the definition of "arson" in the **Model Penal Code**. This is the characteristic definition in modern statutes and is therefore proposed as a standard for prosecution, courts and corrections. **Arson UCR 8** (see entry) includes only burning offenses. See Appendix B for problems in national crime classification and complete set of tentatively proposed national categories for post-arrest offense statistics.

Some statutes include in arson burning or destruction for any unlawful purpose, such as concealing evidence of a crime. In statutes that have not been recently revised "arson" is usually restricted to unlawful burning of property. Damage caused by explosion is separately codified.

arson   UCR 8   In Uniform Crime Reports terminology, the burning or attempted burning of property with or without intent to defraud.

annotation

The UCR category includes offenses of burning one's own property, the property of other persons, and public property. The exclusion from law enforcement data of destruction of property by explosion alone, and other actions often but not always designated "arson" in penal codes, maintains the uniformity of UCR arrest data. See **arson** for recommendation for post-arrest offense data.

Through 1978, this UCR category was used only to classify data on arrests for arson offenses. As of January 1979, by Congressional mandate, arson was declared a "Part I offense," that is, a crime type for which reported occurrences as well as arrests are to be published.

However, in tabulating offenses known to police, i.e., Part I offenses, special reporting conventions are applied to arson. When two or more UCR Part I offenses occur in the same criminal episode and one of these is arson, the arson is counted and tabulated, as is the most serious of the other offenses. In all other circumstances, only the single most serious Part I offense is counted.

This special procedure for arson offenses is employed in order to provide maximum possible data on the occurrence of arson, as mandated, and at the same time maintain historical comparability in published data on occurrences of the other Part I offenses.

In addition to the number of arsons occurring, data are published on clearances of arsons, amount of loss due to arson, and on arsons of inhabited dwellings versus other arsons.

See also **Crime Index.**

assault   *recommended statistical terminology*   Unlawful intentional inflicting, or attempted or threatened inflicting, of injury upon the person of another.

defining features of recommended national category and recommended subcategories

assault

unlawful intentional inflicting of bodily injury

or

attempting or threatening the above act

   aggravated assault

   unlawful intentional inflicting of serious bodily injury

   or

   unlawful threat or attempt to inflict bodily injury or death

   by means of a deadly or dangerous weapon

   with or without actual infliction of any injury

   simple assault

   unlawful intentional inflicting of less than serious bodily injury

   without a deadly or dangerous weapon

   or

   attempt or threat to inflict bodily injury

   without a deadly or dangerous weapon

annotation

"Serious bodily injury" means injury requiring treatment beyond simple first aid, such as broken bones, cuts requiring stitches, all internal injuries, etc.

The above categories, which are used in UCR reporting, are also recommended for prosecution, courts and corrections statistics. See Appendix B for problems in national crime classification and complete set of tentatively proposed national categories for post-arrest offense statistics. See also **aggravated assault UCR 4a–d** and **simple assault UCR 9**.

Historically, "assault" meant only the attempt or threat to inflict injury or constraint on another person. A completed act constituted the separate offense of **battery**: intentional unlawful inflicting of physical violence or constraint upon the person of another. But in modern statistical usage, and in most penal codes, attempted and completed acts are put together under the name, "assault."

The assault group, that is, the group of offenses regularly named "assault" or "battery" is divided into gravity levels in penal codes. The nature of the weapon used and the degree of injury are usually the basic distinguishing features.

While the names "aggravated assault" and "simple assault" are standard terms in data programs, most state penal codes use other words or the labels "first degree," "second degree," etc. to represent the gravity subdivisions of assault (and/or battery). However, almost exactly the same distinction between the more and the less serious crime can be found in every code under the different names, sometimes indicated by classification into felonies and misdemeanors.

Statutory names synonymous or nearly synonymous with "aggravated assault" are: "aggravated assault and battery," "aggravated battery," "assault with intent to kill," "assault with the intent to commit murder or manslaughter," "atrocious assault," "attempted murder," and "felonious assault." **Assault with a deadly weapon (ADW)** (meaning unlawful intentional inflicting, or attempted or threatened inflicting, of injury or death with the use of a deadly weapon) is frequently used in both statistics and statutes.

"Simple assault" is not often distinctively named in statutes since it consists of all assaults not explicitly named and defined as serious.

For the National Crime Survey (**NCS**) classification of assaults, see **personal crimes**.

assault (NCS)   see **personal crimes**

assault on a law enforcement officer   A simple or aggravated assault, where the victim is a law enforcement officer engaged in the performance of his duties.

annotation

The national **UCR** program (see entry) publishes data on "law enforcement officers assaulted." The unit of count is defined as follows: "all assaults on sworn officers who have full arrest powers in which the officer sustained serious injury or in which a weapon was used which could have caused serious injury or death. Also count those sworn officers who were not injured, provided the assault was more than mere verbal abuse or minor resistance to an arrest." Assaults on "off-duty" officers are included, if the officer is acting with official status, or if the attack results from performance of official duty.

This category is not used in UCR summary crime and arrest data and is not recommended for general courts and corrections statistics. See **assault** for general statistical recommendation.

This type of assault is usually distinguished in statutes from other assaults by a separate, higher penalty range. Many statutory definitions of this offense require that the officer be engaged in the performance of his duties at the time of the assault, and that the perpetrator be aware of this fact.

Simple resisting of arrest where the officer's safety is not in danger, does not constitute assault on a law enforcement officer. See **resisting an officer**.

In many jurisdictions a higher penalty is also established for assaults on other government officials, such as firemen and corrections officers.

assigned counsel   see **attorney**

attempt   see **inchoate offense**

attorney *syn* **lawyer** *syn* **counsel** *syn* **advocate**
A person trained in the law, admitted to practice before the bar of a given jurisdiction, and authorized to advise, represent, and act for other persons in legal proceedings.

annotation

An attorney may represent private individuals, corporations, or the government.

The attorney acting on behalf of the government ("the people") in a criminal case is the **prosecutor**. See entry.

The **defense attorney** is the lawyer who advises, represents and acts for the defendant (or, in post-conviction proceedings, the offender). Defense attorneys are categorized for administrative and budgetary purposes with respect to how they are selected and/or compensated:

retained counsel   A defense attorney selected and compensated by the defendant or offender, or by other private person(s).

assigned counsel   A defense attorney assigned by the court on a case-by-case basis to represent in court indigent defendants and offenders, sometimes compensated from public funds but sometimes not compensated at all.

public defender   A defense attorney who is regularly employed and compensated from public funds to represent in court indigent defendants and offenders. See entry for recommended terminology.

When a defendant acts as his or her own defense attorney, he or she is said to be represented **pro se** or **in propria persona.**

AWOL   see **escape**

backlog (court)   The number of cases awaiting disposition in a court which exceed the court's capacity for disposing of them within the period of time considered appropriate.

annotation

Backlog is not the same as pending caseload, which is the number of cases awaiting disposition in a given court (see **caseload (court)**). The pending caseload of a court could be very large but not represent backlog if the rate at which that court can dispose of cases is sufficiently high that the cases can be disposed of within a reasonable period of time.

Backlog can be calculated in relation to any of the administrative units of a court system or in relation to individual judges. It is calculated in various ways in different jurisdictions. There are, very generally speaking, two types of backlog quantifications. One is the number of cases of a given type for which the elapsed time between filing and disposition is exceeding, or is expected to exceed, an explicit, official time limit (see, e.g., **speedy trial**). The other is that portion of a pending caseload which would have to be, but cannot be, disposed of within a given time period to prevent pending caseload from increasing beyond capacity over a series of time periods.

bail   I.   To effect the release of an accused person from custody, in return for a promise that he or she will appear at a place and time specified and submit to the jurisdiction and judgment of the court, guaranteed by a pledge to pay to the court a specified sum of money or property if the person does not appear.   II.   The money or property pledged to the court or actually deposited with the court to effect the release of a person from legal custody.

annotation

Where (I) the action of release is meant, the term **release on bail** is recommended. See **pretrial release**.

A **bail bond** is a document guaranteeing the appearance of the defendant in court as required, and recording the pledge of money or property to be paid to the court if he or she does not appear, which is signed by the person to be released and any other persons acting in his or her behalf.

These other persons are called "sureties." A surety can be either a professional **bail bondsman** (see entry) or a private individual.

The court may or may not require that the pledge of money or property be secured. Pledges may be secured in several ways. The most common way is by employment of a bail bondsman, to whom a nonrefundable fee is paid. In other cases the court can require a deposit of money before the person is released. The requirement can be for the full amount pledged, or for a percentage of the amount pledged.

The amount of the bond, that is, amount of property or money pledged to guarantee appearance, can be changed during the course of proceedings. Bail can be reduced when, for example, the defendant shows that his or her community ties will ensure appearance in court. Bail can be increased when the likelihood that the defendant might abscond increases, as when he or she has been convicted and is awaiting sentencing or has been charged with another crime.

bail bondsman   A person, usually licensed, whose business it is to effect releases on bail for persons charged with offenses and held in custody, by pledging to pay a sum of money if a defendant fails to appear in court as required.

annotation

In most jurisdictions, bail bondsmen must be licensed by the state or local government.

See **bail** and **pretrial release.**

bail forfeiture   see **bail revocation**

bailiff   The court officer whose duties are to keep order in the courtroom and to maintain physical custody of the jury.

annotation

Duties of bailiffs can include seating witnesses, announcing the judge's or other judicial officer's entrance into the courtroom, taking action to prevent or resolve disturbances in the courtroom, and maintaining physical custody of the jury during proceedings in court as well as during sequestration of a jury.

In some jurisdictions the person who performs bailiff and often other duties is called a "court officer." Federal court bailiffs are U.S. marshalls.

bail revocation   The court decision withdrawing the status of release on bail previously conferred upon a defendant.

annotation

Bail status may be revoked if the defendant fails to appear in court when required, or is arrested for another crime, or violates a condition of the bail release, such as a requirement that he or she remain within a certain jurisdiction.

Bail forfeiture is the court decision that the defendant or surety (see **bail**) has lost the right to the money or property pledged to guarantee court appearance or the fulfillment of another obligation, or has lost the right to the sum deposited as security for the pledge, and that the court will retain it.

Neither revocation of bail status nor forfeit of bail is automatic upon failure to appear. Each is a court decision requiring a hearing. Such decisions ordinarily will not be taken unless it appears that the defendant permanently intends to avoid prosecution, sentencing, or execution of a sentence. Further, bail forfeiture will often be reversed and the pledged amount minus court costs will be returned to the defendant or surety if the defendant appears in court within a given period of time.

balance of sentence suspended   *recommended statistical terminology*
A type of sentencing disposition consisting of a sentence to prison or jail, which credits the defendant for time already spent in confinement awaiting adjudication and sentencing, suspends the execution of the time remaining to be served, and results in the release from confinement of the defendant.

annotation

A related disposition is:

sentenced to time served   *recommended statistical terminology*   A sentencing disposition consisting of a sentence to prison or jail, which credits the defendant for an amount of time already spent in confinement equal to the amount of the sentence, and results in release from confinement of the defendant.

These two types of dispositions are functionally equivalent from the defendant perspective, since both provide credit for time previously spent in confinement and result in release of the defendant from confinement at the time of sentencing.

Balance of sentence suspended or sentenced to time served is a subcategory of sentencing dispositions within the larger class **defendant dispositions** (see entry).

battery   see **assault**

bench warrant   *recommended statistical terminology*   A document issued by a court directing that a law enforcement officer bring the person named therein before the court, usually one who has failed to obey a court order or a notice to appear.

annotation

A bench warrant is a special type of **arrest warrant**. A bench warrant is sometimes called an "order for arrest," a "capias" (from Latin: you should seize), and in statutes, an "alias warrant" (a second order issued after a first order has been ineffective). Bench warrants are writs of attachment or arrest from the "bench" of a court in session. In practice they are prepared by the court clerk.

Bench warrants may be issued when a person fails to obey a notice to appear issued in lieu of arrest by a law enforcement officer, fails to respond to a summons or subpoena, fails to obey an order when such failure is contempt of court, and the like.

Bench warrants may also be issued where there has been no failure to obey, such as when a person is first named as a defendant in an indictment, or when issued to transfer an accused person from jail to court for trial.

bifurcated trial   In criminal proceedings, a special two-part trial proceeding in which the issue of guilt is tried in the first step, and if a conviction results, the appropriate sentence or applicable sentencing statute is determined in the second step.

annotation

The two steps of a bifurcated trial generally take place in separate hearings. The second step occurs following the verdict and pronouncement of judgment.

Typical issues in the second step of a bifurcated trial are (1) what sentence to impose (e.g., for capital offense convictions, whether to impose the death penalty), and (2) what statute section should determine the convicted person's sentence, for example, whether or not the convicted person meets the statutory definition of habitual criminal.

bigamy   Unlawful contracting of marriage by a person who, at the time of the marriage, knows himself or herself already to be legally married.

annotation

In many jurisdictions, an unmarried person who knowingly contracts marriage with a person who already is legally married also commits bigamy. In some jurisdictions, cohabitation without legal marriage is also bigamy if one of the persons is legally married to someone else.

In UCR, this offense is included by name in **all other offenses UCR 26**. In the tentatively recommended classification for post-arrest offense reporting "bigamy" is assigned to the "other" category. See Appendix B.

bill of attainder
A law or act which punishes a person without affording him or her a judicial trial as required by the United States Constitution, Article I, Section 9.

annotation

The United States Supreme Court has held that a law or act is invalid as a bill of attainder if it punishes on the basis of some past or permanent characteristic. However, where the law or act imposes burdens or limits benefits on the basis of future events or characteristics, it is not a bill of attainder and therefore valid.

bill of particulars
A specific description which the prosecution sets forth containing the nature, means, character, time and place of a crime as alleged in the complaint or indictment.

annotation

The "bill of particulars" operates as giving notice to the accused of the crimes charged in order for a defense to be prepared.

bill of rights
The first ten amendments to the United States Constitution guaranteeing rights and privileges to the individual.

annotation

The "**bill of rights**" have been made applicable to the states via the Due Process Clause of the 14th Amendment on a case by case, right-by-right basis through selective incorporation as guaranteed by the 5th Amendment to the Constitution.

The following amendments are particularly important in the criminal law and procedure area:

First: "Congress shall make no law respecting an establishment of religion, or prohibiting the free exercise thereof; or abridging the freedom of speech, or of the press; or the right of the people peaceably to assembly, and to petition the Government for a redress of grievances.

Fourth: The right of the people to be secure in their persons, houses, papers, and effects, against unreasonable searches and seizures, shall not be violated, and no Warrants shall issue, but upon probable cause, supported by Oath or affirmation, and particularly describing the place to be searched, and the persons or things to be seized.

Fifth: No person shall be held to answer for a capital, or otherwise infamous crime, unless on a presentment or indictment of a Grand Jury, except in cases arising in the land or naval forces, or in the Militia, when in actual service in time of War or public danger; nor shall any person be subject for the same offence to be twice put in jeopardy of life or limb; nor shall be compelled in any criminal case to be a witness against himself, nor be deprived of life, liberty, or property, without due process of law; nor shall private property be taken for public use, without just compensation.

Sixth: In all criminal prosecutions, the accused shall ejoy the right to a speedy and public trial, by an impartial jury of the State and district wherein the crime shall have been committed, which district shall have been previously ascertained by law, and to be informed of the nature and cause of the accusation; to be confronted with the witnesses against him; to have compulsory process for obtaining witnesses in his favor, and to have the Assistance of Counsel for his defence.

Eighth: Excessive bail shall not be required, nor excessive fines imposed, nor cruel and unusual punishments inflicted.

Tenth: The powers not delegated to the United States by the Constitution, nor prohibited by it to the States, are reserved to the States respectively, or to the people.

bind over   I. To require by judicial authority that a person promise to appear for trial, appear in court as a witness, or keep the peace.   II. *recommended statistical terminology*   The decision by a court of limited jurisdiction requiring that a person charged with a felony appear for trial on that charge in a court of general jurisdiction, as the result of a finding of probable cause at a preliminary hearing held in the limited jurisdiction court.

annotation

The action of a court of limited jurisdiction binding over a felony defendant for trial in a court of general jurisdiction, constitutes for purposes of caseload statistics a disposition of the defendant's case in the limited jurisdiction court. It is recommended that felony cases filed in limited jurisdiction courts for preliminary hearing be counted separately from other limited jurisdiction court caseload in statistical presentations, to provide a proper picture of the interrelationship between limited and general jurisdiction court caseloads.

When a court binds over a defendant for trial he or she may be required to put up **bail** or enter into a "recognizance" (a recorded agreement to appear as required, but without financial stipulations).

The basic meaning of "bind over" is to send forward; the contrasting term is **remand**: to send back. When, for example, the judgment in a case is appealed and a higher court returns the case to a lower court for retrial or other reconsideration, it is said to be remanded.

Defendants are in some jurisdictions said to be "remanded" when they are returned to custody to await trial after a preliminary hearing.

blackmail   see **extortion**

bombing incident   The detonation or attempted detonation of an explosive or incendiary device for a criminal purpose, or with willful disregard of the risk to the person or property of another.

annotation

The FBI Bomb Data Center collects data on events falling within the definition above. Data collected by the Center are published annually by UCR, in the series entitled *Bomb Summary*.

"Bombing incidents" include those instances of arson committed or attempted by means of an explosive or incendiary device. They do not include hoaxes or threats involving fake bombs.

Most penal codes do not systematically separate bomb offenses from other crimes. In criminal proceedings, the offense charged will usually be determined by the criminal purpose, for example, murder, extortion, or arson.

booking   A law enforcement or correctional administrative process officially recording an entry into detention after arrest, and identifying the person, the place, time, and reason for the arrest, and the arresting authority.

annotation

This term is often used to indicate the completion of an arrest, and, depending upon the agency, may be synonymous with arrest as defined in this dictionary in that the booking can be the action that records the fact of arrest and the charge. See **arrest** for recommended terminology.

"Booking" in the narrowest sense means the certification by a detention unit (an area or facility) that it has accepted an identified person into physical custody.

Whether or not fingerprinting occurs at arrest or booking depends upon the practice in a given jurisdiction, which may vary in accord with the type of offense, or the age of the person taken into custody, or other factors. In some states statutes require that certain classes of arrestees be fingerprinted.

bookmaking   see **gambling**

bribery   The giving or offering of anything of value with intent to unlawfully influence a person in the discharge of his duties, and the receiving or asking of anything of value with intent to be unlawfully influenced.

annotation

Giving bribes and receiving bribes are sometimes codified as separate offenses in statutes. The term "bribery" then usually means only the giving or offering of bribes, the soliciting or accepting of bribes being called "corruption."

In UCR, "bribery" is included by name in **all other offenses UCR 26.** This offense is assigned to the "other" category in the tentatively recommended post-arrest offense classification. See Appendix B.

burglary   I. By the narrowest and oldest definition, trespassory breaking and entering of the dwelling house of another in the night-time with the intent to commit a felony.   II. *recommended statistical terminology* Unlawful entry of any fixed structure, vehicle or vessel used for regular residence, industry or business, with or without force, with intent to commit a felony or larceny.

defining features *of recommended national category (definition II)*

unlawful entry of a fixed structure, or a vehicle or vessel used for regular residence, or a vehicle or vessel in a fixed location regularly used for industry or business

with or without force

with intent to commit a felony or larceny

or

attempting the above act

annotation

The above definition (II), which is used in UCR reporting (see **burglary UCR 5)** is also recommended for prosecution, courts and corrections statistics. UCR assists clear definition in this area by giving examples of structures, vehicles and vessels subject to "burglary" and by contrast explicitly classifying thefts from motor vehicles, from buildings open to the public, from recreational vehicles and temporary structures, and from coin-operated devices, as "larceny-theft." See Appendix B for problems in national crime classification and complete set of tentatively proposed national categories for post-arrest offense statistics.

There are more obstacles to capture of comparable data for this crime type than for other major offenses because of the great variation in the manner in which this area of criminal behavior is structured in penal codes.

The behavior which is specifically named as "burglary" may differ a great deal from one state to another:

State A
- breaking and entering (excludes through open door or window)
- the occupied or unoccupied
- dwelling house or sleeping apartment of another
- in the night-time
- with intent to commit a felony or larceny

State B
- entering
- house, room, shop, tenement, apartment, warehouse, store, mill, barn, stable, outhouse, other building, tent, vessel, railroad car, trailer coach, house car, camper used as a dwelling, or mine
- with intent to commit a felony or larceny

However, the fact that particular behavior is not identified as "burglary" in a given state does not mean the behavior is not unlawful, or not identifiable. Acts not called "burglary" will be codified as some other offense(s) under a different name(s), with features which enable it to be identified as belonging to the general crime type of "unlawful entry with intent to commit a crime." State A in the example above has an offense called "breaking and entering," which covers commercial buildings and the like.

The irreconcilable differences usually lie in the precise definitions of crime target, as when one state defines theft from a storage shed or camper as burglary and another state defines such behavior as simple larceny. These borderline cases, however, are of less importance as reported or charged crimes than the relatively clearcut residential and commercial structure burglaries.

For National Crime Survey (NCS) classification of burglaries see **household crimes**.

burglary   UCR 5   *Uniform Crime Reports usage*   Unlawful entry of any fixed structure, vehicle or vessel used for regular residence, industry, or business, with or without force, with intent to commit a felony, or larceny.

annotation

This category is also recommended for use in post-arrest statistics. See **burglary** for defining features and general recommendation.

Burglary is a UCR Crime Index offense. The annual publication *Crime in the United States* presents data both on reported occurrences of burglary offenses and on arrests relating to such offenses. See **Crime Index**.

In UCR data reporting burglary is subdivided as follows:
5.a. forcible entry
5.b. unlawful entry—no force
5.c. attempted forcible entry

Unlawful entry accompanied by the commission or attempted commission of forcible rape, robbery, or aggravated assault (which includes attempted murder), or by the commission of criminal homicide is classified as the "more serious" offense, in accordance with UCR conventions. Unlawful entry without intent to commit a felony or larceny is classified as **all other offenses UCR 26.**

UCR gives as examples of burglary the "offenses locally known as burglary (any degree); unlawful entry with intent to commit a larceny or felony; breaking and entering with intent to commit a larceny; housebreaking; safe-cracking; and all attempts at these offenses."

capacity   In criminal justice usage, the legal ability of a person to commit a criminal act; the mental and physical ability to act with purpose and to be aware of the certain, probable or possible results of one's conduct.

annotation

In most criminal codes, capacity is defined by listing those conditions which establish incapacity to commit a crime. Among the stated bases for incapacity are extreme youth, idiocy, insanity, involuntary intoxication, unconsciousness, and duress.

Whether a person possesses "capacity" in the sense described above at the time of an act or during judicial proceedings determines whether prosecution is legally possible (e.g., children cannot be prosecuted), whether prosecution must halt (e.g., the defendant is found **incompetent to stand trial**), and sometimes the nature of the finding, as in **not guilty by reason of insanity.**

See also **culpability**, which also has to do with mental states, but in relation to the manner in which an act is committed.

In corrections terminology, "capacity" has a very different sense. There, the term is used in relation to the number of persons who can be housed in correctional facilities, as determined by a variety of measures. See **institutional capacity.**

capital offense   I. A criminal offense punishable by death.   II. In some penal codes, an offense which may be punishable by death or by imprisonment for life.

career criminal   In prosecutorial and law enforcement usage, a person having a past record of multiple arrests or convictions for serious crimes, or an unusually large number of arrests or convictions for crimes of varying degrees of seriousness.

annotation

This term has a formal status in management systems for allocating prosecutorial resources and setting priorities in case scheduling in order that defendants and cases warranting special attention be dealt with effectively and speedily. The exact definition varies among different agencies.

Professional criminal is a popular name for a person who has made crime his or her livelihood, that is, a person who depends upon criminal activities for at least a substantial portion of his or her income, and who has developed special, related skills.

Statutorily defined **habitual offenders** fit the definition of "career criminal."

case   At the level of police or prosecutorial investigation, a set of circumstances under investigation involving one or more persons; at subsequent steps in criminal proceedings, a charging document alleging the commission of one or more crimes, or a single defendant charged with one or more crimes; in juvenile or correctional proceedings, a person who is the object of agency action.

annotation

"Case" should not be used in interstate or national information exchange without explicit definition.

In general usage a **court case** is an action brought before a court for adjudication; a set of facts which is the occasion for the exercise of the jurisdiction of a court, and which is handled by the court as a procedural unit. In civil proceedings case counts are usually based on the filings of complaints or petitions. In statistics describing criminal proceedings "case" usually means a single charging document filed in a court containing one or more charges against one or more defendants and constituting the unit of action in court activity following the filing. However, the charges in two or more charging documents are sometimes combined, or the charges or defendants in one charging document separated, for purposes of adjudication. See **criminal case, trial court case, appellate court case, appeal case, request to appeal case, postconviction remedy,** and **sentence review** for recommendations.

From the prosecutorial and correctional perspectives, the defendant may be the entity which is counted: no matter what the dispositions of the various charges against a defendant may be in proceedings involving more than one charge, the disposition of the person is a separate type of fact of significance to prosecutorial effectiveness, corrections caseloads and the affected individual. See **defendant dispositions.**

caseload (corrections)   The total number of clients registered with a correctional agency or agent on a given date or during a specified time period, often divided into active supervisory cases and inactive cases, thus distinguishing between clients with whom contact is regular, and those with whom it is not.

annotation

In corrections, "caseload" usually refers to those persons for whom a probation or parole agency has supervisorial responsibility. See **supervised probation** and **parole supervision.** Caseload movement data are a prominent feature of corrections statistics. See **parole agency caseload entries and removals** and **probation supervisory population movement.**

Persons in the custody of a confinement facility are generally not called "caseloads." However, a correctional counselor within a confinement facility is sometimes considered to have a caseload if his responsibilities are limited to a specific group of inmates.

A correctional agency caseload is, of course, usually only a portion of its total "workload," which includes case investigations, services to confined persons or their families, individual parole program planning and the like. See **probation workload** for example.

caseload (court)   The number of cases requiring judicial action at a certain time, or the number of cases acted upon in a given court during a given time period.

annotation

A model court caseload statistical system has recently been developed by the National Court Statistics Project under Bureau of Justice Statistics sponsorship. The model was developed as part of the State Court Caseload Statistics program, to encourage development of fully comparable cross-jurisdictional caseload data. A term list outline of the complete model classification scheme for general caseload inventory and for case and defendant manner of disposition is presented in Appendix E of this volume. The full model, including recommended tabulation procedures, is presented in the publications *State Court Model Annual Report* (see bibliography, under "National Center for State Courts") and *State Court Model Statistical Dictionary* (see bibliography, under "U.S. Department of Justice").

In statistical presentations of court caseload data, the basic quantities presented are the number of cases filed during a given reporting period (see **filing**), the number of cases disposed of during the period (see **court disposition**), and the number of **cases pending**, that is, filed and not yet disposed of, at both the beginning and end of the period. These four basic quantities: beginning pending, filings, dispositions, end pending, are in the terminology of the NCSP model called the "court caseload inventory".

The difference, if any, between the number of cases pending at the beginning of a reporting period and the number pending at its end is one measure of the adequacy of a court's resources in relation to cases requiring adjudication (see **backlog (court)**).

The basic caseload inventory categories are normally subdivided, according to type of case (e.g., civil vs. criminal), type of filing (e.g., new vs. reopened cases), and for disposed cases according to the manner in which the case was disposed of (e.g., with trial vs. without trial). For criminal cases, further subdivisions usually also identify, at a minimum, whether or not cases terminated with the conviction of a defendant.

Court caseload does not represent all court activity. It is limited to that portion of the court's work which concerns matters identified as "cases" by the court's regular procedures, usually matters involving some controversy requiring a judicial determination. The term "workload" is used to refer to the entire range of a court's work, including cases and "non-case" matters.

Caseload may be calculated with respect to an entire court system, a given type of court, an administrative subdivision of a court, or a particular judge or tribunal.

certification   see **transfer to adult court**

certiorari   see **writ**

change of venue   The movement of a case from the jurisdiction of one court to that of another court which has the same subject matter jurisdictional authority but is in a different geographic location.

annotation

An example of a change of venue is a case which is transferred from a court of general jurisdiction in one city, county, or district to a court of general jurisdiction in a different city, county or district within a given state.

The most frequent reason for a change of venue is a judicial determination that an impartial jury cannot be found within a particular geographic jurisdiction, usually because of widely publicized prejudicial statements concerning the events which are the basis for the case.

See also **jurisdiction**.

charge   In criminal justice usage, an allegation that a specified person(s) has committed a specific offense, recorded in a functional document such as a record of an arrest, a complaint, information or indictment, or a judgment of conviction.

annotation

Because the basic accounting unit in criminal justice data is usually the case or the defendant, and because a given court case (or arrest and prosecution of a given defendant) can involve more than one charge, aggregate data relating to charges usually do not represent total criminal justice agency activity in response to total alleged crimes or offense convictions. See **filing**.

For example, one arrest can incorporate multiple charges, but tabulations of arrests usually report only the most serious charge (generally the offense having the highest penalty). Thus a table displaying total arrests in a certain jurisdiction during a certain period, subclassified by type of offense, reports less than the total number of charges made in that place and time.

Charging documents entered in the record of a court to initiate criminal proceedings also often contain more than one charge. Each of the allegations of an offense in the charging document is called a **count**. This word is usually used as part of a phrase indicating the particular type of offense, as "the defendant is charged with one count of robbery," or "convicted of three counts of theft." Statistics could be developed to show the disposition of each charge (count) at various points in criminal proceedings because each is a separable unit of prosecutorial and judicial activity, but such statistical presentations are uncommon.

charging document   *recommended statistical terminology*   A formal written accusation submitted to a court, alleging that a specified person(s) has committed a specific offense(s).

annotation

For prosecution and court statistics, the filing of a charging document in a court is the recommended unit of count for reporting the initiation of a criminal case. See **filing** for recommended statistical usages.

In misdemeanor cases the **complaint** may be the only charging document filed. In felony cases, prosecution usually commences with an accusation called a "complaint" filed in a lower court. If **probable cause** is found by a magistrate or grand jury, an accusation called an **information** or **indictment** will be filed in the felony trial court. See entries for further information.

check fraud   The issuance or passing of a check, draft, or money order that is legal as a formal document, signed by the legal account holder but with the foreknowledge that the bank or depository will refuse to honor it because of insufficient funds or closed account.

annotation

In UCR arrest reporting this crime is classified as **fraud UCR 11.** See **fraud offenses** for general statistical recommendation.

Instances of check fraud are often called "NSF checks," "nonsufficient funds checks," "insufficient funds," and "bad checks."

When the printed check is illegally created or signed by a person other than the legal account holder the offense is **forgery** (see entry).

chief of police   *recommended statistical terminology*   A law enforcement officer who is the appointed or elected head of a municipal police department, department of public safety, or special authority or district police unit.

annotation

"Chief of police" usually refers to the head of a local, municipal police department but the title is also used for the heads of agencies organized to serve other jurisdictions. "Director" or "superintendent" may be the title for the head of a public safety department or division. "Commissioner" usually refers to one of several persons sitting on a board or commission intended to direct police agency policy.

See **police department** and **law enforcement officer.**

child abuse   see **dependency**

child neglect   see **dependency**

citation (appear)   *recommended statistical terminology*   A written order issued by a law enforcement officer directing an alleged offender to appear in a specific court at a specified time in order to answer a criminal charge, and not permitting forfeit of bail as an alternative to court appearance.

defining features

alleged commission of a criminal offense

order issued by a law enforcement officer in lieu of arrest and booking

requiring appearance in designated court at specific time to answer criminal charge

forfeit of bail not a legal alternative to appearance

annotation

Although this type of citation is classified as an arrest in many jurisdictions the use of this data item provides for distinction between arrests in which the subject is booked or otherwise registered on law enforcement premises, and those where no transport of the suspect is necessary. See **arrest** for recommended data system usage of that term.

Citation (forfeit) is recommended as the name for those written orders where payment of money is expected to be forfeited as an alternative to the requirement of a court appearance. Such orders are often issued for **infractions** (see entry), meaning "non-criminal" offenses. The term "citation (forfeit)" is suggested in order to provide complete classificatory terminology for data systems that process both information relating to criminal charges and information concerning minor vehicle code or other violations that are explicitly defined or treated as non-criminal offenses.

In some jurisdictions forfeiting money in lieu of court appearance results in the recording of a plea of guilty to the offense charged.

In some jurisdictions a citation permitting a forfeit in lieu of court appearance and signed by a law enforcement officer is called a "summons." This usage is not recommended for national level data. See **summons**.

citation (forfeit)   see **citation (appear)**

civil commitment   I. In general usage, the action of a judicial officer or administrative body ordering a person to be placed in an institution or program for custody, treatment or protection, usually one administered by a health service.   II. *recommended criminal justice statistical terminology*   A non-penal commitment to a treatment facility resulting from findings made during criminal proceedings, either before or after a judgment.

annotation

A civil commitment made in the course of disposing of a case initiated by a criminal charge is usually not considered a judgment for purposes of statistical description of criminal defendant or case outcomes. In a criminal case the judgment is **acquittal** or **conviction**. (See also **defendant dispositions**.)

In criminal proceedings (definition II), a civil commitment may follow a court determination that an alleged offender cannot be prosecuted because **incompetent to stand trial** or because **not guilty by reason of insanity**. It may also follow, for example, a successful criminal prosecution for a drug law violation, where the offender is committed to a special institution for the treatment of drug addiction, instead of a penal institution. The federal Narcotics Addict Rehabilitation Act provides for non-penal commitments to treatment facilities as dispositions of alleged or convicted drug offenders.

Although a person may be deprived of liberty by a civil commitment, it is in principle not done for the purpose of punishment, but rather for the welfare of the subject or others. A civil commitment to a medical facility ordinarily follows civil proceedings that have determined that the subject is a danger to self or to others, or cannot care for himself or herself because of mental disability.

The term is also used to refer to court-ordered jailing of a person who refuses to obey a court order issued in the course of a civil suit.

civil contempt   see **contempt of court**

clearance   In Uniform Crime Reports terminology, the event where a known occurrence of a Part I offense is followed by an arrest or other decision which indicates a solved crime at the police level of reporting.

annotation

In the UCR vocabulary, a known offense (see **offenses known to police**) is "cleared" or "solved" (1) when a law enforcement agency has charged at least one person with the offense, or (2) when a suspect has been identified and located and an arrest is justified, but action is prevented by circumstances outside law enforcement control.

Thus, two types of clearances are distinguished:

clearance by arrest   All instances where a known offense is solved by the arrest and charging of at least one person, the summoning, citing or notifying of at least one person, or the citing of a juvenile to appear before juvenile authorities, in connection to the offense.

clearance by exceptional means   All cases where police know the identity and location of a suspect and have information to support arrest, charging, and prosecution, but are prevented from taking action by circumstances outside police control (for example, the suspect is dead, the suspect is already in custody in the same or other jurisdiction, or the victim of the offense has refused cooperation in prosecution).

However, in UCR published data, both types of clearances have been tabulated under the cover term "offenses cleared by arrest."

A related key UCR term is:

clearance rate   In UCR publications, the number of offenses cleared divided by the number of offenses known to police, expressed as a percent.

The national UCR program publishes annually tabulations of clearances and clearance rates for all **Part I offenses**.

A UCR "clearance" does not necessarily indicate the closing of a case from the law enforcement operations standpoint. Although a "clearance by arrest" or by "exceptional means" may have been recorded for UCR reporting, active investigation will continue, for example, where a crime has been cleared by the arrest of one suspect but a second suspect is still being sought.

Conversely, the closing of a police case may or may not indicate a "clearance." Where, for example, investigation of all available leads has not resulted in the identification of a suspect, a not cleared case may be filed inactive or closed pending new information.

clemency   In criminal justice usage the name for the type of executive or legislative action where the severity of punishment of a single person or a group of persons is reduced or the punishment stopped, or a person is exempted from prosecution for certain actions.

annotation

Grounds for clemency include mitigating circumstances, postconviction evidence of innocence, dubious guilt, illness of prisoner, reformation, services to the state, turning state's evidence, reasons of state, the need to restore civil rights, and corrections of unduly severe sentences or injustices stemming from imperfections in penal law or the application of it.

The chief forms of clemency are pardons (full and conditional), amnesties, commutations, reduced sentences, reprieves and remissions of fines and forfeitures. In actual use the meanings of these terms overlap. For example, in some jurisdictions a particular kind of pardon may be called "executive clemency," or a given kind of commutation a "pardon." Informational definitions emphasizing the basic distinctions that are usually, but not always, made are as follows:

full pardon   An executive act completely and unconditionally absolving a person from all consequences of a crime and conviction. This act is sometimes called an "absolute pardon," and can imply that guilt itself is "blotted out." It is an "act of forgiveness" and is accompanied, generally, by restoration of civil rights. American law tends to use this executive remedy, instead of judicial proceedings, when serious doubt of guilt or evidence of innocence arises after conviction.

conditional pardon   An executive act releasing a person from punishment, contingent upon his or her performance or non-performance of specified acts.

amnesty   A kind of pardon granted by a sovereign authority, often before any indictment, trial or conviction, to a group of persons who have committed offenses against the government, which not only frees them from punishment, but has the effect of removing all legal recognition that the offenses occurred. A "pardon" is distinct from an amnesty in that the former applies to only one person, and does not necessarily include the abolition of all legal recognition that the offense occurred. An amnesty is sometimes called a "general pardon" because it applies to all offenders of a given class, or all offenses against a given statute or during a certain time period. The sovereign authority may be executive or legislative.

commutation (of sentence)   An executive act changing a punishment from a greater to a lesser penalty; in correctional usage, a reduction of the term of confinement resulting in immediate release or reduction of remaining time to be served; also, the change from a sentence of death to a term of imprisonment. Commutation does not, generally, connote "forgiveness." It is often used to shorten an excessively and unusually long sentence. Commutation can occur with respect to groups of prisoners, though with a different impact on the term of confinement of each single prisoner.

reduced sentence   A sentence to confinement of which the time duration has been shortened by judicial action; also, a reduced fine or other material penalty. Reduction of sentence can occur at many process points, beginning with the sentencing disposition after conviction.

reprieve   An executive act temporarily suspending the execution of a sentence, usually a death sentence. A reprieve differs from other suspensions of sentence not only in that it almost always applies to temporary withdrawing of a death sentence, but also in that it is usually an act of clemency intended to provide the prisoner with time to secure amelioration of the sentence.

See "terminations" under **prison/parole population movement,** for data terminology for clemency actions.

cohort   In statistics, the group of individuals having one or more statistical factors in common in a demographic study.

annotation

A time factor (e.g., all those admitted to prison on a certain date or within a given year) is implicitly or explicitly present in all person cohorts. Other factors frequently employed in corrections statistics are type of offense, type of correctional treatment program, and time served in confinement.

Basic cohorts pertinent to analyses of correctional population behavior are:

sentencing cohort   The group of individuals who have received a sentencing disposition within a given time period.

admission cohort   The group of individuals who have been committed to a confinement facility, or the group who have been placed on parole, or the group who have been placed on probation within a given time period.

departure cohort   The group of individuals who have been released from a confinement facility, or the group discharged from parole, or the group discharged from probation within a given time period.

"Cohort" has a different usage in law enforcement. See **perpetrator**.

commercial burglary (NCS)   see **commercial crimes**

commercial crimes   In National Crime Survey (NCS) terminology, a summary offense category consisting of:

> commercial robbery
>> completed
>> attempted
> commercial burglary
>> completed
>> attempted

annotation

The NCS commercial crime categories were used for presentation of data from the Commercial Survey of Victimization. This component of NCS was discontinued after the 1976 data collection year. Terminology is presented in this dictionary for the convenience of those wishing to compare the classification scheme employed for published NCS data with those of other statistical programs.

The two major subcategories of commercial crimes employed in NCS data presentation are:

commercial robbery   The theft or attempted theft of money or property from a commercial establishment, by force or threat of force.

Commercial robberies were not restricted to those occurring at the premises of a commercial establishment. Robbery or attempted robbery of sales or delivery personnel, for example, where the property involved was that of the commercial establishment, was also classified as commercial robbery.

Robberies from persons are classified as **personal crimes**. See that entry.

commercial burglary   The unlawful or forcible entry or attempted forcible entry of a commercial establishment, usually, but not necessarily, attended by a theft.

Burglaries of households are classified as **household crimes**. See that entry.

commercial robbery (NCS)   see **commercial crimes**

commercial sex offenses   see **sex offenses**

commitment   *recommended statistical terminology*   The action of a judicial officer ordering that a person subject to judicial proceedings be placed in a particular kind of confinement or residential facility, for a specific reason authorized by law; also, the result of the action, the admission to the facility.

annotation

The various types of commitments are usually designated by a phrase indicating the reason for or the result of the commitment, for example, "diagnostic commitment" or "jail commitment." See **placement** for a term of related meaning.

In terminology recommended for describing the final court dispositions of convicted persons commitments are subtypes of **defendant dispositions** and consist of **jail commitments, prison commitments** and **residential commitments.** The admissions to correctional institutions resulting from these court actions are usually called, in correctional terminology, "court commitments," or **new court commitments** where applicable. (See entries.)

Note that a given instance of a commitment as a court disposition does not necessarily imply that the committed person will be received by the designated correctional agency. For example, the sentence may be appealed or the correctional facility may be overcrowded and unable to admit new prisoners.

In civil proceedings, "commitment" usually refers to involuntary commitment of a person to a mental health facility, and may be called a "civil commitment" to distinguish it from confinement ordered as a penalty for a crime. However, **civil commitments** (see entry) often result from findings made during the adjudication of a criminal case.

Both criminal and civil proceedings may also employ the **diagnostic commitment** (see entry), where a person is sent to a correctional or medical facility for study and observation, with the resulting findings reported to the court for use in making a final disposition of the person.

commutation (of sentence)   see **clemency**

complaining witness   see **witness**

complaint   I. In general criminal justice usage, any accusation that a person(s) has committed an offense(s), received by or originating from a law enforcement or prosecutorial agency, or received by a court.   II. In judicial process usage, a formal document submitted to the court by a prosecutor, law enforcement officer, or other person, alleging that a specified person(s) has committed a specified offense(s) and requesting prosecution.

annotation

A complaint in sense (II) is a type of charging document and initiates a criminal case. See **filing** and **charging document** for recommended statistical terminology.

Most jurisdictions call the charging document filed in a misdemeanor case or at the first step of a felony case a "complaint," and the document filed to initiate trial proceedings at the second step of a felony case an "information," but a few reverse this usage. In some jurisdictions the document filed to bind over a defendant until a grand jury decides whether or not to issue an indictment is also called a "complaint."

complaint denied   see **prosecutorial screening decision**

complaint granted   see **prosecutorial screening decision**

complaint modified   see **prosecutorial screening decision**

complaint requested   see **prosecutorial screening decision**

complicity   Any conduct on the part of a person other than the chief actor in the commission of a crime, in which the person intentionally or knowingly serves to further the intent to commit the crime, aids in the commission of the crime, or assists the person who has committed the crime to avoid prosecution or to escape from justice.

annotation

Complicity is the name of a pattern of behavior, and not the name of an offense. Where complicity occurs before or during the commission of a given crime the chargeable offense is usually that crime. Where the complicity occurs only after the commission of a crime, some penal codes have established a separate chargeable offense carrying a lesser penalty.

Complicity may be characterized according to the nature of the behavior and its relation to the commission of the crime. See **parties to offenses** and **inchoate offense**.

compounding a criminal offense   Unlawful agreement by a person to forebear or cease prosecution, or assistance in prosecution, in return for reparation or any other payment of money or thing of value.

annotation

Depending upon the jurisdiction, a compounder can be a victim, witness or prosecuting attorney who accepts payment to refrain from assisting in prosecution, or the offender who pays or offers to pay someone who can prevent or hinder prosecution. In some states, the only "compounding" offense is compounding a felony.

However, formally authorized payment of reparation or restitution to a victim is a legitimate alternative to prosecution in some jurisdictions.

computer crime   A popular name for crimes committed by use of a computer or crimes involving misuse or destruction of computer equipment or computerized information, sometimes specifically theft committed by means of manipulation of a computerized financial transaction system, or the use of computer services with intent to avoid payment.

annotation

The special kinds of crimes which can be committed in relation to computer systems have rarely been codified in penal statutes. However, conventional theft provisions often do not adequately cover losses that can occur in relation to these systems. Electronically recorded information, for example, can be stolen without any tangible object being lost. One state has dealt with this problem by establishing a type of crime called "offenses against intellectual property," and other crimes relating to unauthorized modification of computer equipment or supplies, and unauthorized access to computers and computer systems.

concurrent sentence   see **consecutive sentence**

concurring opinion   see **opinion**

conditionally suspended sentence   see **suspended sentence**

conditional pardon   see **clemency**

conditional release   *recommended statistical terminology*   The release by executive decision from a federal or state correctional facility, of a prisoner who has not served his or her full sentence and whose freedom is contingent upon obeying specified rules of behavior.

annotation

In this terminology the class "conditional release" includes only those instances where return to a prison can occur at the discretion of an executive agency (usually a **paroling authority**) if the subject violates the stated conditions of behavior. Releases by judicial authority, with return, if any, also decided by court action, are not members of this class. These latter are final exits from the state corrections perspective, since all corrections agency jurisdiction over the subject is terminated.

Conditional releases as defined here consist mainly of **releases to parole** and **mandatory supervised releases.** They are in contrast to the category **provisional exits** where return is expected. They are also in contrast to exits from prison to probation supervision by a state agency and releases to probation administered directly by a court. The latter is usually treated as a final prison/parole system exit in state data.

See **parole agency caseload entries and removals** and **prison/parole population movement** for the uses of these categories in data structures.

confidence game   A popular name for false representation to obtain money or any other thing of value, where deception is accomplished through the trust placed by the victim in the character of the offender.

annotation

This offense is included by name in **fraud UCR 11**, but the term is not used in statutes. See **fraud offenses** for general statistical recommendation.

"Swindle" is sometimes used as a synonym for the above term but a distinction is often made:

swindle   Intentional false representation to obtain money or any other thing of value, where deception is accomplished through the victim's belief in the validity of some statement or object presented by the offender.

Trust in a person, as opposed to belief in the validity of some statement or object, distinguishes a confidence game from a swindle.

confinement   In correctional terminology, physical restriction of a person to a clearly defined area from which he or she is lawfully forbidden to depart and from which departure is usually constrained by architectural barriers and/or guards or other custodians.

annotation

No universal and empirically exact division between "confinement" and "nonconfinement" as mutually exclusive types of **correctional facilities** has been established. Some facilities are clearly bounded by walls or fences within which the inmates must remain, unless departing under escort. Other facilities contain some "locked up" persons and other persons permitted to leave unaccompanied, or have doors or gates that can be secured but in fact are left open.

In the definitional language in this dictionary **confinement facility** means a facility in which all or a large majority of the prisoners are not free to depart at any time, which is almost universally a feature of those facilities called "prisons," "jails," and "pre-arraignment lockups."

When "confinement" is used to characterize sentences or pretrial detention it is relatively unambiguous. Commitment to prison and detention in jail awaiting trial almost always entail confinement in the strictest sense of the word, that is, incarceration in a place with physical and custodial barriers to departure.

Note that "incarceration" is a near-synonym for "confinement," but usually has the specific meaning of confinement in a jail or prison, not confinement in a pre-arraignment lockup, hospital or other facility not intended for the serving of sentences.

See also **correctional facility (adult).**

consecutive sentence   *recommended statistical terminology*   A sentence that is one of two or more sentences imposed at the same time, after conviction for more than one offense, and which is served in sequence with the other sentences; or, a new sentence for a new conviction, imposed upon a person already under sentence(s) for a previous offense(s), which is added to a previous sentence(s), thus increasing the maximum time the offender may be confined or under supervision.

annotation

Consecutive sentences are served one after the other; concurrent sentences are served at the same time:

concurrent sentence   *recommended statistical terminology*   A sentence that is one of two or more sentences imposed at the same time after conviction for more than one offense and to be served at the same time; or, a new sentence imposed upon a person already under sentence(s) for a previous offense(s), to be served at the same time as one or more of the previous sentences.

A "multiple sentence" is two or more concurrent or consecutive sentences, or a combination of both types. It is possible for a person to be serving one of a set of consecutive sentences while also serving time on a concurrent sentence.

See also **maximum sentence.**

consolidated trial   see **trial**

conspiracy   see **inchoate offense**

consumer fraud   Deception of the public with respect to the cost, quality, purity, safety, durability, performance, effectiveness, dependability, availability and adequacy of choice relating to goods or services offered or furnished, and with respect to credit or other matters relating to terms of sales.

annotation

The above term, like **white-collar crime** (see entry), is not amenable to strict definition. Its chief use is as a generic term indicating the focus of crime prevention or law enforcement activities associated with consumer affairs agencies. Particular instances of "consumer fraud" are prosecuted as types of fraud designated in statutes under a variety of names.

This type of crime is also occasionally called "commercial crime," but see also **commercial crimes** for a different usage in National Crime Survey data.

contempt of court   Intentionally obstructing a court in the administration of justice, or acting in a way calculated to lessen its authority or dignity, or failing to obey its lawful orders.

annotation

Flight to avoid prosecution or to avoid confinement following conviction is usually prosecuted as contempt of court. See also **escape** for contrast.

A **criminal contempt** is an offense against the court. A fine or confinement can be imposed for the purpose of punishment.

A **civil contempt** is an offense against the party in whose behalf the mandate of the court was issued. A penalty of fine or confinement can be imposed. The purpose of the penalty is to enforce the court's original order, and the penalty can be avoided by compliance with that order.

Contempt offenses are also characterized as "direct contempt," when committed in the immediate presence of the court and "indirect contempt," usually representing failure or refusal to obey a lawful order, injunction, or decree of the court.

"Contempt of court" is included by name in **all other offenses UCR 26.**

contract parole   see **mutual agreement program**

contributing to the delinquency of a minor   The offense committed by an adult who in any manner causes, encourages or aids a juvenile to commit a crime or status offense.

annotation

The "status offense" will often consist of entering a place where liquor is served, a place where pornography is sold or displayed, a place of gambling, or a place of prostitution. In a few instances, if the unlawful behavior is sexual, a minor can be charged with contributing to the delinquency of another minor.

In UCR, this offense is included in **all other offenses UCR 26.**

conviction   *recommended statistical terminology*   The judgment of a court, based on the verdict of a jury or judicial officer, or on the guilty plea or nolo contendere plea of the defendant, that the defendant is guilty of the offense(s) with which he or she has been charged.

annotation

Acquittal is the other type of **judgment** in criminal proceedings (see entries).

"Conviction" is a major descriptive category in statistics concerning dispositions of cases or defendants in court proceedings. From the point of view of accounting for the results of court activity a conviction is a type of **court disposition** in that it indicates completion of an important stage of a case. However, from the defendant tracking perspective the sentencing disposition is the more final judicial disposition of a convicted person. See **defendant dispositions** for a classification of permanent and provisional exits of defendants from the adjudicatory process.

Where general comparisons between dispositions of defendants and related court caseload activity are needed, it is recommended that defendants convicted without trial, as the result of a guilty or nolo contendere plea be counted separately from defendants convicted at trial.

"Conviction" should not be used as a synonym for "guilty verdict" in statistical presentations, since a guilty verdict can be rejected by the court in its judgment, and thus need not result in a judgment of conviction. See **verdict**.

A **conviction rate** is the number of persons convicted, expressed as a percent of any of a variety of base populations, such as persons arrested or persons tried, or persons released from incarceration during a given time period.

In prosecution management statistics a conviction rate is the number of defendants convicted expressed as a percent of the number of defendants tried in a given court, or by a given agency or prosecutor, minus cases dismissed before trial. Some prosecutorial agencies calculate a **guilty rate**: the number of defendants convicted expressed as a percent of defendant cases filed in a given court, or by a given agency or prosecutor.

The recidivism rate of a correctional population is usually defined as the percent of persons released from incarceration or previously or currently under supervision who are convicted of a new offense within a given time period. See also **recidivism.**

coram nobis   see **writ**

correctional agency   *recommended statistical terminology*   A federal, state, or local criminal or juvenile justice agency, under a single administrative authority, of which the principal functions are the intake screening, supervision, custody, confinement, treatment, or pre-sentencing or predisposition investigation of alleged or adjudicated adult offenders, youthful offenders, delinquents, or status offenders.

annotation

In the statistical terminology recommended for **adult** and **youthful offender** services and facilities in this dictionary, correctional agency is a subtype of **criminal justice agency**. Subtypes of correctional agency include **probation agency, parole agency**, and agencies that administer **correctional facilities (adult)**.

The identification and classification of adult correctional agencies for statistical purposes requires numerous refinements and reporting conventions designed for specific data presentation purposes. The following conventions are recommended as standard national practice from which deviations should be indicated:

1. Private and military agencies are excluded.
2. Agencies of which the sole function is the care of dependent juveniles are excluded.
3. A correctional agency that administers more than one correctional facility is counted as a single agency.

4. All administratively separate agencies are classified and counted separately. This applies even if they perform only one function. Thus a paroling authority detached from the agency that administers parole supervision is a separate agency.

5. For summary statistics, when classifying agencies by specific function, the same agency may be counted more than once. Thus a given probation agency having a broad range of responsibilities could be counted once under adult probation agencies, a second time under juvenile probation agencies, and a third time under **intake** units. A **sheriff's department** could be counted as both a **law enforcement agency** and a correctional agency, depending upon the purpose of the presentation.

6. Compound names should be used in statistical publications for single agencies which perform functions often assigned to two agencies, for example "adult probation/parole agency."

In national Bureau of Justice Statistics publications on correctional agency characteristics each administrative unit serving a discrete geographical area is counted as a separate agency. Thus, for example, a state level parole agency with 10 separate service offices in 10 separate geographical jurisdictions is counted as 10 agencies (or could be counted as 11 agencies if there is a central administration which is separate from the district offices).

correctional day program   *recommended statistical terminology*   A

publicly financed and operated nonresidential educational or treatment program for persons required by a judicial officer to participate.

annotation

This term is provided to account for the dispositions of persons who are not committed to a correctional facility, but who are required by a court to attend a day program designed for a correctional purpose. When such a category is needed for data presentations, it should include all government programs specifically intended for a correctional clientele, whether or not the program is conducted in publicly or privately owned premises.

correctional facility (adult)   *recommended statistical terminology*   A

building or part thereof, set of buildings, or area enclosing a set of buildings or structures, operated by a government agency for the physical custody, or custody and treatment, of sentenced persons or persons subject to criminal proceedings.

annotation

Although this term is used in some official contexts to represent only confinement facilities for committed offenders, such as prisons and other "correctional institutions," it is here proposed as the generic name for all government facilities in which alleged or adjudicated adult offenders are confined (full-time physical custody) or reside (occupation at night).

The adult facility classification structure and descriptors recommended in the first edition of this dictionary have not been substantively changed. Nomenclature has been changed, and **juvenile facility** terminology is dealt with separately (see that entry).

There continues to be a lack of consensus on correctional facility nomenclature, but publications concerning prisoners in adult facilities do continue to utilize, explicitly or implicitly, the same distinguishing features for classification. Standard descriptors are therefore again recommended for the characterization of adult correctional facilities:

primary attributes	descriptors
A. intended age group	1. adult
	2. youthful offender
B. type of custody	1. confinement
	2. residential
C. reason for custody	1. detention pending adjudication or sentencing
	2. commitment by sentence
	3. diagnostic commitment
	4. voluntary referral (subject accepts referral to residential facility by agency or court)
D. upper limit of custodial authority	1. limited to 48 hours or until first court session after arrest
	2. not limited to 48 hours
E. level of government administering facility	1. federal
	2. state
	3. local
F. sex	1. male
	2. female
G. number of inmates or residents	• average daily population

Notes on descriptors:

Adult vs. **youthful offender.** "Adult" in this context means one whose age is such that he or she can be prosecuted for committing a crime. "Youthful offender" means one who has been put in a special facility or program because his or her age is between the limits specified in a statute providing such dispositions for young adults. See also individual entries.

Confinement vs. **residential.** "Confinement" in this context means 24 hour physical restriction of all or most of the facility population to a clearly defined area from which they are forbidden to depart, cannot easily depart because of physical barriers and/or guards, and do not lawfully depart without being in the custody of an official. (Some confinement facilities send selected prisoners out on work furloughs or study releases. See **full-time temporary release.**) "Residential" means that the facility population occupies the premises at night (with or without restriction) and is obliged to do so, but is authorized to leave the facility regularly or frequently during the day. See also **confinement.**

Detention, commitment, diagnostic commitment. "Detention" here means confinement or residential custody pending adjudication or sentencing. "Commitment" means confinement or residential custody resulting from a sentence. "Diagnostic commitment" means confinement for observation and study pending judgment or sentencing. See also individual entries.

Note that the descriptors "detention" and "commitment" which together with level of government administration are used to define the class "jails," can be employed to further subdivide jails into those that hold both detained and committed (sentenced) persons, and those, such as county farms, camps and the like, that hold only committed persons.

Voluntary referrals are technically not in custody, but the descriptor is needed to account for the judicial status of all persons in residential (community) facilities.

Custodial authority **limited to 48 hours or first court session** vs. custodial authority **not limited to 48 hours**. This distinction, characterizing facilities by upper limit of authority, separates those facilities used only for very short term detention from those used for longer term detention and for confinement of sentenced offenders. No other distinctions on the basis of limit of custodial authority are provided here. While it would be extremely useful for some purposes to be able to further subdivide correctional facilities on this basis, such a division is not at this time feasible for national level data.

The traditional distinction between facilities authorized to hold persons sentenced to a year or less and those authorized to hold persons for more than a year is operable and useful only within states. Even at the state level there are several substantial exceptions to this rule, as in Massachusetts, where all facilities serving the jail function are authorized to hold persons with sentences greater than one year. In many other states where the distinction is generally operative, there are one or two facilities with authority to hold people for somewhat longer periods. The national level statistical practice therefore divides facilities into prisons and jails in accord with level of government, classifying state administered facilities as "prisons," and locally administered facilities as "jails." There are five jurisdictions (Delaware, Connecticut, Vermont, Rhode Island and Hawaii) in which all adult confinement facilities are administered at the state level. In current national level classifications, these jurisdictions are not considered to have any jails.

For definitions of **state** vs. **local** level of government, see **level of government**.

It is recommended that these standard descriptors be used to describe and classify public correctional facilities in interstate and national exchange of statistical information intended for general users. The descriptors are intended to serve as the basic elements of official facility class names and definitions, and also as the focus of further distinctions and reporting conventions. One or more of the descriptors for each attribute may pertain to a given facility, such as male/female, or detention/commitment. Proportions of, for example, inmates or residents characterized by type of custody or reason for custody may also characterize facilities, that is, determine the place of a facility in a given classification scheme. These kinds of problems cannot be resolved by universally applied rules. Reporting convention decisions should be explained in each publication.

It is important to note that this approach separates the more resolvable problem of establishing classification features, that is, descriptors, from the very difficult problem of finding acceptable, unambiguous and convenient short names for types of correctional facilities. Whether a given facility is for convenience called a "prison," or a "correctional institution," is not important as long as official communications use the basic standard descriptors, in addition to short names, when describing and classifying facilities.

There are a number of other correctional facility attributes that are sometimes considered basic. These include security level, location, available rehabilitation programs, drug involvement, actual or prescribed length of stay, age distribution, and probation or parole status of the residents in non-confinement facilities. These are treated as secondary because of the difficulty of establishing names and category definitions consistently and reliably applicable to all jurisdictions. It is recommended that data presentations employing descriptors for these attributes as classification features be accompanied by explicit definitions of their meaning in the jurisdiction(s) originating the data.

A general purpose classification scheme is offered below, utilizing attributes (A) through (D).

Adult correctional facility general purpose classification:

name	descriptors
prison common names: prison, penitentiary, correctional institution, federal or state correctional facility, conservation camp	• adult • confinement • committed (sentenced) • state government administration • custodial authority of facility not limited to a maximum of 48 hour detention
jail common names: jail, county farm, honor farm, work camp, road camp	• adult • confinement • adults detained pending adjudication or sentencing and/or committed adults • local government administration • custodial authority of facility not limited to a maximum of 48 hour detention
lockup (prearraignment lockup)	• adult or juvenile • confinement • persons detained pending pretrial release consideration, return to another jurisdiction, other immediate disposition • custodial authority of facility limited to 48 hour detention or until first court session after arrest
residential facility other names: community facility, halfway house, residential treatment center	• adult • residential • adults detained pending adjudication (including judgment withheld) and committed (sentenced) adults

correctional facility (juvenile)   see **juvenile facility**

corrections   A generic term which includes all government agencies, facilities, programs, procedures, personnel, and techniques concerned with the intake, custody, confinement, supervision, or treatment, or pre-sentencing or pre-disposition investigation of alleged or adjudicated adult offenders, delinquents, or status offenders.

annotation

See Appendix A for lists of classificatory terms relating to corrections agencies, personnel and processes.

counsel   see attorney

count   see charge

count (prisoner)   I.   In published summary data, usually the number of inmates present in a given facility or facility system on a regular, specified day of the year, quarter or month.   II.   In management usage, the daily, weekly, or other periodic tally of inmates present in a particular facility.

annotation

In accordance with some reporting conventions the prisoner "count" may include persons who are in hospital, or otherwise temporarily absent from the facility with official reason and approval. In NPS counts of prison populations, prisoners under the jurisdiction of a given state correctional facility system are counted as inmates in that system even if they are permanently housed (in physical custody) in a prison in another state. See **custody** for further information.

counterfeiting   The manufacture or attempted manufacture of a copy or imitation of a negotiable instrument with value set by law or convention, or the possession of such a copy without authorization, with the intent to defraud by claiming the genuineness of the copy.

annotation

See **fraud offenses** for general statistical recommendation. See also **forgery and counterfeiting UCR 10.**

In statutes counterfeiting is included within the definition of forgery. Where a distinction is made, it rests on the fact that a counterfeiting presupposes the prior existence of an officially issued item of value which provides a model for the perpetrator. Examples include currency, coins, postage stamps, ration stamps, food stamps, bearer bonds, etc. This kind of model is absent in a forgery.

court   *recommended statistical terminology*   An agency or unit of the judicial branch of government, authorized or established by statute or constitution, and consisting of one or more judicial officers, which has the authority to decide upon cases, controversies in law, and disputed matters of fact brought before it.

annotation

"Court," "judge," and "bench" are used interchangeably in many contexts; often "the court" should be read as "the judge" or "the judicial officer."

In statistical reporting, the unit considered to be a single "court" is usually an administrative unit having a statutorily specified geographical jurisdiction (often coinciding with a political subdivision of a state, such as a county) and a statutorily specified subject matter jurisdiction. See **jurisdiction**.

There are two basic types of courts: those having original jurisdiction to make decisions regarding matters of fact and law, and those having appellate jurisdiction to review issues of law in connection with decisions made in specific cases previously adjudicated by other courts and decisions made by administrative agencies. However, individual courts are frequently authorized to exercise both original and appellate jurisdiction, depending upon the subject matter of individual cases. For statistical purposes, these courts are classified according to their primary function; as trial courts if they primarily hear cases from the beginning, and as appellate courts if they primarily perform appellate reviews of court or administrative agency decisions.

In most states there are two levels of trial court: those with limited (special) jurisdiction and those with general jurisdiction. In about half of the states there are two levels of appellate court: intermediate appellate courts and courts of last resort. Whether a given court deals with criminal cases only depends upon the structure of the court system of a given state; overall, most courts handle both civil and criminal matters.

trial court   *recommended statistical terminology*   A court of which the primary function is to hear and decide cases.

court of limited (special) jurisdiction   *recommended statistical terminology*   A trial court having original jurisdiction over only that subject matter specifically assigned to it by law. (Limited jurisdiction courts go by such names as "municipal court," "justice court," "magistrate court," "family court," "probate court," and "traffic court.")

court of general jurisdiction   *recommended statistical terminology*   A trial court having original jurisdiction over all subject matter not specifically assigned to a court of limited jurisdiction. Courts of general trial jurisdiction frequently also are given jurisdiction over certain kinds of appeal matters. (These courts are usually called "superior courts," "district courts" or "circuit courts.")

Note that the actual contrast between the two types of trial courts for national data reporting purposes is between courts having precisely limited, narrow jurisdiction and courts having nearly unlimited jurisdiction. (Within a given state the range of authority of each court is, of course, exactly defined.)

In describing criminal proceedings the difference between limited and general jurisdiction is important. In most states there is a limited jurisdiction court (or "lower" court) with authority to try misdemeanor cases and, sometimes, felonies with penalties below a certain limit, and to conduct pretrial proceedings in felony cases generally, including the initial setting of **bail** and the **preliminary hearing** (probable cause determination). The general jurisdiction court (or "higher" court) has jurisdiction over all felony trial matters and hears appeals of limited jurisdiction court case judgments or decisions.

appellate court   *recommended statistical terminology*   A court of which the primary function is to review the judgments of other courts and of administrative agencies.

intermediate appellate court   *recommended statistical terminology*
An appellate court of which the primary function is to review the judgments
of trial courts and the decisions of administrative agencies, and whose decisions are in turn usually reviewable by a higher appellate court in the same
state.

court of last resort   *recommended statistical terminology*   An appellate court having final jurisdiction over appeals within a given state.

The division of authority between the two kinds of appellate courts differs
slightly from state to state. The subject matter jurisdiction of intermediate
appellate courts may be specified by law, or may be determined by the court
of last resort.

Although the court of last resort has final jurisdiction over appeals within a
given state judicial system, issues of law may exist in some cases that permit
subsequent appeal to a federal court.

A classification of courts utilizing the extent of felony jurisdiction and other
distinguishing features significant to the understanding of criminal case procedure or steps and dispositions (though not effective as a court caseload
reporting classification) is as follows:

court of limited jurisdiction ("lower court")

1. no felony trial jurisdiction, or trial jurisdiction limited to less than all
   felonies
2. may or may not hear appeals
3. not necessarily a court of record

court of general jurisdiction ("higher" or "superior court")

1. trial jurisdiction over all felonies
2. may or may not hear appeals
3. court of record

appellate court

1. no criminal trial jurisdiction
2. hears appeals
3. court of record

For detailed information on current court classification and statistical reporting conventions see the Bureau of Justice Statistics series *Expenditure
and Employment Data for the Criminal Justice System.*

court administrator   The official responsible for supervising and performing administrative tasks for a given court(s).

annotation

The duties of a court administrator depend upon the size of the court. They
may include assisting the **presiding judge** in administrative duties; other personnel, budget and administrative tasks; and statistical reporting. In some
small courts, the court administrator also performs some of the duties of a
court clerk, such as assigning case numbers, notifying all parties in a case of
dates of court hearings, and assigning cases to the court calendar.

Courts which have a court administrator usually do not also have an **administrative judge.**

court calendar   The court schedule; the list of events comprising the daily or weekly work of a court, including the assignment of the time and place for each hearing or other item of business, or the list of matters which will be taken up in a given court term.

annotation

To "calendar" a case is to place it upon the court schedule.

Some data systems have a category of court case dispositions called **off-calendar,** meaning all those cases which have not reached judgment or other definite conclusion such as dismissal, but for other reasons (both within and without the control of the court) cannot be scheduled.

A word which is sometimes used in place of "calendar" is "docket," but this term has a different range of meaning: A **docket,** in the basic usage, is a brief record of all the important court actions in a case from its beginning to its conclusion.

court case   see **case**

court caseload inventory   see **caseload (court)**

court clerk   *syn*   **clerk of the court**   An elected or appointed court officer responsible for maintaining the written records of the court and for supervising or performing the clerical tasks necessary for conducting judicial business; also, any employee of a court whose principal duties are to assist the court clerk in performing the clerical tasks necessary for conducting judicial business.

annotation

The typical duties of a court clerk are receiving documents to be filed in the court record, assigning case numbers, scheduling cases on the court calendar, entering judgments and orders in the court record, preparing writs and warrants, and keeping the court records and seal.

court decision   In popular usage, any official determination made by a judicial officer; in special judicial usages, any of several specific kinds of determinations made by particular courts.

annotation

An example of a more limited meaning is the usage of "decisions" to indicate determinations made by appellate courts, as opposed to those made by trial courts.

When "decision" is used in the broadest sense it may refer to a judgment, decree, or finding, and occasionally a court order or opinion, all of which normally have distinctive meanings in official usage:

judgment   The judicial determination or sentence of a court upon a matter within its jurisdiction; the final conclusion of a court as to matters of fact and law. In criminal proceedings, the judicial determination of guilt or nonguilt. See **judgment.**

decree   The sentence or order of the court in civil proceedings making a determination about the issues of fact and law in a case and stating the relative duties and rights of the concerned parties, also called a "judgment" in some usages.

finding   Commonly, a decision by a judicial officer or a jury as to a matter of fact; occasionally used to mean a decision by a judicial officer as to a matter of law, that is, a "judgment."

court order   A mandate, command, or direction issued by a judicial officer or a court, specifying actions to be taken to implement a judgment.

opinion   The statement by a court or judicial officer of the final decision made in a matter before the court and the reasons for the decision. See **opinion.**

court disposition   For statistical reporting purposes, generally, the judicial decision terminating proceedings in a case before judgment is reached, or the judgment; the data items representing the outcome of judicial proceedings and the manner in which the outcome was arrived at.

annotation

"Court disposition" can in criminal justice contexts mean either the immediate result of prosecution (conviction, acquittal or dismissal) or the final result in the sense of sentencing disposition when the judgment is conviction. See **defendant dispositions** for recommended terminology for criminal justice purposes, including a categorization of sentencing dispositions.

Current summary state level court activity statistics describe dispositions with respect to both final outcome of court activity and the type of process which led to the outcome in cases that went to trial. There is variation in the level of detail offered and some terminological variation but the major categories in criminal proceedings are almost always:

> jury trial
> > conviction
> > acquittal
> nonjury trial
> > conviction
> > acquittal
> dismissal/nolle prosequi
> guilty plea
> other disposition

A model court caseload statistical system has recently been developed by the National Court Statistics Project, under Bureau of Justice Statistics sponsorship. The model provides an extensive recommended classification scheme for statistical presentation of trial court case and defendant disposition data, grouped under the heading "manner of disposition, trial court case." The portion of the recommended classification concerning criminal case manner of disposition is:

criminal manner of disposition

> jury trial (number of cases in which a jury trial was begun)
> > conviction (number of defendants in cases where jury trial was begun)
> > > guilty plea (number of defendants convicted on guilty plea after jury trial was begun)
> > acquittal (number of defendants not convicted where jury trial was begun)
> > dismissed (number of defendants disposed of by dismissal of charges after jury trial was begun)

non-jury trial (number of cases in which non-jury trial was begun)
   conviction (number of defendants, as above)
     guilty plea (number of defendants, as above)
    acquittal (number of defendants, as above)
     dismissed (number of defendants, as above)
dismissed/nolle prosequi (number of defendants, where dismissal or nolle occurred before any trial was begun)
bound over (number of defendants, felony preliminaries)
transferred (number of defendants)
guilty pleas (number of defendants convicted on guilty plea before any trial was begun)
bail forfeiture (number of defendants)
other manner of disposition (number of defendants)

In this model classification, as in most state and local court activity statistics, a primary focus is on the method by which cases and defendants are disposed, since the different types of judicial processes have different impacts on the time and resources needed to reach a disposition. The case and defendant disposition counts of the model system are independent and will not sum, both because there may be more than one defendant in a case and because defendants in multiple-defendant cases are counted when they are disposed of, even if the case as a whole has not reached a disposition.

A term list outline of the complete model classification scheme for general court caseload inventory and for case and defendant manner of disposition is presented in Appendix E of this volume.

court of general jurisdiction   see **court**

court of last resort   see **court**

court of limited jurisdiction   see **court**

court of record   A court in which a complete and permanent record of all proceedings or specified types of proceedings is kept.

annotation

Felony trial courts are courts of record. Trial proceedings are supposed to be recorded verbatim. The record, usually in the form of a stenotype or shorthand representation of what has been said and done, but sometimes stored on audiotape, is not necessarily transcribed. The court reporter may store such material in the original form and it will not be converted into a typed transcript unless the record pertaining to a case is requested.

See **court** for recommendations concerning classification of courts.

court order   A mandate, command, or direction issued by a judicial officer in the exercise of his judicial authority.

annotation

A court order is sometimes viewed as a **judgment,** but it is rather the mechanism by which the court, having reached conclusions as to matters of fact and law in a controversy, directs that the actions implementing the judgment occur. Writs and injunctions are orders. See **writ.** See also **court decision.**

court order release from prison   *recommended statistical terminology*   A provisional exit by judicial authority from a prison facility system of a prisoner who has not served his or her full sentence, whose freedom is conditioned upon an appeal, a special writ, or other special legal proceedings.

annotation

This data item in prison/parole population movement statistics does not represent nonprovisional exits resulting from judicial action, such as court ordered reduced sentences and court administered probation after imprisonment (see **split sentence**). A court ordered reduced sentence is a final exit from a state prison system. Court administered probation also removes the subject from the state correctional population.

See **prison/parole population movement** for the use of this category in a model data structure.

court probation   *recommended statistical terminology*   A criminal court requirement that a defendant or offender fulfill specified conditions of behavior in lieu of a sentence to confinement, but without assignment to a probation agency's supervisory caseload.

annotation

This type of **grant of probation** (see entry) is variously called "unsupervised probation," "summary probation," or "informal probation." These terms are also used with other meanings in some jurisdictions.

In this terminology, court probation is a type of **defendant disposition**.

Court probation is used as a sentencing disposition by some courts to avoid unnecessary supervisory activity and expense in appropriate cases. Court probation does not, however, amount to an unconditional release. As in all instances of grants of probation, the court retains jurisdiction over the case, and probation status can be revoked. The typical probation violation that will cause the court to reconsider probationary status and sentence the person to confinement is re-appearance in court charged with a new offense, or a new conviction.

For statistical purposes cases directly and solely under judicial control should be distinguished from those registered in probation agency files as part of the caseload for which they are responsible. The former are not part of **probation supervisory caseload** or population movement. Although supervision by a judge might be said to be "inactive," this term should be reserved to mean "inactive supervision" by a probationary agency. See **supervised probation**.

See also **suspended sentence** for a term used with the same or with contrasting meaning.

This terminology is not recommended for juvenile case data, where the disposition alternatives are more complex. Probation suspension of juveniles is frequently performed by an officer of the juvenile court, rather than by a probation agency or separate probation subunit within the court system.

court reporter   A person present during judicial proceedings, who records all testimony and other oral statements made during the proceedings.

annotation

Court reporters are usually present in the courtroom during court sessions. They may also be present during other judicial proceedings held outside the courtroom, e.g., in the judge's chambers.

In some jurisdictions, court reporters are also responsible for exhibits introduced into evidence during a trial.

Some jurisdictions use audio recording and transcription by a typing pool instead of court reporters.

courtesy supervision   Supervision by the correctional agency of one jurisdiction, of a person placed on probation by a court or on parole by a paroling authority in another jurisdiction, by informal agreement between agencies.

annotation

Courtesy supervision occurs when a receiving agency agrees to supervise a probationer or parolee through arrangements made without reference to statutory or administratively promulgated rules (such as **interstate compacts**) for the exchange of supervisees.

The kind of case handled in this fashion is usually one where the offense is not grave, and the practical and rehabilitative needs of the probationer or parolee are best served by residence in a jurisdiction other than the one where adjudication occurred.

These informal exchanges are often at the local level, as between one county and another. Local exchanges can also be the subject of regular, formal agreements.

See also **supervised probation, parole supervision** and **interstate compact.**

credit card fraud   The use or attempted use of a credit card in order to obtain goods or services with the intent to avoid payment.

annotation

In UCR arrest reporting credit card fraud is classified as **fraud UCR 11**. See **fraud offenses** for general statistical recommendation.

This category is used in some statistical presentations because of the frequency and impact of this type of criminal behavior. However, credit card fraud is rarely codified as such in statutes, the offense being covered by the broadly defined fraud type offenses.

The unlawful acquisition of a credit card is a **theft** type crime (see entry). Unlawful manufacture is **forgery** (see entry).

crime   *syn*   **criminal offense**   *recommended statistical terminology*
An act committed or omitted in violation of a law forbidding or commanding it for which the possible penalties for an adult upon conviction include incarceration, for which a corporation can be penalized by fine or forfeit, or for which a juvenile can be adjudged delinquent or transferred to criminal court for prosecution.

defining features

act specifically prohibited by law, or

failure to perform an act specifically required by law

adult punishable upon conviction by one or more of several penalties, including incarceration, or

corporation punishable by a fine or forfeitures, or

juvenile subject to adjudication for a delinquent act

annotation

The basic legal definition of crime is all punishable acts, whatever the nature of the penalty.

However, the above definition limits "crime" to those actions for which incarceration is a possible penalty. This is in keeping with the usual practice in crime statistics, where, for example, traffic offenses for which the only penalties are fines or loss of driving privileges are not included.

Some penal codes explicitly define a class of very minor offenses, usually called **infractions** (see entry), "violations" or "petty offenses," or designated as the most minor type of misdemeanor, for which no imprisonment or only a very brief period of imprisonment is a possible penalty. This type of distinction assists in arriving at comparable crime data among different jurisdictions, but not being universally applied does not guarantee consistency.

In most jurisdictions felonies and misdemeanors are the two major classes of crimes. However, there is enough inconsistency to create problems in national level crime data. See **felony** for more information about statistical reporting.

Delinquent acts, which can be reported as such when the age of the suspect or perpetrator is known, are technically not "crimes" from some points of view because juveniles cannot ordinarily be prosecuted in a criminal court. See **delinquency**. Nevertheless, the usual reporting convention for law enforcement crime counts is to classify acts committed by juveniles according to standard crime type, without regard to the age/status of the perpetrator.

It should be noted that in some contexts the meaning of "offense" is not clear. This word, in the broadest legal usage, means crimes, delinquent acts, status offenses, infractions, and the like, and also civil (private) wrongs or injuries, and faults.

Crime Index   *syn*   Index of Crime   In Uniform Crime Reports terminology, a set of numbers indicating the volume, fluctuation and distribution of crimes reported to local law enforcement agencies, for the United States as a whole and for its geographical subdivisions, based on counts of reported occurrences of UCR Index Crimes.

annotation

The UCR Index Crimes are **murder and nonnegligent manslaughter UCR 1a, forcible rape UCR 2, robbery UCR 3, aggravated assault UCR 4a–d, burglary UCR 5, larceny-theft UCR 6, motor vehicle theft UCR 7,** and **arson UCR 8**. See entries for definitions of individual offense terms.

All of the UCR Part I Offenses, with the exception of **negligent manslaughter UCR 1b** (involuntary manslaughter) are Index Crimes. Negligent manslaughter is the only Part I Offense not having the feature of specific criminal intent. See **Part I Offenses.**

In the national UCR annual publication *Crime in the United States,* Index Crime data are presented in the form of numbers, rates, or percentage changes in relation to areas, population and periods of time. Crime rates are presented separately for total Index Crimes, for the subcategories "crimes of violence," and "crimes against property," and for the individual offenses in the set. The subcategories are composed of:

crimes of violence	**crimes against property**
syn **violent crime**	*syn* **property crime**
murder and nonnegligent (voluntary) manslaughter	burglary larceny-theft
forcible rape	motor vehicle theft
robbery	arson (as of 1979);
aggravated assault	see entry for conventions

In national UCR reports the **crime rate** is the number of Crime Index offenses known to police, per 100,000 population.

In some state-level UCR publications, crime rates are based on a different population unit, typically 1,000 persons.

crime rate   see **Crime Index**

crimes against property   see **Crime Index**

crime score   A number assigned from an established scale, signifying the seriousness of a given offense with respect to personal injury or damage to property.

annotation

Crime scores and defendant scores are primarily used by prosecutorial agencies in selecting cases which need particularly intensive pretrial preparation, and in assuring similar treatment of cases having similar scores.

A **defendant score** is a number assigned from an established scale, signifying the seriousness of the prior criminal history of the alleged offender.

Defendant scores are calculated on such bases as the number of prior arrests and convictions and the type of offense.

crimes of violence   see **Crime Index**

criminal case   *recommended statistical terminology*   A case initiated in a court by the filing of a single charging document containing one or more criminal accusations against one or more identified persons.

annotation

The choice between the "criminal case," as defined above, and the defendant as the fundamental unit of activity is the basic reporting convention decision in describing court criminal caseload activity. The above recommendation, that the **charging document (complaint, information,** or **indictment)** be used as the basic unit of count for criminal cases is in accord with existing usage in the majority of states regarding court caseload data. It also reflects the usage of the model court caseload statistical system developed by the National Court Statistics Project under Bureau of Justice Statistics sponsorship, where "criminal case" is a major category within trial court caseload. A term list outline of the complete model classification scheme is presented in Appendix E of this volume.

Where the purposes of data presentations include the linking of court filings and/or dispositions to dispositions of persons arrested or detained, or those placed under correctional supervision or committed to confinement, there is a need for court activity data utilizing the defendant as the unit of count, since the person is the unit underlying the data for comparison.

See **defendant dispositions** for a data structure linking court data to corrections data.

criminal contempt   see **contempt of court**

criminal homicide   *recommended statistical terminology*   The causing of the death of another person without legal justification or excuse.

annotation

"Criminal homicide" is a summary category, not a single codified offense. The term, in law, embraces all homicides where the perpetrator is found to have intentionally killed someone without legal justification, or to have accidentally killed someone as a consequence of reckless or grossly negligent conduct. For UCR usage for police level reporting see **criminal homicide UCR 1.**

The following classification structure and terminology is proposed for use in reporting offense data at prosecution, courts and corrections levels where more detail on the type of homicide is available than at the law enforcement reporting level. The offense names and definitions reflect the most common usage and the traditional basic distinctions. See Appendix B for problems in national crime classification and complete set of tentatively proposed national categories for post-arrest offense statistics.

defining features *of recommended national categories and tentatively recommended subcategories*

criminal willful homicide   (equivalent to UCR category 1a, murder and nonnegligent manslaughter)

intentionally causing the death of another person

without legal justification

or

causing the death of another

while committing or attempting to commit another crime

    murder   (UCR term is "murder")

    intentionally causing the death of another person

    without extreme provocation or legal justification

    or

    causing the death of another

    while committing or attempting to commit another crime

voluntary manslaughter   (UCR term is "nonnegligent manslaughter")
intentionally causing the death of another

with provocation that a reasonable person would find extreme

without legal justification

involuntary manslaughter   (UCR term is "negligent manslaughter" or "manslaughter by negligence")

causing the death of another person

without intent to cause death

with recklessness or gross negligence, including by reckless or grossly negligent operation of a motor vehicle

UCR collects and publishes data on negligent (involuntary) manslaughter in its reported crime totals, but excludes vehicular negligent manslaughter from published reported crime data and excludes the entire category from **Crime Index** tabulations. Arrests on vehicular manslaughter charges, however, are included under "negligent manslaughter" in UCR arrest tabulations.

Vehicular manslaughter, causing the death of another by grossly negligent operation of a motor vehicle, is a distinguishable type of involuntary manslaughter in some penal codes, and is often a separate category in statistical presentations.

Classificatory terminology in the area of criminal homicide presents many problems.

"Homicide" which means any killing of one person by another, is often used in statistical publications when **criminal homicide** is meant.

"Willful homicide," which means the intentional causing of the death of another person, with or without legal justification, is often used when **criminal willful homicide** is meant: The legal term "willful" embraces murder and voluntary manslaughter, both of which are criminal, and justifiable homicide, which is not criminal. (The logically contrasting type of homicide, "unintentional," includes both involuntary manslaughter, which is criminal, and those entirely accidental homicides which lack any element of gross or criminal negligence, and are thus noncriminal.)

In state statutes the names and content of the subclasses of criminal homicide vary, and the elements of the offense pertaining to **culpability** are variously defined.

Most, though not all, state codes contain a statutory provision such that the killing of another person while the perpetrator is committing or attempting to commit another crime constitutes an offense of murder. In some of these states the killing of another while committing or attempting any crime constitutes murder. In others the commission or attempt of a felony, or one of a named subset of all felonies is necessary to constitute murder. In still other states there is, in addition to a "felony murder" provision, a provision making killing pursuant to a misdemeanor an offense of manslaughter.

Two terms that refer only to homicides which are not crimes, and which appear in statutes and elsewhere indicating defenses to charges of criminal homicide, are:

excusable homicide   The intentional but justifiable causing of the death of another, or the unintentional causing of the death of another by accident or misadventure, without gross negligence.

justifiable homicide   The intentional causing of the death of another in the legal performance of an official duty or in circumstances defined by law as constituting legal justification.

criminal homicide   UCR 1   In Uniform Crime Reports terminology, the name of the UCR category which includes and is limited to all offenses of causing the death of another person without justification or excuse.

annotation

See **criminal homicide** for discussion of problems in this area of terminology and recommended terminology for prosecution, courts and corrections levels offense statistics.

In UCR data reporting and in UCR publications, criminal homicide is subdivided as follows:

murder and nonnegligent manslaughter (criminal willful homicide) UCR 1a

manslaughter by negligence (involuntary manslaughter)   UCR 1b

In UCR statistics, 1a and 1b together constitute the **Part I offense**, "criminal homicide," but 1b is not a **Crime Index** offense.

See **murder and nonnegligent manslaughter UCR 1a**, and **negligent manslaughter UCR 1b** for definitions.

criminal incident   In National Crime Survey terminology, a criminal event involving one or more victims and one or more offenders.

annotation

In NCS terminology a critical distinction is made between a "criminal incident" and a "victimization." The procedures by which data are compiled relating to these two units of count differ significantly. Only one "criminal incident" is recorded for any continuous sequence of criminal behavior, even though it may contain acts which constitute two or more NCS offenses or involve two or more distinct victims. But one "victimization" is recorded for each distinct person or household harmed as a result of a given criminal incident. Thus, for example, an incident in which two persons were robbed will be recorded as one "criminal incident" of "personal robbery," but two "victimizations." See **victimization** for further discussion.

The NCS offense categories have many subsets and sub-subsets. For these classification structures see the entries for the major categories: **personal crimes** and **household crimes**.

See also **NCS**.

criminal justice   In the strictest sense, the criminal (penal) law, the law of criminal procedure, and that array of procedures and activities having to do with the enforcement of this body of law.

annotation

The federal Crime Control Act of 1973 defines this term as part of a longer phrase, as follows: " 'Law enforcement and criminal justice' means any activity pertaining to crime prevention, control or reduction or the enforcement of the criminal law, including, but not limited to police efforts to prevent, control, or reduce crime or to apprehend criminals, activities of courts having criminal jurisdiction and related agencies (including prosecutorial and defender services), activities of corrections, probation, or parole authorities, and programs relating to the prevention, control, or reduction of juvenile delinquency or narcotic addiction.''

This statutory definition is designed to fit the needs of the federal program of assistance to state and local justice agencies. It extends the scope of meaning of the term to include activities not directly related to law enforcement, yet also attempting to reduce crime, such as educational or rehabilitative programs intended to favorably alter the personal or social characteristics of particular persons.

The "administration of criminal justice" is the performing of "criminal justice functions," that is, required criminal justice activities. See **criminal justice agency**, definition (II) for an official definition of the "administration of criminal justice," and definition (I) for a model list of "criminal justice functions."

The "criminal justice system" is, in ordinary usage, the aggregate of all operating and administrative or technical support agencies that perform criminal justice functions. However, different governmental or research purposes require different definitions of this "system." The basic divisions of the operational aspect of criminal justice are **law enforcement, courts** and **corrections**. See entries.

The basic difference between criminal law and civil law is that the former establishes penalties, usually fines or deprivation of liberty, for behavior that is thought to injure society ("crimes"); the latter provides principles and methods for resolving disputes between private or corporate persons ("private wrongs"). Also, in criminal proceedings a higher standard of proof is required to decide guilt, that is, responsibility. The distinction is not perfect: "Punitive damages," for example, can be awarded in a civil case, but this does occur within a different rationale.

criminal justice agency   *the first of the following definitions is a model indicating the necessary general components of any description of this class of agencies and the usage of the term in this dictionary. The other two describe current official usages.*

I.   *model definition*   Any court with criminal jurisdiction and any government agency or identifiable subunit which defends indigents, or which has as its principal duty(s) the performance of criminal justice functions (prevention, detection, and investigation of crime; the apprehension, detention and prosecution of alleged offenders; the confinement or official correctional supervision of accused or convicted persons, or the administrative or technical support of these functions) as authorized and required by statute or executive order.

The above model definition, which for the sake of clarity limits the scope of the class, "criminal justice agencies," to those agencies which primarily perform major criminal justice duties, sets forth the meaning of this term when used elsewhere in this dictionary. Overall, it is narrower than any national official definition.

The feature "authorized and required . . ." is included to distinguish government agencies, which are required to perform duties, from private agencies, which are only permitted to perform criminal justice functions.

The five major subclasses of criminal justice agencies as defined for use in this dictionary are **law enforcement agency, prosecution agency, public**

defender agency, court, and **correctional agency.** Excluded are all non-government entities, such as private agencies maintaining rehabilitation programs, or private security forces; agencies of which the jurisdiction is limited solely to juveniles; and government agencies of which the law enforcement activities are incidental to their major activities, such as forestry or fish and game departments and port authorities. However, special law enforcement sub-units of non-law enforcement agencies are included. Any administratively separate information system or identifiable subunit thereof of which the principal function is to provide technical support for operating criminal justice agencies is included. Any publicly administered office or legal aid clinic which defends indigents is included.

Statistical publications should indicate whether the model definition, or any of the several official alternatives, or a uniquely necessary definition is being used in the publication. In many cases it is also necessary to further specify what is meant by "government agency or subunit," "principal duty (or function)," and "criminal justice (or justice) functions." It is also necessary to indicate whether criminal justice agencies which operate more than one facility or operate at more than one location are counted as a single agency or whether each facility or location is counted separately.

See the entries **private security agency** and **private rehabilitation agency** for further information.

II. *Bureau of Justice Statistics (BJS) "Justice Agencies in the United States" (definition of "criminal and civil justice agency")*   "All courts, civil attorney agencies and any other governmental agency or subunit that defends indigents or of which the principal functions or activities consist of the prevention, detection, and investigation of crime; the apprehension, detention, and prosecution of alleged offenders; the confinement or official correction supervision of accused or convicted persons; or the administrative or technical support of the above functions."

The agency survey covers, in addition to criminal justice agencies, all courts and certain other agencies such as those providing legal services to governments because such agencies frequently have mixed jurisdiction and cannot consistently provide separate budget, manpower, and caseload data for civil vs. criminal and juvenile vs. adult functions.

III. *BJS series, "Expenditure and Employment Data for the Criminal Justice System"*   In this series the focus is on the collection of cost data concerning criminal and civil justice functions, and not on agency budgets per se. For employment data, the scope of the operational definition is nearly the same as the Justice Agencies definition, since data are limited to government agency personnel. Expenditure data additionally include public expenditure for the defense of indigents performed by privately administered legal aid societies or by court-appointed or private counsel, and for the operation of private facilities housing juveniles and adult female offenders.

The "Agencies" and "Expenditure" definitions (II and III) represent a compromise between the need for strict definition by criminal justice function and the practical problems of large scale national data collection, which requires comprehensive and consistent coverage to ensure comparability across jurisdictions. For precise and detailed descriptions of the scope of these two data programs see the definitions sections in the BJS publication *Justice Agencies in the United States, Summary Report 1980* and series *Expenditure and Employment Data for the Criminal Justice System.*

criminal mischief *syn* **malicious mischief**   Intentionally destroying or damaging, or attempting to destroy or damage, the property of another without his consent, usually by a means other than burning.

annotation

The above reflects the usual content of statutory definitions.

This kind of behavior is in popular and occasionally official usage called "vandalism." Specific instances include breaking school windows, slashing tires, and defacing public or private property of any kind.

For law enforcement statistical usage, see **vandalism UCR 14.** This offense is assigned to the "other" category in the tentatively recommended post-arrest offense classification. See Appendix B.

criminal offense   see **crime**

criminal proceedings   The regular and orderly steps, as directed or authorized by statute or a court of law, taken to determine whether an adult accused of a crime is guilty or not guilty.

annotation

In summary reports on trial and appellate court activity with respect to criminal cases, statistical descriptions of proceedings begin with the filing of a charging document and end with the (1) manner of disposition of the charge(s) (dismissal, guilty plea, jury trial or nonjury trial) (2) outcome (conviction or acquittal), and (3) disposition of appeals, if any.

For purposes of describing the flow of criminal cases and defendants through the criminal justice process from the prosecutorial and correctional perspective, data items representing a greater range of steps are necessary. See Appendix A under "law enforcement and court process terms" for a list of statistical terms defined in this dictionary which, if applicable to the procedures in a given jurisdiction, can be used as units of count at key process points. See **defendant dispositions** for a listing of data items representing the various ways in which defendants may exit the judicial process.

criminal willful homicide   see **criminal homicide**

culpability   I. Blameworthiness; responsibility in some sense for an event or situation deserving of moral blame.   II. In Model Penal Code (MPC) usage, a state of mind on the part of one who is committing an act, which makes him or her potentially subject to prosecution for that act.

annotation

Some kind of culpability in the latter sense above is an element in all crimes defined in the style of the **Model Penal Code,** which is the basis for many substantial revisions of state penal codes since its publication.

MPC divides culpability into four ways of acting: purposely, knowingly, recklessly, and negligently. Brief versions of the MPC definitions of the four key terms are as follows:

To act **purposely** is to consciously desire one's conduct to produce a particular result.

To act **knowingly** is to be aware that one's conduct is almost certain to cause a particular result.

To act **recklessly** is to be aware that one's conduct is likely to produce a given result, but to act with conscious disregard of the risk.

To act **negligently** is to act without awareness that one's conduct is likely to cause a particular result, when one should be aware of the risk.

These differences sometimes distinguish between offenses (murder is purposeful killing; involuntary manslaughter is often defined as negligent killing) and sometimes between degrees of an offense (arson, first degree: purposeful burning; arson, second degree: reckless burning).

The ability of data originators to make these distinctions has impact on criminal justice statistics. For example, the law enforcement level must report some crimes before sufficient information is available to determine whether an act was purposeful (intentional), reckless, or negligent. Thus, for example, murder often cannot be distinguished from voluntary manslaughter in crimes known to police.

See also **capacity**, which is a related concept but which is an attribute of persons, not acts, that determines whether or not they can be prosecuted and/or convicted of a crime.

curfew and loitering laws—(juveniles)   UCR 28
In Uniform Crime Reports terminology, the name of the UCR offense category used to record and report arrests made for violations of curfew and loitering laws regulating the behavior of juveniles.

annotation

These violations are ordinarily **status offenses**. See **delinquency**.

curfew violation
The offense of being found in a public place after a specified hour of the evening, usually established in a local ordinance applying only to persons under a specified age.

annotation

Conduct such as loitering may be included in what can be charged or counted as a curfew violation. If the statute or ordinance applies only to juveniles then it is a **status offense**. See **delinquency**.

current parole eligibility date
see **eligible for parole**

custody
Legal or physical control of a person or thing; legal, supervisory or physical responsibility for a person or thing.

annotation

The nonstatistical meaning of "custody" is broad. It ranges from the clearest legal and physical control and responsibility, as when an arrested person is in the custody of a police officer, to physical control without legal jurisdiction, as when a jail holds prisoners in its custody who are legally under the jurisdiction of a state prison system. "Custody" also applies to physical objects, such as evidence taken into custody by law enforcement investigators.

In constructing classifications of correctional caseloads and population movement and in interpreting such data it is necessary to distinguish between three types of custody of persons:

jurisdiction (corrections) *syn* **jurisdictional control (corrections)** The authority to confine or release a person, to remove a person from or return a person to a correctional caseload, or to otherwise direct or set conditions for behavior.

supervisory custody (corrections) Responsibility for supervision of a probationer, parolee or other member of a non-incarcerated correctional caseload.

physical custody (corrections) Direct control of and responsibility for the body of a confined person.

The distinction between jurisdictional control and physical custody is necessary in describing what is being counted in prison population statistics, where the statistician has a choice between counting populations for which a correctional agency has legal responsibility, that is, jurisdiction; and populations under their immediate control, that is, persons in their physical custody over whom they may or may not have jurisdiction. See, for example, "new entries" under **prison/parole population movement.**

National Prisoner Statistics (NPS) usage is that a "State prison system has jurisdiction over a person if it retains the legal power to incarcerate the person in one of its own prisons . . . jurisdiction is not determined by an inmate's physical location; jurisdiction is determined by the legal authority controlling him."

The term "supervisory custody" is necessary to represent the type of custodial responsibility assigned to probation agencies, which have neither full jurisdictional control over their clients nor immediate physical control over their persons. Parole agencies may have only supervisory custody of their caseloads, or may have jurisdictional control also, depending upon whether the paroling authority and the field service function are in a single agency. A judicial officer who places a person on probation, but without assignment to an agency caseload, may be said to have both jurisdiction and supervisory custody of the probationer if he sets probation conditions and requires the subject to report compliance to him.

See also **supervision.**

D.A.   see **prosecutor**

dangerous person   In law enforcement usage, a person who, when at large, is believed likely to cause serious harm to himself or herself or to others.

annotation

While there is no uniform definition of this term in police usage, the stated grounds for believing that a person is dangerous are usually evidence of past violent behavior and, of course, actual infliction of injury. Simple resisting of arrest is not grounds for considering a person dangerous.

Terms such as **habitual offender** and **career criminal** refer to the repetitiveness of criminal behavior, and do not necessarily in any given case indicate that an element of violence is included.

"Dangerousness" may be taken into account in determining whether a person will be committed to confinement after conviction for an offense. Use of weapons and/or inflicting of injury are **aggravating circumstances** (see entry). These can cause the offender to receive a more severe penalty as provided by statute or by judicial decision.

"Dangerous to self or others" is a technical term in many mental health statutes relating to civil commitments to confinement.

deadly weapon   An instrument designed to inflict serious bodily injury or death, or capable of being used for such a purpose.

annotation

A statutory distinction is sometimes made between a "deadly" weapon, that is, one specifically designed to cause serious injury or death, for example a gun, and a **dangerous weapon,** that is, one capable under certain circumstances of causing serious injury or death, for example a knife. However, in many criminal codes and in general usage the two are merged. For example, an automobile is not designed to cause injury or death but it may be considered to satisfy the "deadly weapon" criterion for an aggravated assault charge.

The essential distinction being made in statutory and other crime definitions making use of the feature "deadly or dangerous" weapons (e.g., armed robbery vs. strongarm robbery) is between the presence or absence of an instrument which, if used by the perpetrator, would greatly increase the likelihood that serious injury or death would result.

dead time   see **time served**

death sentence   see **prison commitment**

decree   see **court decision**

defamation   Intentional causing or attempting to cause damage to the reputation of another, by communicating false or distorted information about his actions, motives, or character.

annotation

Defamation is not always a single codified offense. A statutory distinction is often made between **slander,** which is defamation by spoken communication, and **libel,** which is defamation by any non-spoken communication, most commonly by some written or printed matter.

Defamation is not a criminal offense in all jurisdictions. Defamation can, however, always be a cause of action in a civil suit. Criminal defamation is assigned to the "other" category in the tentatively recommended post-arrest classification. See Appendix B.

defendant   *recommended statistical terminology*   In criminal justice usage, a person formally accused of an offense(s) by the filing in court of a charging document.

annotation

For statistical purposes, a person becomes a defendant when the formal accusation is entered into the record of the court (see **filing**) and remains a defendant until the prosecutor withdraws the prosecution, or the court dismisses the case or otherwise determines that judgment will not be pronounced, or the court pronounces judgment (acquittal or conviction). See **defendant dispositions** for a data structure for the reporting of defendant exits from the adjudicatory process.

A **co-defendant** is one of two or more persons named in a single charging document or tried in the same trial proceeding.

In civil proceedings, the defendant is the person against whom relief or recovery is sought in a civil action or suit, the one who defends against or denies a complaint or charge.

See also **offender.**

defendant dispositions   *recommended statistical terminology*   The class of prosecutorial or judicial actions which terminate or provisionally halt proceedings regarding a given defendant in a criminal case after charges have been filed in court.

annotation

This term is proposed for criminal justice defendant data presentations as a substitute for "court disposition," which has more than one official meaning. "Provisionally" is used in the definition to indicate the contingent nature of the dispositions such as probation, which are frequently categorized as final although further judicial action will be necessary if the conditions are violated.

The recommendation that there be such a class of data items, and the choice of name, stem from the need to describe the outcomes of court activity from the prosecutorial and/or correctional points of view where the individual defendant's changes in legal status must be accounted for. (See **arrestee dispositions** for pre-filing dispositions.)

As the data structures and terminologies in actual case or offender tracking or history systems indicate, this is a complex data area. Disposition names vary from one jurisdiction to another and quite often the same terms are used with different meanings. Also, most of the court decisions that appear as single defendant dispositions also occur in combination, and different combinations are favored in different jurisdictions.

In order to provide terminology for the full range of commonly distinguishable types of defendant dispositions, a model data structure is proposed, followed by comment on the problems posed by the fact that the disposition types are not mutually exclusive in practice.

This model defendant data structure differs in several significant respects from the proposed structure for case and defendant "manner of disposition" developed by the National Court Statistics Project (see Appendix E). The differences are essentially the result of a difference of focus, and do not imply any basic incompatibility. The NCSP model is a portion of their model general court caseload statistical system. The major purpose of that system is to measure court activity relevant to court management concerns. The defendant dispositions are characterized by means of a relatively small number of general categories. The disposition points recognized correspond to those generally utilized for caseload statistics, and the disposition type categories are subdivided according to procedural distinctions reflecting differences in court workload.

The purpose of the model data structure presented here, by contrast, is to clearly identify the ways in which defendants exit the judicial process, and the impact of final judicial determinations upon defendants and upon correctional agency caseloads/populations. In order to achieve this purpose, the focus has been placed on the defendant alone. The data items cover all distinguishable decisions having potentially different impacts on the defendant, with relatively little consideration given to procedural differences (e.g., trial vs. no trial) which do not closely relate to differing consequences for the defendant.

The data items are limited to those indicating a final or potentially final court determination regarding the defendant. Dispositions which are intermediate from the defendant perspective, that is, where the court definitely intends to take subsequent action regarding the defendant, are excluded.

Parenthetical information has been added to aid the reader in establishing relationships between this data structure and the NCSP model.

defendant dispositions   (asterisk indicates term is fully defined and discussed in an individual dictionary entry)

pre-judgment:

* **no true bill***   grand jury rejects all charges against defendant (pretrial)
* **nolle prosequi***   prosecutor declares that he will not pursue the case (pretrial)
* **dismissal***   court dismisses all charges against defendant (may be subdivided as: pretrial, during jury trial, during non-jury trial)
* **transfer to juvenile court***   (pretrial)
* **adjudication withheld***   court suspends adjudication conditional upon defendant behavior (may be subdivided as: pretrial, during jury trial, during non-jury trial)
  * **with referral to probation or other criminal justice agency**
  * **with referral to noncriminal justice agency**
  * **with no referral**
* **incompetent to stand trial***   defendant found legally incapable of defense (pretrial)
* **civil commitment***   adjudication suspended or terminated and defendant placed in noncriminal justice facility for care or treatment (may be subdivided as: pretrial, during jury trial, during non-jury trial)

at or post-judgment:

* **acquittal***   (may be subdivided as: following jury trial, following non-jury trial)
* **not guilty by reason of insanity***   (may be subdivided as: following jury trial, following non-jury trial)
* **civil commitment***   as above

  (**conviction*** may be subdivided as: following guilty plea without trial, following jury trial, following non-jury trial)

(sentencing dispositions:)

- **sentencing postponed***   pronouncement of any other sentencing disposition postponed by court contingent upon defendant behavior
- **suspended sentence***
  - **unconditionally suspended sentence**   sentence pronounced but defendant permanently discharged from court jurisdiction
  - **conditionally suspended sentence**   sentence pronounced but execution suspended contingent upon defendant behavior
- **balance of sentence suspended* or sentenced to time served**   defendant released at time of sentencing disposition after previous confinement
- **grant of probation***   defendant placed in probation status
  - **court probation***   no assignment to probation agency caseload
  - **supervised probation***   defendant assigned to active or inactive probation agency caseload
- **restitution***   defendant required to compensate victim or provide community service
- **fine*, forfeit, court costs**
- **residential commitment***   defendant required to reside in halfway house, group home, etc.
- **jail commitment***
- **prison commitment***
  - **definite term**   single time value specified by court
  - **minimum-maximum term**   range of time specified by court or automatic application of statute
  - **life term**   with or without possibility of parole
  - **death sentence**

Detailed reporting conventions must be established when aggregating data on defendant dispositions in any system because a defendant charged with more than one offense can receive a different disposition for each charge. Also, components of a given defendant disposition on even a single charge must be ignored when the disposition combines alternatives and the data are intended to be expressed on a level of generality permitting cross-jurisdictional comparisons. For example, the combination "probation with jail" is common enough and important enough to perhaps be given separate, primary item status in national level data but the combination "probation with restitution" might not be so rated.

At this point in the development of statistical programs the only feasible reporting convention is "record most serious disposition/severe sentence," without regard to less serious dispositions that the defendant may have received relating to the same case. This method, of course, involves elaborate rank ordering decisions as to which dispositions are the more serious, unless the contrast is simple as in prison vs. straight probation. There is also a loss of information in that it is not possible to identify the sentence or other disposition received in relation to specific crimes with which the defendant may have been charged.

The following list suggests which defendant disposition categories might be collectible for national level data at this time. These are the categories typical in current state and local statistical publications.

generalized defendant disposition classification

pre-judgment:

dismissal/nolle prosequi
 —pretrial
 —jury trial
 —non-jury trial

adjudication withheld
 —pretrial
 —jury trial
 —non-jury trial

other off-calendar (transfers, fugitives, etc.)
 —pretrial
 —jury trial
 —non-jury trial

judgment or post-judgment:

acquittal
 —jury trial
 —non-jury trial

conviction

 unconditionally suspended sentence
  —guilty plea (pretrial only)
  —jury trial
  —non-jury trial

 fine/forfeit/court costs
  —guilty plea (pretrial only)
  —jury trial
  —non-jury trial

 probation or conditionally suspended sentence
  —guilty plea (pretrial only)
  —jury trial
  —non-jury trial

 probation with jail
  —guilty plea (pretrial only)
  —jury trial
  —non-jury trial

 jail commitment
  —guilty plea (pretrial only)
  —jury trial
  —non-jury trial

 prison commitment
  —guilty plea (pretrial only)
  —jury trial
  —non-jury trial

defense attorney   see **attorney**

delinquency   In the broadest usage, juvenile actions or conduct in violation of criminal law, juvenile status offenses, and other juvenile misbehavior.

annotation

Common usage of this term frequently includes not only criminal offenses (see **crime**), but also status offenses, and may include violations of accepted conventions of behavior, or "tendencies" to engage in such conduct. Thus it is too often used in connection with unspecified numbers of undefined juvenile offenses, or to describe police workloads that relate to street activity as opposed to arrests and charges, or to describe an unmeasured amount of misbehavior believed to be characteristic of a given population, often in the absence of any statutory definition of the misbehavior.

Its use as a summary term for combined counts of delinquent acts and status offenses is especially uninformative: the most serious crimes are classed with the most minor misconduct.

Specific terms that should be used in national level statistical reporting are defined below. Note that the decision to recommend the use of "delinquent act" and "delinquent" to refer to events and cases where a violation of a penal code is charged, is based on majority usage, and the fact that no more acceptable terms are available, even though some states use such terms to refer also to behavior that is an offense only for minors (status offenses).

delinquent act   *recommended statistical terminology*   An act committed by a juvenile for which an adult could be prosecuted in a criminal court, but for which a juvenile can be adjudicated in a juvenile court, or prosecuted in a court having criminal jurisdiction if the juvenile court transfers jurisdiction: generally, a "felony or misdemeanor level offense" in states employing those terms.

delinquent   *recommended statistical terminology*   A juvenile who has been adjudged by a judicial officer of a juvenile court to have committed a delinquent act.

status offense   *recommended statistical terminology*   An act or conduct which is declared by statute to be an offense, but only when committed or engaged in by a juvenile, and which can be adjudicated only by a juvenile court.

status offender   *recommended statistical terminology*   A juvenile who has been adjudged by a judicial officer of a juvenile court to have committed a status offense. (In some jurisdictions a status offender who commits repeated status offenses can be adjudged a delinquent. These should not be counted as delinquents in interstate or national information exchange concerning offenses, as opposed to adjudications.)

Juveniles alleged, but not adjudged to have committed delinquent acts should be described as **alleged delinquents.**

Juveniles alleged, but not adjudged to have committed status offenses should be described as **alleged status offenders.**

Juvenile cases and judgments are often characterized by the word describing the person instead of the offense or condition. Thus the possible **juvenile court judgments** (see entry) are in data publications often described as delinquent, status offender, and **dependent** (see **dependency**).

In the oldest juvenile codes, no distinction was made between delinquent acts and status offenses, or, respectively, criminal behavior and non-criminal behavior. The recent legislative trend has been to separate delinquents from status offenders. Despite variation in statutory classification, basic court record information usually permits differentiation of status offenses from delinquent acts for the purposes of statistical reporting. Since the range of behavior covered by the two may extend from murder to truancy, statistical reporting should maintain separate categories.

Typical status offenses are violation of curfew, running away from home, truancy, possession of an alcoholic beverage, "incorrigibility," "having delinquent tendencies," "leading an immoral life," and being "in need of supervision" (see **PINS/CHINS/JINS/MINS**).

"Status offense" ordinarily refers to juvenile conduct, but the term has also been used to refer to adults who were charged with the status offense of being vagrant or an addict.

The National Center for Juvenile Justice study, *Juvenile Court Organization and Status Offenses: A Statutory Profile,* describes the various state codifications of juvenile offenses.

delinquent   see **delinquency**

delinquent act   see **delinquency**

dependency   The state of being dependent for proper care upon the community instead of one's family or guardians.

annotation

"Dependency" in practice is used to mean the legal status which is the result of a court finding, and also the condition of "dependency" or willful neglect or abuse which is the reason for the finding.

Dependency is not an offense. A usage is recommended here in order to provide a complete classification for all **juvenile court judgments** in interstate data reporting:

dependent   *syn*   **dependent and neglected**   *recommended statistical terminology*   A juvenile over whom a juvenile court has assumed jurisdiction and legal control because his or her care by parent, guardian or custodian has not met a legal standard of proper care.

The other juvenile court judgments are **delinquent** and **status offender** (see **delinquency**).

A given child alleged or adjudged to be in a condition of "dependency" may be called, in statute and/or in practice, a "dependent of the court," a "dependent and neglected child," a "neglected child," or an "abused child." These child welfare terms have special, different meanings in different jurisdictions and contexts: In "aid for dependent children," "dependent" means that the parent cannot financially support the child and the label is an administrative description not indicating a court judgment of dependency. In one state the meaning of "neglected child" may be limited to children whose custodians have been formally adjudged guilty of "willful neglect," "abandonment," or "criminal nonsupport." But elsewhere it may include children toward whom the court has assumed or could assume the authority of parent, for any reason ranging from willful "child abuse" to inadvertent "child neglect."

The words "neglect" or "neglected" are usually employed with broad reference in statutory terminology in describing situations where a child lacks proper care, including those where he suffers psychological or physical damage for any reason. Among the related adult offenses are "criminal nonsupport," "neglect of a minor," and the like, where the adult willfully fails to provide for the child.

"Child abuse" is not a common statutory term; such behavior is often codified as "assault on a child," or is described as "physical abuse" in legal language stating reasons for a juvenile court to assume jurisdiction and remove the minor from parental care. On the other hand, "child abuse" is the standard name in the behavioral sciences for a pattern of parental behavior that includes physical abuse of a child.

dependent   see **dependency**

dependent and neglected   see **dependency**

deputy sheriff   *recommended statistical terminology*   A local law enforcement officer employed by a county sheriff's department.

annotation

For national level law enforcement data, sheriff's department personnel whose permanent duties are primarily custodial or concerned with civil processes should be excluded from this class.

See **sheriff's department** and **law enforcement officer.**

detainee   Usually, a person held in local, very short term confinement while awaiting consideration for pretrial release or first appearance for arraignment.

annotation

The term is also used to refer to all persons held in physical custody for lengthy periods while awaiting trial and judgment. Such persons may also be called "detentioners." See **detention.**

detainer (corrections)   An official notice from a government agency to a correctional agency requesting that an identified person wanted by the first agency, but subject to the correctional agency's jurisdiction, not be released or discharged without notification to the first agency and opportunity to respond.

annotation

The placing of a detainer is often, but not always, subsequent to the issuing of a warrant. Typical reasons for detainers include that the person is wanted for trial in the requesting jurisdiction or is wanted to serve a sentence.

A detainer is notification of the existence of a warrant or other official procedural document and cannot be legally ignored by the recipient custodial agency. Methods of implementation of detainers, and the various states' and prisoners' rights and obligations relating to the implementation, are the subject of interstate agreements on detainers, usually codified in statute.

Temporary release from a prison to other custody for trial with return expected is recorded as an "authorized provisional exit" in population movement data. See **prison/parole population movement.**

detention   The legally authorized confinement of a person subject to criminal or juvenile court proceedings, until the point of commitment to a correctional facility or until release.

annotation

"Detention" describes the custodial status (reason for custody) of persons held in confinement after arrest or while awaiting the completion of judicial proceedings. See **pretrial detention** for statistical terminology. See also **pre-arraignment lockup** and **jail**.

Release from detention can occur prior to trial (see **pretrial release**), or after trial or adjudication as a result of a dismissal of the case, an acquittal, or a sentencing disposition that does not require confinement.

The contrasting type of confinement is that resulting from **commitment** after judgment. See entry.

detention center   see **juvenile facility**

detention hearing   *recommended statistical terminology*   In juvenile justice usage, a hearing by a judicial officer of a juvenile court to determine whether a juvenile is to be detained, continue to be detained, or be released, while juvenile proceedings in the case are pending.

annotation

A detention hearing must be held to determine the lawfulness of the authority under which a juvenile is confined if detention is to continue for longer than a specified time period (usually 48 hours).

A juvenile whose detention is not to be continued is usually released to the custody of parent(s) or guardian(s), but in some jurisdictions provision is also made for the setting of bail, as in adult criminal proceedings.

In some jurisdictions, a decision to detain can only be made after a petition has been filed in juvenile court. In others, the decision to detain can be made while the intake investigation is proceeding, before a decision has actually been made whether to file a petition.

If the juvenile is detained, a detention hearing decision must precede an **adjudicatory hearing.**

See **pretrial release** for the parallel adult process.

determinate sentence   see **indeterminate sentence**

detoxification center   A public or private facility for the short-term medical treatment of acutely intoxicated persons, or drug or alcohol abusers, often functioning as an alternative to jail for persons who have been taken into custody.

diagnosis or classification center   *recommended statistical terminology*   A functional unit within a correctional or medical facility, or a separate facility, which contains persons held in custody for the purpose of determining whether criminal proceedings should continue or the appropriate sentencing or treatment disposition, or which correctional facility or program is appropriate for a committed offender.

annotation

Diagnosis and classification centers are often established as special units within larger state or local correctional facilities, with one or two such centers serving the courts and correctional facility systems of an entire state, but some are housed in facilities entirely separate from other institutions.

Persons may be sent to these centers by the court (see **diagnostic commitment**) before court disposition of the case. They may also be placed in a center after a court disposition of commitment to the jurisdiction of a correctional agency. The agency then decides which of available alternative facilities and programs is most appropriate for the offender.

Parolees returned to prison for alleged or confirmed parole violations may also be placed in diagnostic facilities for study and/or reclassification.

diagnostic commitment   *recommended statistical terminology*   The action of a court ordering a person subject to criminal or juvenile proceedings to be temporarily placed in a confinement facility, for study and evaluation of his or her personal history and characteristics, usually as a preliminary to a sentencing disposition, juvenile court disposition, or other disposition of the case.

annotation

This kind of commitment is usually a provisional one which will be followed by a final **defendant disposition** (see entry), and thus is not a key unit of count in summary statistics.

It is usually a commitment to confinement either in a restrictive correctional facility or as an inpatient in a public or private medical facility. It may occur before judgment and thus be unrelated to any determination of guilt.

Diagnostic commitments have various purposes. A court may commit a person for study and observation to determine if he or she is competent to be tried, or, if he or she has been found **incompetent to stand trial** or found **not guilty by reason of insanity** (see entries), to determine whether the person is a danger to self or others.

There is also the diagnostic commitment to advise the court as to what kind of correctional program is most suitable for a person who has been convicted of a crime or adjudged to be a delinquent or status offender. In such an instance the key findings may be whether to confine the person at all, or, given that confinement is necessary, what program is most appropriate. This kind of determination is often made for presentation to the court in a **presentence** (adult) or **predisposition** (juvenile) **report** (see **presentence investigation** and **predisposition investigation**).

The assignment of an offender by a **correctional agency** to a diagnosis and classification center for study after a sentence of commitment to prison is not called a diagnostic commitment in this terminology, since the assignment does not represent a basic status change for the subject.

See also **diagnosis or classification center.**

directed verdict   see **verdict**

discharge   In criminal justice usage, to release from confinement or supervision, or to release from a legal status imposing an obligation upon the subject person.

annotation

This term is used with various meanings in criminal justice statistical publications, often without definition. Its use without qualification is not recommended. Preferred terms are listed under **defendant dispositions, parole agency caseload entries and removals, probation supervisory population movement** and **prison/parole population movement.**

A "discharge" from prison or parole is most often, though not always, understood to mean a final separation from the jurisdiction of the correctional agency. "Discharge" from probation may mean a satisfactory termination or a revocation of the probation status (see preferred terms as above). In court disposition data some kinds of sentencing dispositions are sometimes called "conditional discharges," meaning that the persons are released from punishment contingent upon fulfilling obligations stated by the court. See also **suspended sentence.**

discretionary review   see **appeal case**

dismissal   I. In judicial proceedings generally, the disposal of an action, suit, motion or the like without trial of the issues; the termination of the adjudication of a case before the case reaches judgment.   II. *recommended criminal justice statistical terminology*   The decision by a court to terminate adjudication of all outstanding charges in a criminal case, or all outstanding charges against a given defendant in a criminal case, thus terminating court action in the case and permanently or provisionally terminating court jurisdiction over the defendant in relation to those charges.

annotation

"Dismissal" or "dismissed" is a major descriptive category in statistics concerning dispositions of cases and defendants in court proceedings. Although dismissals can be subcategorized by nature in various ways, they are usually presented as a single category of case or defendant dispositions in statistical reports. Dismissals and instances where the prosecutor declines to pursue the case are often combined under the label "dismissed/nolle prosequi" (see **nolle prosequi**).

A dismissal of a defendant case is a data item in the class **defendant dispositions** (see entry). See also **adjudication withheld** for another kind of provisional termination of adjudication.

Where general comparisons between dispositions of defendants and related court caseload activity are needed, it is recommended that defendants whose cases are dismissed prior to trial be counted separately from those where dismissal occurs after a trial has begun.

In criminal proceedings, a dismissal of a given charge or entire case can be initiated by motion of the defense or prosecution, or on the court's own motion. The common reasons for dismissals include insufficient evidence to support arrest or prosecution (see **probable cause**), evidence illegally obtained, errors in the conduct of the proceedings or failure to proceed as quickly as required, and failure of the jury to agree on a verdict. See **illegal search and seizure, dismissal for want of prosecution, mistrial, hung jury,** and **dismissal in the interest of justice** for examples.

With respect to the possibility of reopening the case, **dismissals with prejudice** (no subsequent prosecution possible) are distinguished from **dismissals without prejudice** (reopening possible).

dismissal for want of prosecution   In criminal proceedings, the judicial termination of a case against a defendant, occurring after the filing of a charging document but before the beginning of a trial, on grounds that prosecution has not been continued.

annotation

A court may dismiss a case for want of prosecution on the motion of the defense or on its own motion.

In some jurisdictions, such dismissals are automatic in cases which have not been brought to trial within a specified period of time following the filing of a charging document, unless a defendant has waived the right to have the trial during the period. See **speedy trial.**

Nolle prosequi, by contrast, is a termination of a case against a defendant by formal notice given by the prosecution that it does not intend to continue. See entry.

dismissal in the interest of justice   In criminal proceedings, the judicial termination of a case against a defendant, on the grounds that the ends of justice would not be served by continuing prosecution.

disorderly conduct   UCR 24   In Uniform Crime Reports terminology, the name of the UCR category used to record and report arrests for committing a breach of the peace.

annotation

UCR includes, as examples, the following offenses or groups of offenses in this category:

> Affray
> Unlawful assembly
> Disturbing the peace
> Disturbing meetings
> Disorderly conduct in State institutions, at court, at fairs, on trains, or public conveyances, etc.
> Prize fights
> Blasphemy, profanity, and obscene language
> Desecrating flag
> Refusing to assist an officer
> All attempts to commit any of the above

Note that unlawful assembly, which is listed by UCR as an example of disorderly conduct, is in a few states the name given to behavior elsewhere commonly called "riot." In UCR "riot" is placed in **all other offenses UCR 26.**

See **disturbing the peace** for a general recommendation for prosecution, courts and corrections statistics.

disposition   In criminal justice usage, the action by a criminal or juvenile justice agency which signifies that a portion of the justice process is complete and jurisdiction is terminated or transferred to another agency; or which signifies that a decision has been reached on one aspect of a case and a different aspect comes under consideration, requiring a different kind of decision.

annotation

The above definition indicates the broadest meaning of the term, which reflects the basic sense of "to dispose of": to arrange, settle, determine the fate or condition of, or relinquish. It should be noted that most of the important units of count (other than types of crimes) in criminal justice statistics are decisions determining the fate or condition of cases or defendants, made by police, prosecutors, the courts and corrections agencies.

Since some data presentation purposes require that the case be viewed as the fundamental unit of action and other purposes require that the defendant be the focus, the boundaries and contents of the class, "dispositions," differ among different data systems and programs. There is also variation in the ways that different data systems deal with continuing cases or defendants that do not pass a given major decision point during a given reporting period, cases where the "final" disposition can be altered by subsequent defendant behavior (as in probation revocation), and the like.

For data structures and terminology concerning major types of dispositions, and examples of reporting problems, see **arrestee dispositions, court disposition, defendant dispositions,** and the various prison, parole and probation population movement entries.

disposition hearing   *recommended statistical terminology*   A hearing in juvenile court, conducted after an adjudicatory hearing and subsequent receipt of the report of any predisposition investigation, to determine the most appropriate form of custody and/or treatment for a juvenile who has been adjudged a delinquent, a status offender, or a dependent.

annotation

The possible dispositions of juveniles over whom a court has assumed jurisdiction range from placement of a juvenile on probation or in a foster home to commitment of the juvenile to confinement. See **juvenile disposition.**

In the juvenile justice process, the disposition hearing occurs after an **adjudicatory hearing** and **juvenile court judgment** and terminates with the **juvenile disposition.**

A **transfer hearing** (see entry) is not a disposition hearing.

dissenting opinion   see **opinion**

district attorney   see **prosecutor**

disturbing the peace   *tentatively recommended national category for prosecution, courts and corrections statistics*   Unlawful interruption of the peace, quiet or order of a community, including offenses called "disorderly conduct," "vagrancy," "loitering," "unlawful assembly," and "riot."

annotation

See Appendix B for problems in national crime classification and complete set of tentatively proposed national categories for post-arrest offense statistics.

This category combines crime types separated at the law enforcement reporting level (see **disorderly conduct UCR 24, vagrancy UCR 25, all other offenses UCR 26** and **curfew and loitering laws—(juveniles) UCR 28**), on the grounds that detailed subclassification will not capture nationally comparable data at prosecution, courts and corrections levels. State penal codes define much the same array of actions and behaviors as criminal, but group the distinct offenses in various ways and name them differently, overall expressing the common offense elements in quite different structures.

Most jurisdictions have a statutory offense called "disorderly conduct" or an article or chapter called "disturbance of the peace" or "offenses against public order." Acts which commonly constitute the offense or offense group are: public fighting, violent behavior in public, use of offensive or abusive language or making offensive gestures in public, making unreasonable noise, disrupting religious or other public meetings, and failing to move on or to disperse in accordance with police order.

"Riot" is particularly difficult to distinguish from "disorderly conduct" at a state-to-state comparability level. One of the critical distinctions is often quantitative, as when riot is defined as "disorderly conduct" by a group of persons, and the critical number of persons depends upon the jurisdiction ("three or more," "seven or more," etc.). See **riot**.

Offenses named as "loitering" or "vagrancy," or described in language indicating that they are of these general crime types are placed in the "disturbing the peace" category because their elements are included in the "disorderly conduct" or "disturbing the public order" sections of most penal laws.

diversion   I.   In the broadest usage, any procedure which (a) substitutes non-entry for official entry into the justice process, or (b) substitutes the suspension of criminal or juvenile proceedings for continuation, or (c) substitutes lesser supervision or referral to a non-justice agency or no supervision for conventional supervision, or (d) substitutes any kind of non-confinement status for confinement.   II.   *Standards and Goals definition*   The official suspension of criminal or juvenile proceedings against an alleged offender at any point after a recorded justice system intake but before the entering of a judgment, and referral of that person to a treatment or care program administered by a non-justice or private agency, or no referral.

annotation

Definition (I) represents the actual span of usage of the term, though some of the included actions, such as probation instead of confinement, are conventional alternatives to incarceration that were employed before the term "diversion" was used in the justice vocabulary.

Definition (II) is that recommended by the Task Force on Corrections of the National Advisory Commission on Criminal Justice Standards and Goals, (pages 73–4 of the volume *Corrections*, issued January 23, 1973). It strategically narrows the meaning of the term. The Commission's definition requires:

- That adequate grounds for alleging the commission of an offense exist.
- That an official system entry be recorded (arrest, referral to juvenile intake agency or appearance in court).
- That judicial proceedings be halted or at least suspended after entry and before judgment.
- That the alternative to continuation of proceedings be referral to non-justice supervision of treatment, or no referral.

The definition thus excludes from the meaning of "diversion" actions that preclude formal system intake, all pre-conviction dispositions involving referral or assignment to criminal justice agency programs, and all post-conviction dispositions generally.

Statistical terminology covering the range of actions relevant to any definition of adult diversion is included in the model data reporting structures for **arrestee dispositions** and **defendant dispositions**. Three subtypes of **prosecution withheld** and **adjudication withheld** are provided: (1) With referral to probation or other criminal justice agency, (2) with referral to a non-criminal justice agency, and (3) no referral. These, together with the appropriate sentencing dispositions also listed under defendant dispositions, constitute the data items needed to produce summary statistics concerning "diversion" of arrested adults in the broadest usage. A selection of items from the total set can be used to describe more narrowly defined "diversion" procedures.

In national level data presentations using this (or any other) statistical terminology the type of criminal or juvenile justice agency causing the diversion, the process point in criminal or juvenile proceedings at which diversion occurs, and the type of agency or program to which the subject is diverted (if a referral is made) should be identified.

For bibliographical purposes The National Institute of Law Enforcement and Criminal Justice (now the National Institute of Justice) defines diversion as "a process which limits penetration of youth into the juvenile justice system. This is achieved by termination of contacts with the system and referral to nonsystem agencies or through informal processing by system personnel. The diversion process occurs at any point between apprehension and adjudication." (*Juvenile Diversion, 2nd Edition, A select bibliography.* April, 1977.) This definition coincides with the task force definition, except for the feature "informal processing by system personnel."

Some agencies call an interview determining whether or not a defendant is eligible for a diversion program a "pretrial release" interview. This term is not recommended as the name of a diversion eligibility screening process, because the common meaning of **pretrial release** (see entry) is a release operative only until adjudication is completed. These latter releases are for the purpose of granting freedom while awaiting the conclusion of judicial proceedings, not for the purpose of avoiding such proceedings.

In many definitions of "diversion," a distinction is made between "entry" and "penetration." In such contexts, "entry" means first officially noticed intake into the justice system through arrest, referral to a probation agency, or complaint to a court. "Penetration" means a case disposition after entry that continues direct justice system control (or continues and intensifies it) by moving the person to the next process step, such as commencement of prosecution, or a disposition that causes the person to be placed under supervision or in confinement as opposed to no supervision or no confinement.

docket   see **court calendar**

driving under the influence   *recommended statistical terminology*   Unlawful operation of any motor vehicle while under the influence of alcohol or a controlled substance(s) or drug.

annotation

This category is recommended for post-arrest offense data. It is used in UCR reporting (see **driving under the influence UCR 21**). See Appendix B for problems in national crime classification and complete set of tentatively proposed national categories for post-arrest offense statistics.

Common abbreviations used in data systems to label this offense are: DUI, "driving under the influence," and DWI, "driving while intoxicated."

This behavior may be codified as a single statutory offense, as separate subsections of a statutory offense, or as two or more separate statutory offenses. Where a distinction is made, it is most commonly between:

driving under the influence of alcohol, also called **drunk driving**   The operation of any motor vehicle after having consumed a quantity of alcohol sufficient to potentially interfere with the ability to maintain safe operation.

driving under the influence of drugs   The operation of any motor vehicle while attention or ability is impaired through the intake of a narcotic drug or an incapacitating quantity of another drug.

The Uniform Offense Classifications of the National Crime Information Center (NCIC) classify separately "driving under the influence drugs" and "driving under influence liquor." In UCR arrest data "driving under the influence" is a single category.

In most jurisdictions an offense can be charged regardless of whether the operation of the vehicle was observed to be reckless. An offense of "driving under the influence of alcohol" is usually charged on the basis of evidence from a test for blood alcohol level, administered within a reasonable time after arrest. The maximum permissible amount of alcohol in the blood is specified by statute, usually as a percentage. In the absence of objective ways to measure some forms of drug intoxication, the offense may be charged in certain jurisdictions if the suspect can be determined to be addicted to a drug.

Whether a given instance of this type of offense is a felony or misdemeanor usually depends on whether bodily injury to another person results (often called "felony drunk driving"), and whether the person has previously been convicted of the same offense.

driving under the influence   UCR 21   In Uniform Crime Reports terminology, the name of the UCR category used to record and report arrests for offenses of driving or operating any vehicle or common carrier while drunk or under the influence of liquor or drugs.

annotation

In most jurisdictions, a test for blood alcohol level is used to determine whether a person is under the influence of liquor. The maximum permissible amount of alcohol in the blood is specified by statute, usually as a percentage.

See **driving under the influence** for general recommendation.

driving under the influence of alcohol   see **driving under the influence**

driving under the influence of drugs   see **driving under the influence**

drug abuse violations   UCR 18   In Uniform Crime Reports terminology, the name of the UCR category used to record and report arrests for offenses relating to growing, manufacturing, making, possessing, using, selling, or distributing narcotic and dangerous nonnarcotic drugs.

annotation

For reporting of arrests relating to drug offenses the national UCR program requires the following breakdown:

Sale/manufacturing
   a. Opium or cocaine and their derivatives (morphine, heroin, codeine).
   b. Marijuana.
   c. Synthetic narcotics—manufactured narcotics which can cause true drug addiction (Demerol, methadones).
   d. Dangerous nonnarcotic drugs (barbiturates, Benzedrine).

Possession
   e. Opium or cocaine and their derivatives (morphine, heroin, codeine).
   f. Marijuana.
   g. Synthetic narcotics—manufactured narcotics which can cause true drug addiction (Demerol, methadones).
   h. Dangerous nonnarcotic drugs (barbiturates, Benzedrine).

For general recommendation and other classifications of drugs see **drug law violation.**

drug law violation   *recommended statistical terminology*   The unlawful sale, purchase, distribution, manufacture, cultivation, transport, possession, or use of a controlled or prohibited drug, or attempt to commit these acts.

annotation

This category is recommended for post-arrest offense data. It is used in UCR reporting (see **drug abuse violations UCR 18**). See Appendix B for problems in national crime classification and complete set of tentatively proposed national categories for post-arrest offense statistics.

No standard drug offense subcategory terminology and classification is proposed here. The significant distinction between possession for use and all other drug offenses corresponds to standard penal code surface distinctions, but for some drugs the actual discrimination between possession for use and possession for sale depends on the amount found in the possession of the defendant, and the quantitative limits differ from state to state. Penalty ranges for drug violations also differ greatly from state to state.

Subclassifications of drugs vary. UCR collects data on arrests for drug abuse violations utilizing four drug type categories: (1) opium or cocaine and their derivatives (morphine, heroin, codeine), (2) marijuana, (3) synthetic narcotics—manufactured narcotics which can cause true drug addiction (Demerol, methadones), and (4) dangerous nonnarcotic drugs (barbiturates, Benzedrine). The Uniform Offense Classifications list eight drug types: (1) hallucinogens (excluding marijuana), (2) heroin, (3) opium, (4) cocaine, (5) synthetic narcotics, (6) marijuana, (7) amphetamines, and (8) barbiturates.

Definitions of "drug" or "controlled substance" vary slightly. State and federal statutes specify in detail exactly which substances are controlled and most lists are based on the Uniform Controlled Dangerous Substances Act, but the category content is not entirely identical among all jurisdictions.

drunk driving   see **driving under the influence**

drunkenness   UCR 23   In Uniform Crime Reports terminology, the name of the UCR category used to record and report arrests made for offenses of public drunkenness or other public intoxication, except "driving under the influence UCR 21."

annotation

In UCR practice, arrests relating to offenses of drug intoxication are placed in this UCR category. Where the arrest charges include or consist of other drug offenses, the arrests are placed in **drug abuse violations UCR 18.**

See **intoxication** for general recommendation.

due process of law   A right guaranteed by the Fifth, Sixth, and Fourteenth Amendments of the U.S. Constitution, and generally understood, in legal contexts, to mean the due course of legal proceedings according to the rules and forms which have been established for the protection of private rights.

annotation

Due process of law, in criminal proceedings, is generally understood to include the following basic elements: a law creating and defining the offense, an impartial tribunal having jurisdictional authority over the case, accusation in proper form, notice and opportunity to defend, trial according to established procedure, and discharge from all restraints or obligations unless convicted.

element of the offense   Any conduct, circumstance, condition, or state of mind which in combination with other conduct, circumstances, conditions, or states of mind constitutes an unlawful act.

annotation

The same element is often a key element of more than one offense. Penal codes usually organize offenses sharing many key elements into one numbered section, sometimes with subsections labelled by decimal points and numbers, or by letters, describing individual offenses. In this dictionary the sets of "defining features" used to clarify the definitions of many offenses are usually equivalent to the sets of "elements of the offense" traditionally used to define those crimes in legal practice.

A major class in summary offense statistics will sometimes consist of what is seen as "one" offense, such as burglary or kidnapping. That is, each member of the class has almost exactly the same set of offense elements. But often summary offense statistics place in one major class those offense types which share only one or two key element(s), for example, "crimes of violence."

The fact that key elements may be shared throughout a series of otherwise strategically different offenses permits alternative ways of classifying related offenses, and thus major categories may not be the same in all penal codes or statistical classifications. For example, "assault with intent to kill" may be classified as attempted murder or as a subtype of assault.

See also **included offense**.

eligible for parole   The status of a person committed to the jurisdiction of a federal or state prison system and usually in confinement in an institution, who by a combination of such factors as sentence effective date, statutory provisions concerning length of sentence to be served in confinement, time credit deductions, and individual sentence, can legally be considered for release from confinement in prison to parole status.

annotation

In data systems, the **minimum eligible parole date** is the date on which the offender is or was first eligible for parole, as determined at the time of admission to prison or as first set by paroling authority action, depending on the statutes and other rules of the jurisdiction.

The **current parole eligibility date** is that date on which a given offender is currently eligible for parole, which may or may not be the same as the original minimum eligible parole date.

See **paroling authority decisions.**

embezzlement   The misappropriation, misapplication, or illegal disposal of legally entrusted property by the person(s) to whom it was entrusted, with intent to defraud the legal owner or intended beneficiary.

annotation

In some state codes embezzlement is treated as a form of **larceny,** i.e., theft by taking, in others as fraud, i.e., theft by deception.

See **fraud offenses** for general statistical recommendation. See also **embezzlement UCR 12.**

embezzlement   UCR 12   In Uniform Crime Reports terminology, the name of the UCR offense category used to record and report arrests for offenses of "misappropriation or misapplication of money or property entrusted to one's care, custody, or control."

annotation

By UCR reporting convention, arrests in incidents of employee theft are placed in this category since an employee is considered to have been entrusted with the money or property involved.

See **fraud offenses** for general recommendation.

entry to parole   see **release to parole**

escape   *tentatively recommended national category for prosecution, courts and corrections statistics*   The unlawful departure of a lawfully confined person from official custody.

defining features of tentatively recommended national category

unlawful departure of a lawfully confined person from a place of confinement or from custody while being transported

person confined because arrested, charged or convicted of a crime

annotation

This crime type is tentatively recommended as a national category for post-arrest offense statistics. Some penal codes explicitly include failure to return from authorized leave in the offense of "escape," but others do not. However, the distinction between failures to return and escapes as defined above is usually maintained in administrative data. See Appendix B for problems in national crime classification and complete set of tentatively proposed national categories for post-arrest offense statistics.

The National Prisoner Statistics (NPS) program employs the definition of "escape": unlawful departure from physical custody accomplished by breach of physical security, and flight from the custody of correctional personnel while being transported.

In NPS data **AWOL**, that is, failure to return from an authorized temporary absence, is counted separately, and is defined as those instances where the failure to return is formally declared an AWOL in accord with the rules of a given state. Some states do not formally register a person as AWOL until his absence has continued long after the required time of return. A variety of conventions exist with respect to the counting of "walkoffs" or "walkaways" from community correctional centers.

In penal codes, assisting or permitting an escape, or assisting anyone to avoid prosecution or custody are also offenses.

Avoiding prosecution or confinement after being charged with a criminal offense is usually not described as a specific offense in state statutes but is treated as failure to obey a court order (see **contempt of court**). Flight from justice across state lines or the borders of the U.S. to avoid prosecution, custody or confinement, or to avoid giving testimony in criminal proceedings concerning a crime punishable by imprisonment, is a federal offense.

See also **wanted person.**

excusable homicide   see **criminal homicide**

ex-offender   see **offender**

expert witness   see **witness**

expiration of sentence   *recommended statistical terminology*   In correctional usage, the termination of the period of time during which an offender has been required to be under the jurisdiction of a state prison or parole agency as the penalty for an offense.

annotation

This term is meant for use in prison/parole data only.

See "removals" in **parole agency caseload entries and removals** and "terminations" in **prison/parole population movement** for data structure usage.

"Expiration of probationary period" is the equivalent term for probation statistics. See **normal termination** under **probation supervisory population movement**.

A sentence to state correctional jurisdiction is said to have expired when the authority of the agency to confine or release the offender ends. That is, during the time an offender is on parole or has other conditional release status the sentence has not expired, but once the maximum time set by court or statute as the confinement and/or supervisory period has ended, no court or agency can limit that person's freedom without a new prosecution and conviction for a new offense.

Note that it is the maximum time period that cannot be extended. The calendar date on which the sentence is to expire can be altered if the offender escapes or violates conditions of his or her release, thus causing some of the time since sentencing to be considered not valid as **time served** (see entry) in prison or on parole.

Correctional agencies recalculate at various steps in the prison and parole process, the date that marks the end point of the total period of time that the person can be under correctional jurisdiction. This is the **aggregate maximum release date**, the calendar date on which a given offender should be fully discharged on all sentences currently in effect in that jurisdiction.

In states having a mandatory conditional release statute, correctional agencies also calculate the mandatory release date. This date marks the end point of the time that a given person may be incarcerated prior to conditional release, calculated as the length of institutional sentence minus credited good time.

extortion   Unlawfully obtaining or attempting to obtain something of value from another by compelling the other person to deliver it by the threat of eventual physical injury or other harm to that person or his property, or a third person.

annotation

Extortion differs from **robbery** in that in robbery there is an immediate confrontation between offender and victim, and the threatened injury is physical and imminent. Extortion is usually categorized as type of theft offense in penal codes.

Blackmail is the popular name for the kind of extortion where the threat is not physical but relates to exposing some secret or true or alleged fact which would do harm to the personal circumstances of a person, or damage his or her reputation. See also **threat**.

For the tentatively recommended national classification of post-arrest offense data, where kidnapping is the means of accomplishing extortion, the offense should be classified as **kidnapping** (see entry). Other extortions would be counted under "other." See Appendix B.

extradition   The surrender by one state to another of an individual accused or convicted of an offense in the second state.

annotation

Extradition usually occurs upon a demand in the form of a warrant issued by a court in the state or country wishing to obtain custody of the individual.

The delivery of the person to the state having jurisdiction to try or punish him or her will occur under executive or judicial authorization of the state in which the person is located at the time of the demand.

eyewitness   see **witness**

facilitation   see **inchoate offense**

facility   Generally, a structure or location built or established to serve a particular purpose.

annotation

In much correctional usage a basic distinction is made between **public facilities**, those used for programs operated by a government agency, and **private facilities**, those used for programs operated by a private agency. The distinction rests on immediate managerial responsibility, not on source of funding. Many private facility programs are wholly or in part supported by public funds.

A "contract facility" is a public or private facility which by special contract houses, supervises or treats persons under the jurisdiction of a court or correctional agency.

For classification information, see **correctional facility (adult)** and **juvenile facility.**

false imprisonment   see **kidnapping**

federal law enforcement agency   see **law enforcement agency**

federal law enforcement officer   see **law enforcement officer**

felony   A criminal offense punishable by death, or by incarceration in a prison facility.

annotation

In most jurisdictions felonies are one of the two major classes of crimes, the other being **misdemeanors**. The distinctive feature of the felony class is that although the upper limit of potential penalties depends upon the particular crime and ranges from as little as two years of confinement to death or life imprisonment, the lower limit for the entire class is relatively unvarying, usually one year.

The above terminology is recommended as the starting point for national level statistical usage because of the extent to which the felony/misdemeanor distinction, even though not consistent in detail among states, is meaningful, as described below. Statistics employing felony-misdemeanor distinctions and intended for national use should, however, present full definitions of these terms and any reporting conventions adopted in connection with them.

Felonies are not distinguished from misdemeanors in the same way in all jurisdictions. Most states define as a felony any offense for which the possible punishment is a year or more in a state prison, but a few states use the term "misdemeanor" to name offenses that can be punished by up to two or even five years incarceration. Time is, also, not the only consideration. One state defines a felony as "any crime for which an offender may be sentenced to death or imprisonment at hard labor." Further, even where two states employ the same "year or more" distinction, the same criminal act may be a felony in one and a misdemeanor in the other.

The felony-misdemeanor distinction does, however, reflect certain differences nationwide with a sufficient degree of consistency to produce meaningful statistics. The most serious crimes are never "misdemeanors," the most minor offenses are never "felonies." The class, "felony," is usually defined as the type of offense, and the only type, that can be punished by commitment to a prison, that is, a correctional facility having the custodial authority to hold persons with sentences of up to life. Further, the distinction regularly corresponds to differences in court processes: historically, misdemeanors were tried in lower courts and felonies in higher courts. This difference still underlies current procedural structure; the more serious felonies are tried in courts of general jurisdiction. (See **court**.)

Data displays should account for the many cases that enter the courts system as felonies and are disposed of as if they were misdemeanors, or are formally declared to be misdemeanors.

See **infraction** for recommended usage concerning offenses for which incarceration is not usually a permitted penalty.

FI   see **field interview**

field interrogation   see **field interview**

field interview   In law enforcement usage, generally, any contact between a private citizen and a law enforcement officer acting in his official capacity, whether or not relating to suspicion of criminal activity.

annotation

This term, and more or less equivalent terms such as "FI," "field contact," "field inquiry," "field stop," and "stop" are common law enforcement working vocabulary. The precise definitions are specific to a given local jurisdiction.

Field interrogation has a narrower meaning in law enforcement usage: the questioning by an officer in the field of a person who has come under direct suspicion in relation to a particular criminal event.

If an arrest is not made a **field interrogation report** (FI report or FIR) may result from a field interrogation. It identifies the person questioned and describes the circumstances of the contact. It is used as a source of information on modus operandi, on the whereabouts of suspects at the time of a crime, and other matters relevant to crime investigation. FI reports are temporary records.

filing   I. *recommended general court caseload statistical terminology* The initiation of a case in court by formal submission to the court of a document alleging the facts of a matter and requesting relief.   II. *recommended criminal justice statistical terminology*   The initiation of a criminal case in a court by formal submission to the court of a charging document, alleging that one or more named persons have committed one or more specified criminal offenses.

annotation

In the broadest usage, "filing" refers to the entering of any document into the official record of a court. The recommended definitions in I and II restrict usage to refer to events with potential major significance for national statistics: those filings which initiate a court case.

Definition I above reflects the usage of the model court caseload statistical system developed by the National Court Statistics Project under Bureau of Justice Statistics sponsorship, and is also the usual statistical usage of the term in connection with total court caseload.

Definition II specifically characterizes the criminal court case within the general definition of "case." It identifies the point at which the formal adjudication of a criminal case begins, and is the unit of count recommended for use in statistics describing the criminal case subset of total court caseload. In offender tracking data, the "filing" is also the process step at which critical counts are made.

Charging documents are variously called **complaints, informations** and **indictments** (see entries), depending upon the jurisdiction, the level of court and the originator of the accusation.

The single or several charges in a given charging document will ordinarily relate to one criminal event or a series of related criminal events, and constitute one unit of action in court as charge(s) are adjudicated. However, charges and defendants initially named in one document are sometimes later separated for trial or other purposes. Also, in offender-based transaction statistics and some other kinds of case flow data, the basic accounting unit is the defendant. Data presentations dealing with criminal case workload and flow should provide complete explanations of reporting conventions concerning filings.

In misdemeanor cases the initial document, usually called a "complaint," is ordinarily the only charging document filed. In felony cases one charging document will be filed to initiate the **preliminary hearing** on **probable cause**, and if the defendant is thereafter held to answer the felony charge, a second document may be filed to initiate the trial stage in a higher court. Thus, in a two level court jurisdiction, the initiation of a felony case could be counted twice. The second document may be called an "information," if it is filed by decision of the prosecutor, and will be called an "indictment," if filed by decision of a grand jury. (In some jurisdictions all felony accusations filed in a higher court are grand jury indictments.)

It is recommended that filings and dispositions of felony cases in courts of limited jurisdiction be counted separately from other caseload in those courts, to provide a proper picture of the interrelationship between limited and general jurisdiction court caseloads.

final plea   see **plea**

finding   see **court decision**

fine   The penalty imposed upon a convicted person by a court, requiring that he or she pay a specified sum of money to the court.

annotation

The recommended statistical category for **defendant dispositions** (see entry) is **fine, forfeit, court costs**, that is, all financial penalties imposed upon a defendant in a criminal case. Such penalties are often combined with other sentencing dispositions such as a grant of probation, or a jail or prison commitment.

While the requirement that a convicted person pay court costs is technically not a fine, such requirements are generally treated as fines in data programs.

A "forfeit" is something to which the right is lost by failure to perform an obligation or by commission of a crime. Bail is forfeited if the defendant does not appear for trial.

forcible rape   see **sex offenses**

forcible rape   UCR 2   *Uniform Crime Reports usage*   Sexual intercourse or attempted sexual intercourse with a female against her will, by force or threat of force.

annotation

See **sex offenses** for defining features and for general recommendation concerning prosecution, courts and corrections offense statistics.

Forcible rape is a UCR Crime Index offense. The UCR annual publication *Crime in the United States* presents data both on the occurrence of forcible rape offenses and on arrests relating to such offenses. See **Crime Index**.

In UCR data reporting, forcible rape is subdivided as follows:

2.a.   rape by force
2.b.   attempt to commit forcible rape

forfeit   see **fine**

forgery   The creation or alteration of a written or printed document, which if validly executed would constitute a record of a legally binding transaction, with the intent to defraud by affirming it to be the act of an unknowing second person; also the creation of an art object with intent to misrepresent the identity of the creator.

annotation

See **fraud offenses** for general statistical recommendation. See also **forgery and counterfeiting UCR 10**.

In statutes counterfeiting is included within the definition of forgery. Where a distinction is made, it rests on the fact that forged materials are of relevance to the legal affairs of specific persons while counterfeited materials, most typically money, have intrinsic value set by social convention or governmental authority. See **counterfeiting**.

forgery and counterfeiting   UCR 10   In Uniform Crime Reports terminology, the name of the UCR offense category used to record and report arrests for offenses of making, manufacturing, altering, possessing, selling, or distributing, or attempting to make, manufacture, alter, sell, distribute, or receive "anything false in the semblance of that which is true."

annotation

UCR provides the following list of offenses as examples of the content of this category:

Altering or forging public and other records.
Making, altering, forging, or counterfeiting bills, notes, drafts, tickets, checks, credit cards, etc.
Forging wills, deeds, notes, bonds, seals, trademarks, etc.
Counterfeiting coins, plates, banknotes, checks, etc.
Possessing or uttering forged or counterfeited instruments.
Erasures.
Signing the name of another or fictitious person with intent to defraud.
Using forged labels.
Possession, manufacture, etc., of counterfeiting apparatus.
Selling goods with altered, forged, or counterfeited trademarks.
All attempts to commit the above.

See **fraud offenses** for general recommendation.

fraud   UCR 11   In Uniform Crime Reports terminology, the name of the UCR offense category used to record and report arrests for offenses of conversion or obtaining of money or other thing of value by false pretenses, except forgery, counterfeiting and embezzlement.

annotation

Arrests for the fraud type offenses of forgery and counterfeiting are placed in **forgery and counterfeiting UCR 10**. Arrests for embezzlement are placed in **embezzlement UCR 12**.

See **fraud offenses** for general recommendation.

fraud offenses   *tentatively recommended national category for prosecution, courts and corrections statistics*   The crime type comprising offenses sharing the elements of practice of deceit or intentional misrepresentation of fact, with the intent of unlawfully depriving a person of his property or legal rights.

defining features *of tentatively recommended national category*

unlawfully depriving a person of his property or legal rights

by means of deceit or intentional misrepresentation

without damage to property or injury or threatened injury to persons

or

attempting or preparing to attempt the above offense

annotation

The phrase "preparing to attempt" in the above set of defining features is intended to embrace counterfeiting and forgery, both of which offenses comprise the making, possessing or altering of something in preparation for an attempt to defraud. A variety of offenses commonly separated in statistics (see list below) are placed together in this recommended broad category because research into penal codes and statistical practice indicates that the distinctions are not workable on a national basis. Different subdivisions of fraud are employed in different systems and the data capture capacity of all of them is questionable. (See Appendix B for a complete set of recommended and tentatively recommended national categories for post-arrest offense data, and for discussion of problems.)

Simple theft by taking (theft by stealth) and some types of theft by deception are often integrated in penal codes, but a great variety of other deception offenses are usually codified separately in relation to particular ways or instruments of using deceit in the commission of a criminal act, and the particular things or services which are the object of the theft. Consequently, offense elements are specified in considerable and different detail in different jurisdictions. Also, the same common offense names are attached to significantly different offenses.

In data systems the term "fraud" or "fraudulent activities" may appear as the name of a class of offenses, but the class typically contains only some of those crimes which share the element of fraud. For example, in Uniform Crime Reporting there is a category, **fraud UCR 11** but **forgery and counterfeiting UCR 10**, and **embezzlement UCR 12**, are separate (see those entries).

Offenses sharing the element of fraud, defined for informational purposes in this dictionary are: **check fraud, confidence game, counterfeiting, credit card fraud, embezzlement, forgery,** and swindle (under **confidence game**). All these are included in the tentatively recommended "fraud offenses" category.

fugitive   see **wanted person**

full opinion   see **opinion**

full pardon   see **clemency**

full-time temporary release   *recommended statistical terminology*   The authorized temporary absence of a prisoner from a confinement facility, for a period of 24 hours or more, for purposes relating to such matters as the prisoner's employment or education, or personal or family welfare.

annotation

This term is proposed for use when it is necessary to distinguish between extended leaves of absence of a full day or more and regular, short absences of part of a day for the same purposes. The regular brief absence is best designated as:

part-time temporary release   *recommended statistical terminology*   The authorized temporary regular absence of a prisoner from a confinement facility, for periods of less than 24 hours, for purposes relating to such matters as employment or education.

These terms are recommended for national level use because the terms "furlough," and "work/study release," and their variants, have been used interchangeably to mean both full- and part-time release.

The part-time release is not counted in national level prison population movement data.

The full-time release is classed as a **provisional exit** as opposed to a **conditional release** (see entries) in prison population movement data, because return from a conditional release depends upon the subject's behavior. See **prison/parole population movement** for a model data structure.

The National Prisoner Statistics definition of "work release," as of 1976, is "A program whose objective is the daytime release of inmates of a correctional institution to enable them to hold a paying job located outside of the physical confines of the institution and independent of the control of correctional authorities." This is probably the common usage, but some agencies have indicated that "work release" is a type of full-time release.

gambling   I. Staking or wagering of money or other thing of value on a game of chance, or on an uncertain event.   II. *tentatively recommended national category for prosecution, courts and corrections statistics*   Offenses relating to unlawful games of chance or wagering systems.

defining features *of tentatively recommended national category (II)*

unlawful making or receiving of wagers on a game of chance or uncertain event, or

operating, or promoting or permitting the operation of, an unlawful game of chance or wagering establishment

annotation

This category is tentatively recommended for post-arrest offense data. It is used in UCR reporting (see **gambling UCR 19**). See Appendix B for problems in national crime classification and complete set of tentatively proposed national categories for post-arrest offense statistics.

Gambling offenses included by name under **gambling UCR 19** are:

bookmaking   An organized, continuous operation for the unlawful receiving and paying off of wagers on uncertain events.

As defined in some penal codes, this offense includes casual operations such as office football pools. Prosecution, however, is highly unlikely in such instances. The usual criminal case relates to a professional operation conducted entirely for the purpose of making profits.

lottery   An unlawful game of chance in which a set amount of money is wagered for a chance to win a set prize.

numbers game, also called **policy**   An unlawful game of chance in which money is wagered on the occurrence of a chosen number and in which a winner is usually paid at odds.

Lotteries and numbers games differ in several ways. Usually in a lottery, a person bets a set amount of money by buying a ticket with a unique number on it. Only one person can bet on that number. The amounts to be won are set in advance. In most lotteries the winning numbers are determined by random selection from the numbers on the printed tickets.

In a numbers game, a person usually bets however much money he chooses on a single number. Any number of people can bet on the same number. The amount to be won is variable, depending on factors such as the amount of the person's bet, the total amount of all bets on the winning number, etc. The winning number is not randomly selected from the numbers bet on, but consists of a set of digits taken from an external source, such as the last three digits of the day's parimutuel gross receipts.

Some versions of all of the above activities except numbers games are legal in some jurisdictions.

gambling   UCR 19   In Uniform Crime Reports terminology, the name of the UCR category used to record and report arrests for offenses relating to promoting, permitting, or engaging in gambling.

annotation

For reporting of arrests relating to gambling offenses UCR requires a breakdown by type of gambling, as follows:

    a. Bookmaking (horse and sport book).
    b. Numbers and lottery.
    c. All other.

See **gambling** for general recommendation and definitions of the subtypes.

good time   In correctional usage, the amount of time deducted from time to be served in prison on a given sentence(s) and/or under correctional agency jurisdiction, at some point after a prisoner's admission to prison, contingent upon good behavior and/or awarded automatically by application of a statute or regulation.

annotation

A variety of names are used for the various types of good time: "mandatory good time," "statutory good time," "gain time," "blood time," "ordinary good time," "earned good time," "industrial good time," "work time," "meritorious good time," and the like.

The basic division is between good time received by automatic implementation of a rule, and good time earned by some kind of well performed service or worthy action.

Application of an automatic good time rule usually reduces the offender's maximum potential term in confinement and/or under correctional jurisdiction, though in many states it reduces the minimum term, and thus the parole eligibility date is affected. Some states have no "good time" provisions. See **time served** and **maximum sentence.**

Good time can be lost by misbehavior, unless awarded under a statute or regulation providing otherwise. Fixed good time is called "vested good time."

Summary descriptions of each state's good time rules can be found in *Parole Systems in the United States* (3rd ed., 1976, National Council on Crime and Delinquency). See also the Bureau of Justice Statistics publication *A National Survey of Parole-Related Legislation* for update on changes to parole and good time rules.

grand jury   *recommended statistical terminology*   A body of persons who have been selected according to law and sworn to hear the evidence against accused persons and determine whether there is sufficient evidence to bring those persons to trial, to investigate criminal activity generally, and to investigate the conduct of public agencies and officials.

annotation

In many states all felony charges must be considered by a grand jury before filing in the trial court. Ordinarily, a member of a prosecutorial agency presents to the grand jury for its consideration a list of charges and evidence related to a specific criminal event. The grand jury may then decide to indict (see **indictment**) or not indict (see **no true bill**).

A trial jury is distinguished from a grand jury in that a trial jury hears a case in order to render a verdict of guilt or nonguilt. A grand jury is asked only to decide whether there is sufficient evidence to cause a person to be brought to trial for a crime. See **trial jury.**

grant of parole   see **release to parole**

grant of probation   *syn*   **probation order**   *recommended statistical terminology*   A court action requiring that a person fulfill certain conditions of behavior for a specified period of time, often with assignment to a probation agency for supervision, either in lieu of prosecution or judgment, or after conviction, usually in lieu of a sentence to confinement.

annotation

The above replaces the 1st edition entry of "probation (sentence)." Probation is not always a sentencing disposition because it can be awarded before or after judgment, a difference in procedure which should be indicated in data presentations.

When probation is awarded before judgment it is in this recommended criminal justice terminology a defendant disposition listed under **adjudication withheld**. When awarded after conviction it is a sentencing disposition. Grants of probation can be subdivided into **court probation** (no correctional agency supervision) and **supervised probation** (active or inactive supervision by a probation agency).

In this terminology the granting of probation after conviction is viewed as a legal procedure distinct from sentence suspension or postponement. But in some jurisdictions, a grant of probation is viewed as a form of **suspended sentence** or **sentencing postponed**, or as an adjunct to such dispositions.

In one sense, a grant of probation is a legal agreement between the court and the defendant or offender, stipulating that as long as the subject meets certain behavioral requirements, the court will not proceed to judgment or will not impose confinement or will impose only a very limited period of confinement as a penalty for violation of the criminal law.

A grant of probation after conviction often includes another kind of sentencing disposition as a condition: a period in jail, payment of restitution in the form of money or public service, a fine, etc. Conditions of probation unique to an individual may also be imposed, such as payment of personal debts. Some courts commit offenders to prison with a period of probationary status, instead of parole, to follow.

The limits of probationary periods are usually set by statute and can be longer than the maximum sentence of confinement, or series of sentences to confinement, provided by law for a given offense(s). Some jurisdictions limit probationary periods for felonies to the maximum possible period of imprisonment for the offense.

See **defendant dispositions** and **probation supervisory population movement** for related classificatory terminology.

group home   see **juvenile facility**

guilty plea   see **plea**

guilty verdict   see **verdict**

habeas corpus   see **writ of habeas corpus**

habitual offender   *syn*   **habitual criminal**   A person sentenced under the provisions of a statute declaring that persons convicted of a given offense, and shown to have previously been convicted of another specified offense(s), shall receive a more severe penalty than that for the current offense alone.

annotation

Briefly, "habitual offenders" are persons punishable by statutory prescription on the basis of a previous separate conviction(s) in addition to the current conviction. The exact meaning of the term varies among jurisdictions depending on the type and number of crimes for which repeated convictions qualify the offender as "habitual."

In popular speech "habitual criminal" and terms such as "professional criminal" are used interchangeably, but the latter has no legal standing. The terms "career criminal" and "repeat offender," however, are acquiring formal status through official use in criminal justice policy statements and program descriptions. See **career criminal**.

In some jurisdictions, a statutorily defined habitual offender is called a "multiple offender."

See also **recidivist**.

halfway house   see **juvenile facility**

hearing   A proceeding in which arguments, witnesses, or evidence are heard by a judicial officer or administrative body.

annotation

In the broadest usage "hearing" refers to anything taking place before a judicial or quasi judicial body exercising decision making powers, in formal or informal circumstances, and including both adversary and non-adversary proceedings.

A trial is, technically, a type of hearing but is rarely referred to as such in criminal proceedings. See **trial**. For hearings in which key steps in criminal proceedings are taken, see **initial appearance, preliminary hearing, arraignment** and **sentencing hearing**. See also **probation revocation** and **parole revocation**.

hijacking   Taking control of a vehicle by the use or threatened use of force or by intimidation; or, taking a vehicle by stealth, without the use or threatened use of force, in order to steal its cargo.

annotation

Hijacking is a popular name for behavior that can constitute any of several statutory offenses. Where an occupant of the vehicle is forced to accompany the perpetrator the chargeable offense can be **kidnapping** or false imprisonment. Where a vehicle is taken by force with intent to permanently deprive the owner of the vehicle or any of its parts or contents the chargeable offense can be **robbery**.

Where a vehicle is taken by stealth the chargeable offense is usually **larceny**, but such an incident is usually recorded in data systems in a separate category of **motor vehicle theft**.

See **kidnapping** for recommendation concerning "hijack" of vehicles containing persons.

hit and run   *tentatively recommended national category for prosecution, courts and corrections statistics*   Unlawful departure by the vehicle operator from the scene of a motor vehicle accident which resulted in injury to a person or damage to property of another.

annotation

This category is tentatively recommended for prosecution, courts and corrections statistics. See Appendix B for problems in national crime classification and complete set of tentatively proposed national categories for post-arrest offense statistics.

The behavior described above is clearly identified in almost all state statutes, although usually under a variety of names other than "hit and run," and sometimes located in a vehicle code or other nonpenal law chapter.

homicide   see **criminal homicide**

household burglary (NCS)   see **household crimes**

household crimes   In National Crime Survey published data, a summary offense category consisting of:

household burglary
  forcible entry
  unlawful entry without force
  attempted forcible entry
household larceny
  completed larceny
    less than $50
    $50 or more
    amount not available
  attempted larceny
motor vehicle theft

annotation

Household crimes, also called "crimes against households," and **personal crimes** are the NCS primary offense categories.

In the NCS program, criminal events are not pre-classified in data collection, either by the survey interviewer or by the respondent. Rather, the determination of whether an event is to be considered a **criminal incident** (see entry) for NCS and its proper classification is made through computerized examination of reported characteristics of the event.

Data are presented in publications with varying levels of detail. The presentation categories for household crimes most generally employed are:

household burglary   The unlawful or forcible entry or attempted forcible entry of a residence, usually, but not necessarily, attended by theft.

In NCS usage, a residence is a separate living quarters which is occupied by a conventional household.

household larceny   The theft or attempted theft of money or property from a residence or its immediate vicinity.

Thefts or attempted thefts from residences which are accompanied by unlawful or forcible entry of the residence are classified as household burglary. Household larceny is limited to those instances where the person committing or attempting the theft had a legal right to be present in or about the residence.

Larceny from a person is classified as a **personal crime**. See that entry.

motor vehicle theft   The stealing or unauthorized taking of a motor vehicle, including attempts at such acts.

The NCS definition of "motor vehicle" is: "Includes automobiles, trucks, motorcycles, and any other motorized vehicles legally allowed on public roads and highways."

Motor vehicle theft is always classified as a household crime in NCS. By NCS convention, a "household," rather than any individual person, is the victim of this crime.

household larceny (NCS)   see **household crimes**

hung jury   A jury which after long deliberation is so irreconcilably divided in opinion that it is unable to reach any verdict.

annotation

The existence of a hung jury can result in the termination of a trial before verdict and judgment, when the court is satisfied that the jury is unlikely to agree upon a verdict within any reasonable period of time. Termination of a trial because of a hung jury usually results in retrial on the original charges, but is occasionally followed by a **dismissal** (see entry) of the charges.

In some jurisdictions, the judicial determination that a hung jury exists is grounds for declaring a **mistrial.**

illegal search and seizure   An act in violation of the Fourth Amendment of the U.S. Constitution: "The right of people to be secure in their persons, houses, papers and effects, against unreasonable searches and seizures, shall not be violated, and no warrants shall issue but upon probable cause, supported by oath or affirmation, and particularly describing the place to be searched and the persons or things to be seized."

annotation

Modern definitions of two of the key terms are:

search   The examination or inspection of a location, vehicle, or person by a law enforcement officer or other person authorized to do so, for the purpose of locating objects relating to or believed to relate to criminal activities, or wanted persons.

seizure   The taking into custody of law, by a law enforcement officer or other person authorized to do so, of objects relating to or believed to relate to criminal activity.

See also **probable cause** and **search warrant.**

Interpretation of the fourth amendment varies. Understanding of the rules governing search and seizure in different jurisdictions requires study of the statutes and case law of each state. In California, searches and seizures are considered to be "reasonable" if made under any of the following circumstances:

1. "With a valid search warrant; or
2. "Incidental to a valid arrest made pursuant to a warrant of arrest or on probable cause (exception: a search warrant is required for materials having possible protection as free speech by the First Amendment); or
3. "By an officer lawfully on the premises (e.g., with probable cause to make an arrest; with consent; to render aid; in hot pursuit of escaping felon; pressing emergency; search of parolee's premises; or on public premises), though no arrest is in fact made, and who sees the evidence or contraband in plain sight; or
4. "By an officer who searches a vehicle with reasonable cause to believe the vehicle contains contraband or evidence of crime even though not incidental to valid arrest (justified because of mobility). This rule is limited to vehicles. Probable cause to believe a search will reveal contraband does not justify a search of a home or personal effects without a warrant, unless the search is incidental to a valid arrest based on probable cause; or
5. "With consent voluntarily obtained."

A judicial officer may determine at a suppression hearing that evidence was obtained by illegal search and seizure. If the evidence is then suppressed, and if it is critical in proving the charge, the prosecution may drop the case and it may be dismissed. If it is not critical, the case may proceed.

inactive supervision   see **supervised probation**

incest   Unlawful sexual intercourse between closely related persons.

annotation

Typically, intercourse is prohibited between ancestors and descendants, between siblings, and between half-siblings, sometimes between aunt and nephew or uncle and niece as well. Frequently the prohibitions are extended to persons related by adoption, in addition to those related by blood.

In some states, a single statute prohibits both sexual intercourse and intermarriage between closely related persons, but in many states these are two separate offenses, sometimes specifying different degrees of relationship. Some states, for example, prohibit marriage between first cousins, although intercourse between such persons would not be incest.

An offense of incest would be classified as "forcible rape," "other violent sex offenses," "statutory rape" or "other nonviolent sex offenses" in the tentatively recommended categories for prosecution, courts and corrections level offense reporting. The decision would depend upon whether force was used, and upon the age and sex of the victim. This splitting of "incest type" offenses parallels the practice in many recently revised penal codes. See **sex offenses** for classification. "Marriage within prohibited degrees" would be placed in the "other" category. See also Appendix B.

In UCR, "incest" is included by name in **sex offenses UCR 17**, and "marriage within prohibited degrees" in **all other offenses UCR 26**.

inchoate offense   *syn*   **anticipatory offense**   An offense which consists of an action or conduct which is a step to the intended commission of another offense.

annotation

Many state penal codes have a chapter entitled "inchoate offenses." In general usage "inchoate" usually carries the meaning of "incomplete, attempted, not fully formed." The criminality of the behavior constituting an inchoate offense arises from the presence of the intent to proceed to completion of a criminal act.

In some cases, when the intended crime is completed, the inchoate offense may also be charged. But the chief purpose of codification of inchoate offenses is to provide for punishment for criminal behavior that does not accomplish a final criminal purpose. The penalties for inchoate offenses usually depend upon the gravity of the intended crime.

Offenses typically listed under this heading in penal codes are:

attempt   The intentional performance of an overt act directed toward the commission of a crime, with intent to commit the crime and ability to do so, but without completion of it.

Attempts are sometimes accorded the same penalties as the completed offenses.

One judicial opinion states that an act must have four characteristics in order to constitute an attempt:

1. It must be a step toward a punishable offense.
2. It must be at least apparently adapted to the purpose intended.
3. It must come close to completion.
4. It must not succeed.

In UCR **Part I offense** data, attempts are counted together with completed crimes, with the exception of "attempted murder" which is counted as **aggravated assault UCR 4a–d.**

A **threat** may be an element of an attempted or completed crime. See entry.

criminal conspiracy   An agreement by two or more persons to commit or to effect the commission of an unlawful act, or to use unlawful means to accomplish an act which is not in itself unlawful, plus some overt act in furtherance of the agreement.

The term "collusion" is used in some contexts to mean certain kinds of conspiracy. Sometimes it means conspiracy to commit fraud; sometimes any conspiracy that involves only two persons.

solicitation to commit a crime   Unlawful intentional asking in any manner of another person(s) to commit a crime.

criminal facilitation   Unlawful conduct on the part of a person by which he or she knowingly aids another person to commit a crime.

In facilitation there is no offense unless a crime has actually been committed by another person. It is generally charged where the defendant acted with a degree of **culpability** less than that required to convict him or her of the substantive crime. Many jurisdictions have no statutory offense of this type.

included offense   *syn*   lesser included offense   An offense which is made up of elements which are a subset of the elements of another offense having a greater statutory penalty, and the occurrence of which is established by the same evidence or by some portion of the evidence which has been offered to establish the occurrence of the greater offense.

annotation

The interpretation of data describing the dispositions of criminal cases requires understanding of the legal concept "included offense" and the related but not equivalent term "reduced charge." The charge(s) of which a defendant is convicted will often not be the same as the charge(s) made in the charging document that initiates criminal proceedings. This type of alteration of charges however, occurs within strict limitations with respect to a given case (proceedings relating to one charging document). The convicted offense must be an included offense to the original charge or a reduced charge that has a logical relation to the evidence of criminal behavior brought forth in connection with the original charge.

The **Model Penal Code** defines "included offense" as an offense which has any of the following characteristics:

a) It is established by proof of the same or less than all the facts required to establish the commission of the greater (charged) offense.

b) It consists of an attempt or solicitation to commit the greater offense or to commit an offense otherwise included in the greater offense.

c) It differs from the greater offense only in the respect that a less serious injury or risk of injury to the same person, property or public interest, or a lesser kind of culpability suffices to establish its commission.

In many jurisdictions it is standard practice for the prosecutor to separately charge all lesser included offenses. However, a person can be found guilty of a lesser included offense even if not specifically charged with it, in any instance where the judge so decides in a nonjury trial or instructs the jury as to the possibility in a jury trial.

When a person is convicted of an included offense in lieu of conviction of the original greater offense, it is sometimes said that he or she was "convicted of a reduced charge."

However, a "reduced charge" is the result of an optional step in criminal proceedings. In practice, a **reduced charge** is a new charge, which is entered by prosecutorial action during the course of proceedings, and which replaces the original greater charge. The reduced charge is then the only one to be considered by judge or jury.

The reduced charge need not be an included offense with respect to the original charge. That is, it can be an offense which has one or more elements which are not elements of the more serious offense.

See also **element of the offense**.

incompetent to stand trial   *recommended statistical terminology*   In criminal proceedings, the finding by a court that a defendant is mentally incapable of understanding the nature of the charges and proceedings against him or her, of consulting with an attorney, and of aiding in his or her own defense.

annotation

This is a type of **defendant disposition** (see entry).

When a court finds that a given defendant is incompetent to stand trial, criminal proceedings against that defendant are suspended until such time as the defendant may be found competent. Frequently, the court will order periodic examination of the defendant to determine whether competency has been regained.

A plea or finding that a defendant is **not guilty by reason of insanity** differs from a finding that a defendant is "incompetent to stand trial." The former is a defense to prosecution on the grounds that the defendant was mentally incompetent at the time that an alleged crime was committed. The latter concerns only the defendant's mental fitness at the time of trial, and is not related to any determination of guilt. See **capacity**.

A finding of "incompetent to stand trial" can be followed by a **civil commitment** (see entry).

indecent exposure   Unlawful intentional, knowing, or reckless exposing to view of the genitals or anus, in a place where another person may be present who is likely to be offended or alarmed by such an act.

annotation

In most jurisdictions an offense will only be charged against a person who is above a certain age or who has attained a certain degree of physical development. In some states, an age limit for the offense is established by statute. Some statutes specify that the act must be performed in a "lewd or lascivious" manner.

This offense would be classified as "other nonviolent sex offenses" in the tentatively recommended categories for post-arrest offense reporting. See **sex offenses**.

This offense is included by name in **sex offenses UCR 17.**

indeterminate sentence   A type of sentence to imprisonment where the commitment, instead of being for a specified single time quantity, such as three years, is for a range of time, such as two to five years, or five years maximum and zero minimum.

annotation

Statutory sentencing structures and actual individual sentences are frequently characterized by the words, "indeterminate" or "indefinite," versus "definite," "determinate," or "flat." This language falsely suggests that there are two clearly contrasting types of sentencing structures and sentences.

In fact, there are as many patterns of time limits, rules automatically modifying time limits, and rules endowing different authorities with different amounts or types of discretion to alter time served in confinement and under correctional jurisdiction, as there are states. Also, some states permit different types of sentence structures to be applied to different offenders or offenses within the same jurisdiction.

Generally, an "indeterminate" sentence will be as defined above, with a paroling authority determining, within limits set by the sentencing judge or by statute, the exact date of release from prison and of termination of correctional jurisdiction.

Where the sentence is **determinate**, a single time quantity is set and this is in effect the maximum. This quantity (and/or the minimum attached by automatically applied rule) is likely to be lower than the limits automatically provided by statute, or set by the court, in the "indeterminate" method. Some degree of paroling authority discretion, "good time" rules, and the like will still usually determine the actual release and termination dates.

The most recent summary description of the sentencing structures of the 50 states is *Parole Systems in the United States* (3rd ed., 1976, National Council on Crime and Delinquency). This area of law and regulation is in transition and the current status in each state can be determined only by inquiring of the individual parole authorities.

For statistical data reporting, one type of maximum sentence figure (meaning maximum potential period of confinement), and sometimes a minimum sentence time value, is calculable for each offender at time of commitment by applying the court sentencing decision and the rules of the jurisdiction to the individual case. See **maximum sentence.**

Index Crimes   see **Crime Index**

indictment   A formal, written accusation submitted to the court by a grand jury, alleging that a specified person(s) has committed a specified offense(s), usually a felony.

annotation

An indictment is the type of charging document which initiates the trial stage of a felony case after **grand jury** consideration. See **charging document** and **filing** for recommended statistical terminology.

The usual procedure is for a prosecutor to present allegations and evidence to a grand jury (often called a "bill of indictment") and for the grand jury, if it agrees that there is sufficient evidence to sustain an accusation(s), to "return an indictment" (also called a "true bill"). The indictment delivered to the court states the facts about the alleged crime as found by the grand jury and cites the penal code sections believed to have been violated.

For the grand jury action rejecting a case, see **no true bill**.

When a grand jury takes notice of an offense on its own initiative and delivers an indictment it is sometimes called a "grand jury original." See also **presentment**.

In some jurisdictions all felony cases must be tried through indictment by a grand jury but in others felony trials will ordinarily be initiated by the filing of an **information** by a prosecutor.

Since "to indict" means "to accuse," "indictment" is sometimes used to mean any accusation of wrongdoing.

information   In criminal justice usage, a formal, written accusation submitted to the court by a prosecutor, alleging that a specified person(s) has committed a specified offense(s).

annotation

An information is a type of charging document and initiates a criminal case. See **filing** and **charging document** for recommended statistical terminology.

This term is usually the name for the accusation filed by the prosecutor to initiate the trial stage of a felony case, but these are also called "affidavits" and "accusations."

In some jurisdictions the prosecutor does not formally initiate felony trials. All felony cases reach the trial court by way of grand jury **indictment** (see entry).

infraction   A violation of state statute or local ordinance punishable by a fine or other penalty, but not by incarceration, or by a specified, unusually limited term of incarceration.

annotation

This term is recommended as the best available name for the type of offense which generally is not viewed as a crime in the sense that instances are not recorded in criminal justice records and not covered in criminal case statistics. This category is not strictly definable as a national level unit of count, but is always distinguishable from the clearcut "criminal" offenses in a given state. **Violation** is also used as a name for this type of offense. This usage is not recommended. See entry.

Some state codes clearly define a specific, named class of offenses not punishable by incarceration, or by a limited period such as up to 15 or up to 30 days. Others do not differentiate so clearly in statute, but in all jurisdictions there is a class comprised of "noncriminal" offenses such as parking violations, minor violations of health and sanitation codes, and the like which are disposed of by **citations (forfeit)** (see **citation (appear)**), administrative hearing, or other essentially non-adversary procedures. Data concerning these offenses are therefore likely to appear only in descriptions of, for example, special traffic court or administrative agency workload.

"Infraction" also appears frequently in correctional contexts as the name for an act contrary to prison regulations. See **infraction (corrections)**.

infraction (corrections)   A statutory offense or a violation of prison or jail administrative regulations committed by an offender while incarcerated or in a temporary release program such as work release.

annotation

This term does not apply to misconduct while on **conditional release** status (see entry). See **parole violation** for contrast.

Alleged infractions of law or institutional rules are recorded in documents usually called "conduct reports" or "disciplinary reports." Opportunity to rebut such allegations is usually offered to the prisoner in a proceeding called an "inmate disciplinary hearing" or similar name.

When it is believed that a crime has been committed a corrections agency usually has a certain amount of discretion regarding the decision to seek a judicial disposition or to treat the matter as an infraction of an institutional rule.

initial appearance   *recommended statistical terminology*   In criminal proceedings, the first appearance of an accused person in the first court having jurisdiction over his or her case.

annotation

Various procedural steps may be taken during a first appearance. In minor misdemeanor cases the first appearance may be the only one, and judgment and penalty, if any, will be determined at that time. When the charge(s) is more serious, the accused at initial appearance may be informed of the charges, a plea may be entered and bail set, or the accused may merely be informed of his or her rights and of the general nature of the proceedings and it may be determined whether he or she has counsel.

The timing of an initial appearance is largely determined by whether the defendant is in custody, and by the laws concerning the maximum period a person can be held in custody without court appearance.

Despite the various possibilities as to what may occur at an initial appearance, it is ordinarily necessary to record the fact and date of the event in management data systems. The information is needed to track cases and defendants, to capture elapsed time information, and generally to differentiate the first court hearing from all other hearings of statistical relevance.

In any given jurisdiction the initial appearance may be characterized by the major step taken in that court at that point. Thus, a first appearance may be called a "preliminary **arraignment**," "**preliminary hearing**," "magistrate's preliminary hearing," or "**presentment**" (see entries).

initial plea   see **plea**

inmate   see **prisoner**

institutional capacity   An officially stated number of inmates which a confinement or residential facility is or was intended to house.

annotation

Institutional capacity is a term of broad possible meaning. The following terms are commonly used to indicate more limited meanings. The definitions provided are intended to represent some typical usages.

design capacity or **bed capacity**   The number of inmates which a correctional facility was originally designed to house, or currently has the capacity to house as a result of later, planned modifications, exclusive of extraordinary arrangements to accommodate overcrowded conditions.

rated capacity   The number of inmates which a correctional facility can house without overcrowding, determined by comparison with some set of explicit standards applied to groups of facilities.

operational capacity or **staff capacity** or **budgeted capacity**   The number of inmates which a correctional facility can house while in conformity with a set of standards relating to what are considered appropriate ratios between staff and inmates and staff and bed capacity. This capacity, determined by administrative decisions relating to such factors as budgetary or personnel limits, is often less than design or rated capacity.

It should be noted that the adjectives "design" and "rated" tend to relate to architectural features. The others, such as "operational," usually represent personnel factors. Exact meanings cannot be determined without knowledge of the criteria employed in different jurisdictions or standard-setting systems.

A long term study of state and local confinement facilities has recently been completed by Abt Associates, of Boston, Massachusetts, for the National Institute of Justice. A special measure of institutional capacity was devised for the study, to provide a standard for comparison of facilities in different jurisdictions. This is the **measured capacity**.

The measured capacity of a facility is the number of persons who can be housed in the facility, allowing a minimum of 60 square feet of floor space per person. The measure is based on the space available in individual housing areas rather than on total housing space for the facility. Any separate area of less than 120 square feet is considered an individual cell housing one person. For larger areas, the total square footage of each area is divided by 60 to determine the number of persons that can be housed in the space.

institutional facility   see **juvenile facility**

insufficient evidence   In criminal proceedings, evidence that is not enough to constitute proof at the level required at a given point in the proceedings.

annotation
See **levels of proof.**

intake   The process by which a juvenile referral is received by personnel of a probation agency, juvenile court or special intake unit, and a decision made to close the case at intake, or refer the juvenile to another agency, or place him or her under some kind of care or supervision, or file a petition in a juvenile court.

annotation

Intake, or "probation screening" or "preliminary screening" is the first step in decisionmaking regarding a juvenile (or parent, in the case of dependency and neglect cases) whose behavior or alleged behavior is in violation of law or could otherwise cause a juvenile court to assume jurisdiction.

What kind of official or government unit makes the intake decision depends on how a given jurisdiction has organized its juvenile services. The screening function is sometimes assigned to probation officers attached to the court, sometimes to individuals or a special unit within a probation agency, or to a separate agency.

Regardless of the location of intake decision authority, actions at three distinct steps of the intake process can be counted in data reporting on juvenile proceedings.

referral to intake   A written request by a law enforcement agency, parent, or other agency or person, that an intake officer or unit take appropriate action concerning a juvenile alleged to have committed a delinquent act or status offense, or alleged to be dependent. These data are not reported by an intake agency; they are the output of another agency, such as a police department, asking an intake officer or unit to consider a case.

referral received   The receipt by an intake officer or unit of a written request in the form of a report or complaint alleging a violation(s) of a statute(s) or requesting that action be taken concerning a dependent child. These data represent the incoming workload of an intake agency, the aggregate of all the referrals to intake made by other agencies and persons.

intake decision   The immediate outcome of the referral of a juvenile case to an intake officer or unit. These data represent the decisions of the intake agency concerning what further actions, if any, will be taken regarding the referred case.

Classification of and terminology for juvenile intake decisions varies greatly among jurisdictions. A typical set of intake decision categories will include: closed at intake, counseled and released, placed on informal probation, referred for testing, referred to another agency, petition filed for formal court action. (In some jurisdictions the prosecutor will review petitions alleging delinquent acts or status offenses after the intake officer or unit has considered the social aspects of the case but before the petition is filed in court, in order to consider the adequacy of the factual basis of the allegations.)

Current data publications usually treat the juvenile court and all of its functionally connected officials, administrative units, or agencies as one unit for purposes of describing screening and adjudicatory activity. In addition to the above dispositions at the point of intake decision, the data presentation will list dispositions of placement on formal probation, placement in a group or foster home, commitment to a juvenile correctional facility, and so on. The summaries may indicate, under "method of handling" or a similar label, whether the disposition was made "unofficially," that is, by the intake officer or unit, or "officially" by the court.

Intake screening decisions that refer the client out of the justice system or away from formal adjudication are now often called **diversion** (see entry).

Data terminology is recommended in this dictionary only for proceedings following the filing of a petition, that is, a request for formal adjudication. See **juvenile petition** and **juvenile court judgment.**

intake decision   see intake

intent   The state of mind or attitude with which an act is carried out; the design, resolve or determination with which a person acts to achieve a certain result.

annotation

"Intent," "purpose," and "motive" appear in general usage as synonyms, but motive does not belong in this group. A **motive** is an inner stimulus that moves a person to act. In a sense, motive precedes an action. Intent is an aspect of an action. In definitions of crimes, intent is the purpose to use a particular means to accomplish a particular result. The difference in meaning is best presented by example: The motive for a murder can be hate or greed (the desire for financial gain). The intent, which makes the action a crime, is the determination to kill. Intent is an element of most offenses. Motive is never an element of an offense.

See also **culpability.**

interlocutory appeal   A request, made at some point before judgment in trial court proceedings, that a court having appellate jurisdiction review a pre-judgment decision of the trial court before judgment is reached.

annotation

Some states permit interlocutory appeals, others do not.

Unlike appeals following completion of trial court proceedings, interlocutory appeals do not challenge the trial court's decision in the case as a whole, but only the correctness of some particular pre-judgment decision. See **appeal.**

The decision being appealed may or may not be one which would have a bearing on the eventual judgment in the case. Where the subject matter of the appeal is such that it would likely have a bearing (for example, an appeal of a decision granting or denying a motion to suppress evidence in a criminal case), the trial court proceedings may be halted pending determination of the appeal.

intermediate appellate court   see court

intermittent sentence   *recommended statistical terminology*   A sentence to periods of confinement interrupted by periods of freedom.

annotation

This term is proposed as a substitute for "weekend sentence," which has come to be used in some jurisdictions to mean regular repeated periods of imprisonment on any specified day or days of the week.

interstate compact   An agreement between two or more states to transfer prisoners, parolees, or probationers from the physical or supervisory custody of one state to the physical or supervisory custody of another, where the correctional agency that first acquired jurisdiction over the person usually retains the legal authority to confine or release the prisoner.

annotation

Interstate compacts providing for the transfer of probationers, parolees or prisoners are formal documents setting forth the conditions under which such transfers may take place and the respective powers and duties of the participating agencies. The rules and procedures are frequently expressed in statutes.

Formal agreements are also executed between local jurisdictions, and both state and local agencies also utilize informal **courtesy supervision** (see entry).

Interstate compacts concerning the transfer of supervisory custody of adult probationers and parolees usually require the receiving state to assume "the duties of visitation and supervision," although the sending state retains jurisdiction (see **custody**), and the probationer or parolee signs an agreement to return to the sending state upon demand and waives all procedure relating to extradition.

Interstate compacts relating to juveniles usually have among their chief purposes, returning runaways or juveniles absconding from supervision to their homes or to community supervision. This kind of transfer is, however, usually done informally.

An interstate compact concerning prisoners may provide for the exchange of prisoners, or for transfer in one direction only, as when state A, having overcrowded institutions, regularly sends some prisoners to state B for housing.

Exchanges aimed at protecting prisoners who have been threatened by other inmates are often done informally.

The National Prisoner Statistics program counts as "transfers from another jurisdiction" only those interstate compact movements where both jurisdiction and physical custody are transferred. See **transfer (corrections)**.

intoxication   *syn*   **public intoxication**   *tentatively recommended national category for prosecution, courts and corrections statistics*   The offense of being in a public place while intoxicated through consumption of alcohol, or intake of a controlled substance or drug.

annotation

This category is tentatively recommended for national post-arrest offense data. It is used in UCR reporting (see **drunkenness UCR 23**). See Appendix B for problems in national crime classification and complete set of tentatively proposed national categories for post-arrest offense statistics.

Public intoxication resulting from alcohol, or "public drunkenness," has been decriminalized in many jurisdictions. That is, the behavior or condition is no longer a penal code violation but is usually treated as a health problem. In other jurisdictions, the statutes explicitly provide law enforcement discretion to treat these cases as health matters or crimes.

Where a person who is publicly intoxicated performs acts which cause a disturbance, he or she may be charged with "disorderly conduct." See **disturbing the peace** for general recommendation.

Operation of a motor vehicle while intoxicated is usually a separate statutory offense. See **driving under the influence.**

involuntary manslaughter   see **criminal homicide**

jail   *recommended statistical terminology*   A confinement facility administered by an agency of local government, typically a law enforcement agency, intended for adults but sometimes also containing juveniles, which holds persons detained pending adjudication and/or persons committed after adjudication, usually those committed on sentences of a year or less.

annotation

In jurisdictions where the basic penalty range division is not the usual one year or less vs. more than a year, some local confinement facilities for sentenced prisoners have the custodial authority to hold persons sentenced for up to several years.

In a number of jurisdictions facilities have been established that hold only arrested persons who are awaiting first appearance in court for arraignment or pretrial release consideration. These are not considered to be jails in this recommended terminology. See **pre-arraignment lockup**.

In five jurisdictions (Delaware, Connecticut, Vermont, Rhode Island and Hawaii), all adult confinement facilities are administered at the state level. Facilities administered by state governments are not classified as jails in this recommended terminology.

See **correctional facility (adult)** for further classification information. See also **felony** and **misdemeanor.**

jail commitment   *recommended statistical terminology*   A sentence of commitment to the jurisdiction of a confinement facility system for adults which is administered by an agency of local government and of which the custodial authority is usually limited to persons sentenced to a year or less of confinement.

annotation

A jail commitment is a type of **sentencing disposition** in the major class **defendant dispositions** (see entries).

A jail commitment is often included as a "condition of probation," meaning that release from jail will be followed by a period of probationary status.

"Jail commitments" in this terminology include commitments to the facilities called "jails," and also those called "county farms," "honor farms," "work camps," "road camps," and the like, if the custodial authority of the facility is sentences of a year or less. For discussion of problems in classificatory definitions of "jails" see **correctional facility (adult).**

joinder   I.   In the broadest usage, the combining of multiple defendants and/or charges for purposes of any legal step or proceeding.   II.   In criminal proceedings, the naming of two or more defendants and/or the listing of two or more charges in a single charging document.

annotation

In criminal proceedings the term "consolidation" is often used to refer to the joining for trial of defendants or charges originally contained in separate charging documents. See "consolidated trial" under the entry **trial**.

"Joinder of defendants," and "joinder of offenses" are used to specify who or what is being joined.

See also **severance**.

joyriding   see **motor vehicle theft**

judge   see **judicial officer**

judge pro tem   *syn*   **judge pro tempore**   A judge who sits in lieu of a regularly appointed or elected judge, and who is appointed with full authority to hear all of the cases scheduled for, and to exercise all functions of, the regular judge.

annotation

A judge pro tem is appointed to substitute for a regular judge who, for example, is on vacation or is ill. Such appointments may be for a day or a week or for up to several months.

Judges pro tem are usually attorneys, retired judges, or judicial officers from other courts.

judgment   I. In the broadest usage, any decision or determination of a court.   II. *recommended criminal justice statistical terminology* The statement of the decision of a court, that the defendant is acquitted or convicted of the offense(s) charged.

annotation

"Judgment" is sometimes used to mean any court decision, such as a judgment of conviction, an acquittal, a court order, or a sentence. Since final judgments of **conviction** or **acquittal** (see entries) are key decisions in criminal cases, the most limited meaning is recommended for criminal justice data terminology.

A **verdict** is not equivalent to a judgment. Although the court must pronounce a judgment of **acquittal** after a "not guilty" verdict is delivered by a jury, the court may decline to follow a "guilty" verdict with a judgment of **conviction**.

Pronouncement of judgment is recommended as a basic process point for counting disposed cases and defendants in general court activity data. See **court disposition**.

The date of a judgment of conviction is an important item in calculations of elapsed time in those jurisdictions where a sentence must be pronounced within a time limit. The count begins the day the judgment is pronounced.

See **juvenile court judgment** for juvenile case decisions. See also **court decision**.

judicial officer   *recommended statistical terminology*   Any person authorized by statute, constitutional provision, or court rule to exercise those powers reserved to the judicial branch of government.

annotation

For national level comparative data the judicial personnel category is necessarily broad. Only in single jurisdictions is it possible to make a distinction on a consistent basis between those judicial officers commonly called "judges" and those known by other titles.

As a general rule, a judge is an official having broad authority granted by statute or constitution. Judges preside over sessions of courts of general jurisdiction. Judges conduct appellate court business.

Other judicial officers receive delegated authority through a court, or in certain cases limited authority by statute. It is also possible to define those officials who are not judges as those whose decisions cannot become court orders without confirmation by a judge. However, distinctions such as these do not apply throughout all states consistently enough to permit a national level division of judicial officers into two clearcut categories.

Judicial officers of all types may have special names indicating particular roles or functions within the modern judicial system, or names that reflect historical roles, derived from long standing tradition. One of the oldest names is **magistrate**, which as a modern official title in the U.S. usually means the judicial officer of a court of limited jurisdiction who sets bail and may conduct misdemeanor trials and felony preliminary (probable cause) hearings. (But the term also appears in legal literature as a synonym for "judge.")

Special names for judges include **appellate judge, trial judge, administrative judge, presiding judge, judge pro tem, special judge** (see those entries). Names for other judicial officers include "justices of the peace," "magistrates," "masters," "commissioners," "referees," "hearing officers" and, collectively, "parajudicial personnel" or "parajudges."

Some of these "parajudges" perform basic functions of the judicial process such as setting bail and hearing certain kinds of cases. Others specialize in or are limited to a particular type of proceeding such as probate, juvenile matters, traffic or domestic relations. Still others are officials such as parole board or commission members and certain probation officers, holding specified, limited judicial powers in relation to the powers and duties of the administrative agencies to which they belong.

The authority of officials known by these titles in any given jurisdiction depends upon the combination of statutory and administrative rules, and customs, governing practice in the particular jurisdiction.

In *Parajudges: Their Role in Today's Court Systems* (National Center for State Courts, Research and Information Service, 1976.), "parajudges" are described as follows: "For the purposes of this report, a parajudge is defined as a master, court commissioner, referee, etc., who participates in the judging or decision-making process but, in most cases, does not make a final judgment. As a rule, he has no original jurisdiction, but receives cases on an assignment basis from the judge(s). Parajudges conduct hearings, analyze evidence, examine witnesses, and submit their report to the court. These reports may contain findings of fact, conclusions of law, and recommendations for disposition. The judge, after reviewing the parajudge's report, issues the court's decree. No parajudicial report becomes the court's order without first receiving the confirmation of a judge. At his discretion, a judge may accept, reject, or modify the parajudge's findings."

jurisdiction   The territory, subject matter, or persons over which lawful authority may be exercised by a court or other justice agency, as determined by statute or constitution.

annotation

An important related term is:

venue   The geographical area within which a court has jurisdiction; the geographical area (municipality, county, etc.) from which a jury is drawn and in which trial is held in a court action.

There are generally two kinds of subject matter jurisdiction for courts:

original jurisdiction   The lawful authority of a court to hear or act upon a case from its beginning and to pass judgment on the law and the facts.

appellate jurisdiction   The lawful authority of a court to review a decision made by a lower court; the lawful authority of a court to hear an appeal from a judgment of a lower court.

A given court can have more than one kind of jurisdiction. From the criminal justice perspective, for example, a court of limited jurisdiction will commonly have trial jurisdiction over misdemeanor cases but only preliminary jurisdiction over felony cases. A court of general jurisdiction will have trial jurisdiction over felony cases and frequently appellate jurisdiction over misdemeanor cases tried in lower courts. An appellate court will have appellate jurisdiction over felony cases and original jurisdiction for the issuance of certain writs, but no trial jurisdiction.

See **court**. For the use of the term in corrections see **custody**.

jurisdiction (corrections)   see **custody**

jury   see **trial jury**

jury panel   The group of persons summoned to appear in court as potential jurors for a particular trial, or the persons selected from the group of potential jurors to sit in the jury box, from which second group those acceptable to the prosecution and the defense are finally chosen as the jury.

annotation

That segment of the population within a given jurisdiction which is summoned for jury duty, and which must appear as potential jurors for a particular trial, is sometimes called the "jury pool."

The group of persons who are asked to sit in the jury box are usually selected by the court clerk by lot. As individuals are dismissed from the box for various reasons, replacements are chosen, also by lot.

See also **trial jury** and **grand jury**.

jury poll   A poll conducted by a judicial officer or by the clerk of the court after a jury has stated its verdict but before that verdict has been entered in the record of the court, asking each juror individually whether the stated verdict is his own verdict.

annotation

A jury poll can be initiated by motion of the prosecution or the defense, or the court. If the poll determines that all or the required portion of jurors do not agree on a verdict, then the jury in some jurisdictions may be sent back for further deliberation, or, in others, discharged.

jury sentencing In criminal proceedings, upon a jury verdict of guilty, the recommendation or determination of a sentence by the jury.

annotation

Jury sentencing occurs only in those jurisdictions which have statutes specifically authorizing it, and usually relates only to crimes punishable by death or by life imprisonment.

When the jury recommends a sentence the court may not necessarily accept it. However, in some jurisdictions the jury, by statute, makes a final determination of sentence.

jury trial see **trial**

justifiable homicide see **criminal homicide**

juvenile In the context of the administration of justice, a person subject to juvenile court proceedings because a statutorily defined event or condition caused by or affecting that person was alleged to have occurred while his or her age was below the statutorily specified age limit of original jurisdiction of a juvenile court.

annotation

Court jurisdiction is determined by age at the time of the event, not at the time of judicial proceedings, and continues in juvenile offender cases until the case is terminated (unless the case is transferred to adult court for prosecution).

The age limit defining the legal categories "juvenile" and "adult" varies among states and also, with respect to specified crimes, within states. The generally applicable age limit within a given state is most often the 18th birthday. In statutes establishing criminal trial court jurisdiction over persons below the standard age for specified crimes (usually violent crimes such as murder or armed robbery) the age limit may be lowered to 16 or even less. These variations in the age factor are small enough to permit data aggregated on the basis of the state definitions of "juvenile" to be comparable for many purposes. However, each state should note its age limit in statistics for general distribution.

Those juvenile cases which originate in juvenile courts and are later transferred to criminal trial courts should be identified as such in **criminal case** processing and **defendant disposition** summary data.

See **delinquency** and **dependency** for reasons for judicial proceedings.

juvenile adjudication see **juvenile court judgment**

juvenile complaint see **juvenile petition**

juvenile court *recommended statistical terminology* The name for the class of courts which have, as all or part of their authority, original jurisdiction over matters concerning persons statutorily defined as juveniles.

annotation

A juvenile court can be a separately established court, a special division of a court, or a special session of a court. Any court with juvenile jurisdiction as defined above should be included in summary counts of juvenile courts regardless of the name and organizational level of the court, and regardless of whether it also has jurisdiction over other kinds of cases, with the exception of traffic courts that hear both adult and juvenile cases.

"Family court" is the name in many court systems for the court or section of a court which adjudicates juveniles. The jurisdiction of a family court extends over all matters concerning the family and its members as a unit, and can encompass appropriate types of civil and criminal, adult and juvenile cases. Family courts may hear cases involving criminal acts (such as child abuse or assault between family members), civil matters (such as adoption or divorce), and juvenile matters. They are called family courts because they specialize in cases which stem from family problems or family issues, or which are limited to members of a given family, although there is no such thing as "family jurisdiction."

Juvenile process terms in this dictionary, roughly in order of occurrence, are:

intake

detention hearing

transfer hearing

    transfer to adult court

adjudicatory hearing

juvenile court judgment

  delinquent

  status offender

  dependent

  petition not sustained

disposition hearing

juvenile disposition

juvenile court judgment   *syn*   juvenile adjudication   *recommended statistical terminology*

The juvenile court decision terminating an adjudicatory hearing, that the juvenile is a delinquent, status offender, or dependent, or that the allegations in the petition are not sustained.

annotation

See **delinquency, dependency,** and **petition not sustained** for definitions of the above four types of court findings. (Terminology relating to status offenders is presented in the **delinquency** entry.)

A judgment that a juvenile has committed a delinquent act is similar to a conviction in a court having criminal jurisdiction, in that a court has made a finding that the juvenile has committed an act that could be prosecuted as a crime if he or she were adult. (The judgments "status offender" and "dependent" have no parallel in criminal proceedings.) "Petition not sustained" is comparable to a dismissal or acquittal. The **juvenile disposition** (see entry) follows the judgment, and in the case of juvenile offenders, is similar to an adult sentencing disposition.

The decision at a **transfer hearing** to transfer a juvenile to an adult court for prosecution is not considered to be a judgment in recommended terminology since it is not an outcome of an **adjudicatory hearing.** See **transfer to adult court.**

juvenile disposition   *recommended statistical terminology*   The decision of a juvenile court, concluding a disposition hearing, that an adjudicated juvenile be committed to a juvenile correctional facility, or placed in a juvenile residence, shelter, or care or treatment program, or required to meet certain standards of conduct, or released.

annotation

A juvenile disposition of an adjudged delinquent or status offender is similar to an adult sentence in that both are decisions that may result in confinement or other restrictions on behavior. Dispositions of dependents, however, are not described as correctional commitments. See **delinquency** and **dependency**.

Probation, commitment to a juvenile correctional facility, and placement in a residence, shelter or care program are types of juvenile dispositions. However, no subclass terminology is proposed in this dictionary because of the complexity and jurisdictional variation of juvenile dispositions. Many jurisdictions have several types of probation, and unique categories of juvenile correctional facility or program commitments. See also **intake.**

A juvenile disposition is not necessarily final since the disposition may include provision for review of the decision by the juvenile court at a specific later date.

The decision at a **transfer hearing** to transfer a juvenile to criminal court for prosecution as an adult is not considered to be a juvenile disposition in this terminology since it is anticipated that proceedings against the juvenile will continue in criminal court. Such a transfer does, however, constitute a disposition of the juvenile's case in the juvenile court. See **transfer to adult court**.

juvenile facility   *syn*   **correctional facility (juvenile)**   A building or part thereof, set of buildings or area enclosing a set of buildings or structures, which is used for the custody and/or care and treatment of juveniles who have been administratively determined to be in need of care or who have been formally alleged or adjudged to be delinquents, status offenders or dependents.

annotation

Juvenile facilities may be operated by public agencies or by private organizations.

The classification of juvenile facilities for the purpose of reporting on the numbers and characteristics of the juveniles confined or resident within them is in a state of transition.

Although the great variation in juvenile facility nomenclature among different states and agencies has created some problems in arriving at nationally comparable data concerning juveniles in care or custody, the major problem in development of valid facility classification and standard terminology is the applicability of the classificatory features.

The fundamental distinctions often underlying classifications of juvenile facilities are nonsecure vs. secure (parallel to adult confinement vs. residential as described in this dictionary), community-based vs. noncommunity-based, detention pending court disposition vs. post-disposition commitment (also represented by short term vs. long term), small population vs. large population, and populations limited to non-delinquents vs. mixed populations including delinquents. In any one jurisdiction distinctions such as these usually have an objective nature, that is, they are mutually understood by the body of professionals legally responsible for daily decisions regarding juvenile dispositions and for the management of facilities.

The national Census of Juvenile Detention and Correctional Facilities, conducted by the U.S. Bureau of the Census for the U.S. Department of Justice, currently employs two pairs of categories for its primary facility classification. The first pair contrasts facilities in relation to the reason why the majority of the facility population is being held in custody:

short-term facilities are those which primarily care for juveniles in detention awaiting adjudication, commitment or placement, and/or those being held for diagnosis or classification.

long-term facilities are those which primarily care for juveniles received following commitment or placement by a juvenile court, those received as voluntary admissions, and/or those on probation or aftercare. (Long-term facilities include open facilities where juveniles on probation or aftercare may be required to reside.)

The second pair of categories contrasts facilities in relation to degree of restrictiveness. This is a multivariate distinction. Generally, an:

open facility is one in which access to the community is relatively frequent, in-house restrictions including physical security features are minimal, and entrances and exits are relatively uncontrolled.

institutional facility is one with relatively little community access and considerable in-house restrictions in the form of physical restrictions and staff controls.

These categories have been used in the publication series, *Children in Custody*, since the 1977 survey.

Additionally a six-part classification scheme is used, subdividing the two main categories of long and short-term facilities:

long-term facility	short-term facility
training school	detention center
ranch, forestry camp, and farm	shelter
halfway house and group home	reception or diagnostic center

The individual juvenile facility types are defined as follows:

training school   "A long-term specialized type of facility that provides strict confinement for its residents."

ranch, forestry camp, and farm   "A long-term residential facility for persons whose behavior does not necessitate the strict confinement of a training school, often allowing them greater contact with the community."

halfway house and group home   "A long-term facility in which residents are allowed extensive contact with the community, such as attending school or holding a job."

detention center   "A short-term facility that provides temporary care in a physically restricting environment for juveniles in custody pending court disposition and, often, for juveniles who are adjudicated delinquent or are awaiting transfer to another jurisdiction."

shelter   "A short-term facility that provides temporary care similar to that of a detention center, but in a physically unrestricting environment."

reception or diagnostic center   "A short-term facility that screens persons committed by the courts and assigns them to appropriate correctional facilities."

juvenile justice agency   A government agency, or subunit thereof, of which the functions are the investigation, supervision, adjudication, care or confinement of juvenile offenders and non-offenders subject to the jurisdiction of a juvenile court; also, in some usages, a private agency providing care and treatment.

annotation

In addition to agencies dealing with alleged and adjudicated delinquents and status offenders, this definition includes agencies that deal only with **dependents**, who have committed no offenses. The class is not parallel to **criminal justice agencies**, which are public agencies, and which are concerned only with persons who have been accused or convicted of crimes.

No recommendation for statistical usage is made here because the functions of adjudication and care or treatment of juveniles are not uniformly organized among different jurisdictions. They are sometimes assigned to special government units, but may also be carried out by agencies with adult jurisdiction, or by private organizations. What should be classified as a juvenile justice agency therefore varies greatly according to the jurisdiction and the purpose of the data presentation.

juvenile parole   see **aftercare**

juvenile petition   *recommended statistical terminology*   A document filed in juvenile court alleging that a juvenile is a delinquent, a status offender, or a dependent, and asking that the court assume jurisdiction over the juvenile, or asking that an alleged delinquent be transferred to a criminal court for prosecution as an adult.

annotation

The unit of count in process data should be "juvenile petitions filed." Petitions may be filed by an intake officer or by a prosecutor (and by a social welfare agent or other government officer in cases of dependency, where the allegations concern the behavior of the adult responsible for the juvenile). In some states private citizens may also file petitions. A petition alleging that a juvenile is a delinquent or status offender is sometimes called a "juvenile complaint."

Filing of a petition results in an **adjudicatory hearing** to determine the truth of the allegations, or a **transfer hearing** to determine if jurisdiction should be waived, or both.

For outcomes of the filing of a petition, see **transfer to adult court** and **juvenile court judgment**.

A juvenile need not have been taken into custody in order for a petition to be filed. See **detention hearing**.

kidnapping   *tentatively recommended national category for prosecution, courts and corrections statistics*   Transportation or confinement of a person without authority of law and without his or her consent, or without the consent of his or her guardian, if a minor.

defining features *of tentatively recommended national category*

unlawful transport or confinement of a person without his or her consent, or

if a minor, without the consent of his or her guardian

including hijack of vehicle containing persons

or

attempting the above act

annotation

This crime type is tentatively recommended as a cross-jurisdictional statistical category because it is needed for arrestee, defendant and convicted person disposition statistics; is not derivable from the UCR or UOC data structures, but is a significant crime type clearly delineated in most penal codes. See Appendix B for problems in national crime classification and complete set of tentatively proposed national categories for post-arrest offense statistics.

The range of behavior indicated above is variously named and codified in different jurisdictions. Some states place unlawful transportation and unlawful confinement without transportation together in a single penal code section and under a single name, as above. Some states, however, have established two or more separate statutory offenses, only one of which has the name "kidnapping." One of the others is often called "forcible detainment" or "false imprisonment." Some version of the unlawful transport type of offense is sometimes called or defined as "abduction."

Statutory definitions of "kidnapping" can be very narrow, as when the elements are unlawful transportation by use of force, with confinement and concealment, for the purpose of extortion. But the range of behavior having to do with unlawful transport and/or confinement extends from narrowly defined kidnapping to abduction for the purpose of compelling marriage and the taking of a child from the parent having legal custody by the parent not having legal custody.

In UCR, kidnapping is included by name in **all other offenses UCR 26**, but is not defined.

larceny *recommended statistical terminology* Unlawful taking or attempted taking of property other than a motor vehicle from the possession of another, by stealth, without force and without deceit, with intent to permanently deprive the owner of the property.

defining features *of recommended national category*

taking away property (excluding self-propelled motorized road vehicles, but including vehicle parts) which the possessor is entitled to retain

property is in the immediate or constructive possession of another (including in his vehicle, or in his premises if open to the public)

excluding taking that requires unlawful entry or force or is accomplished by deception

or

attempting the above act

annotation

The above category, which is used in UCR reporting (see **larceny-theft UCR 6**), is also recommended for prosecution, courts and corrections statistics. **Motor vehicle theft** (see entry) is a separate category. See Appendix B for problems in national crime classification and complete set of tentatively proposed national categories for post-arrest offense statistics.

"Larceny" is the name commonly used for the basic "theft" offense of simple taking by stealth. Taking by force or threat of violence is always a distinct offense in statistical presentations and penal codes. Taking by deceit (fraud) is almost always classified separately in statistics but in statutes is often codified in the same penal code section as theft. See **theft** and **fraud offenses** for further information.

In most statistical offense classifications, thefts of motor vehicles are treated as a separate category, usually called "motor vehicle theft," and the class, "larceny," is restricted to thefts of other property.

For the National Crime Survey (**NCS**) classification of larceny, see **personal crimes** and **household crimes**.

larceny-theft   UCR 6   *Uniform Crime Reports usage*   Unlawful taking, carrying, leading, or riding away by stealth of property, other than a motor vehicle, from the possession or constructive possession of another, including attempts.

annotation

This category is also recommended for use in post-arrest statistics. See **larceny** for defining features and general recommendation.

Larceny-theft is a UCR Crime Index offense. The annual publication presents data both on the occurrence of larceny-theft offenses and on arrests relating to such offenses. See **Crime Index**.

For supplementary UCR data reporting, larceny-theft is subdivided as follows:

(A) pocket picking
(B) purse snatching
(C) shoplifting
(D) thefts from motor vehicles
(E) theft of motor vehicle parts and accessories
(F) theft of bicycles
(G) theft from buildings
(H) theft from coin-operated device or machine
(I) all other larceny

"Larceny-theft UCR 6" excludes thefts of motor vehicles. See **motor vehicle theft UCR 7**.

law enforcement   The generic name for the activities of the agencies responsible for maintaining public order and enforcing the law, particularly the activities of prevention, detection and investigation of crime and the apprehension of criminals.

annotation

The modern preference for "law enforcement" in many official contexts instead of the older term "police" does not represent a difference in meaning. The "police power" is the inherent power of the state to regulate affairs within its jurisdiction in the interests of the safety and welfare of its citizens. A police force or police agency is the body of professional persons to which a government delegates authority to implement its police power.

law enforcement agency   *recommended statistical terminology*   A federal, state, or local criminal justice agency or identifiable subunit of which the principal functions are the prevention, detection, and investigation of crime, and the apprehension of alleged offenders.

annotation

A law enforcement agency is a **criminal justice agency**. An organizational subunit of a larger agency is considered a law enforcement agency in this terminology if its primary activities fit the definition, irrespective of the principal functions of the larger agency. However, agencies that only incidentally perform law enforcement functions, without assigning them to a specific organizational subunit, are not law enforcement agencies.

Examples of agencies included within this definition are state police agencies; state highway patrols; law enforcement subunits within federal or state regulatory agencies, and within port, bridge or transit authorities and special districts; campus police departments of publicly financed colleges and universities; sheriff's departments; and city police departments.

Examples of agencies excluded from this definition are **correctional agencies, courts, prosecution agencies** and subunits thereof; agencies primarily concerned with the protection of natural resources or health, such as forestry or fish and game departments or sanitation inspection units; and special prosecutorial subunits such as the organized crime unit of the U.S. Department of Justice and the prosecutorial units of regulatory agencies.

The subtypes of law enforcement agency are:

federal law enforcement agency   *recommended statistical terminology* A law enforcement agency which is an organizational unit, or subunit, of the federal government.

Examples of federal law enforcement agencies are the Federal Bureau of Investigation, the Secret Service, and the Bureau of Alcohol, Tobacco and Firearms.

Federal agency subunits often called law enforcement agencies, such as the organized crime unit of the U.S. Department of Justice or the enforcement unit of the Internal Revenue Service, are in this terminology classified as **prosecution agencies** because their primary purpose is to try cases in court, although many of their personnel may perform law enforcement duties.

state law enforcement agency   *recommended statistical terminology* A law enforcement agency which is an organizational unit, or subunit, of state government.

This definition includes **state police** agencies, **state highway patrols**, state park rangers, and campus police agencies of colleges and universities which are financed and administered by state government. It includes state agency units which guard property, if the personnel are sworn officers. It does not include agencies such as fish and game or forestry departments of which the law enforcement duties are incidental to their main purposes, and are not assigned to a special unit. However, a special law enforcement subunit of a regulatory or protective agency is classified as a law enforcement agency in this terminology.

local law enforcement agency   *recommended statistical terminology* A law enforcement agency which is an organizational unit, or subunit, of local government.

This definition includes **sheriff's departments** with criminal law enforcement duties, **police departments**, and campus police agencies of colleges and universities which are financed and administered by local city and community college districts. It does not include campus police of educational institutions which are privately financed or administered. It includes law enforcement units administered by special district limited purpose units of government, such as port and bridge authorities.

See also **level of government.**

law enforcement officer   I. In some usages, any government employee who is an officer sworn to carry out law enforcement duties, whether or not employed by an agency or identifiable subunit which primarily performs law enforcement functions.   II. *recommended statistical terminology*   An employee of a law enforcement agency who is an officer sworn to carry out law enforcement duties.

annotation

"Sworn personnel" are persons formally authorized to make arrests while acting within the scope of explicit legal authority.

Definition (II) above is recommended for use in national level general data. The class includes sworn investigative personnel of identifiable special law enforcement subunits of some non-criminal justice agencies, such as federal or state regulatory agencies. It excludes employees of **courts** and **correctional agencies** who perform law enforcement duties, and employees of those non-criminal justice agencies or subunits whose law enforcement activities are incidental to their primary functions.

"Police officer" and "peace officer" are often used when "law enforcement officer" as defined in (II) above is meant. The use of these titles in interstate and national information exchange is not recommended. "Police officer" often has a narrower meaning: a sworn officer employed by a local police department. "Peace officer" often has a broader meaning, as in definition (I) above, being used to designate prison guards, parole officers, probation officers, court personnel, forest rangers, and game wardens in addition to law enforcement agency personnel. It is recommended that where such a broad category is used in statistical data presentations, careful consideration be given to the choice of terms to be used and explicit definitions be provided for all terms.

Terminology is presented below for subtypes of law enforcement officer, distinguished by level of government. (See **law enforcement agency** for corresponding definitions of agency types.) Each level has a variety of subtype names and borderline cases.

federal law enforcement officer   *recommended statistical terminology* An employee of a federal law enforcement agency who is an officer sworn to carry out law enforcement duties.

Examples of this class are agents of the Federal Bureau of Investigation and the Bureau of Alcohol, Tobacco and Firearms, and the investigative staff of federal organized crime units and tax law enforcement units.

state law enforcement officer   *recommended statistical terminology* An employee of a state law enforcement agency who is an officer sworn to carry out law enforcement duties.

Examples of this class are **state police officers, state highway patrol officers,** and state park police. For national level general data, this class should include those campus police officers who are employees of state university campus police and state college police agencies. Private campus police are excluded.

local law enforcement officer   *recommended statistical terminology*   An employee of a local law enforcement agency who is an officer sworn to carry out law enforcement duties.

Examples of this class are **sheriffs, deputy sheriffs, chiefs of police,** city police officers, and sworn personnel of law enforcement subunits of port and transit authorities. For national level general data, this class should include campus police officers who are employees of local city and community college districts. Private campus police are excluded.

lawyer   see **attorney**

lesser included offense   see **included offense**

level of government   The federal, state or local location of administrative authority or funding responsibility of a given agency.

annotation

Within the broad categories of federal, state and local, the level of government is often characterized in greater detail in order to provide for classification of agencies of special purpose units of government. Since many factors can be involved in establishing more detailed categories, the particular classification structure that should be used depends on the purpose of the data presentation.

In this dictionary **law enforcement agencies** and **correctional facilities (adult)** are classified as federal, state or local, in accord with the location of administrative authority.

"Local" means any level of government that is not clearly federal or state. Local agencies are those belonging to "units of general local government" (which in federal statutes dealing with criminal justice matters means general purpose subdivisions of a state) and agencies or subagencies that are parts of special purpose units of government: special regional agencies, independent school districts, port authorities, and the like.

The Bureau of Justice Statistics series, *Expenditure and Employment Data for the Criminal Justice System*, classifies criminal justice activities of general purpose governments broadly as federal, state, and local. "Local" is further subdivided into county, municipal, and township jurisdiction. Data for law enforcement activities of special purpose units of government (bridge, port, airport, tunnel authorities, independent school districts, etc.) are presented separately.

Courts are characterized in this dictionary and in most statistical publications with respect to their subject matter jurisdiction, rather than by level of government. See **court.**

Reporting conventions must also be established regarding state level agencies that are divided into distinct units serving different geographical areas. These can be counted as one agency or as several, depending upon the purpose of a given statistical compilation.

levels of proof   The degrees of certainty required at different stages in the criminal justice process.

annotation

The common names and characterizations of the different degrees of certainty are presented below. To investigate requires "suspicion." To question or superficially search a suspect requires something more than suspicion but less than probable cause. To arrest and prosecute requires "probable cause." To convict requires "proof beyond a reasonable doubt."

suspicion   Opinion based on slight evidence, upon facts or circumstances which are somewhat less than reasonable grounds to believe something.

probable cause   A set of facts and circumstances which would induce a reasonably intelligent and prudent person to believe that a crime had been committed and that a particular person had committed it; reasonable grounds to make or believe an accusation. (See entry also.)

The evidence sufficient to establish probable cause at the time of arrest, and thus to justify the lawfulness of the arrest can be less than that required to support prosecution. Thus, an arrest can be lawful even though charges are later dismissed at a preliminary hearing for lack of probable cause.

proof beyond a reasonable doubt   Proof that does not amount to absolute certainty but leaves no reasonable doubt that the defendant committed the alleged crime(s), that is, a standard of proof in which evidence offered in court to prove an alleged set of facts must preclude every reasonable hypothesis except that one which it supports, that of the defendant's guilt.

In civil cases the judgment rests on the balance of weight of the evidence. The less strict standard of proof is **preponderance of the evidence**: the evidence offered in court to prove an alleged set of facts must be of better quality and amount, of greater weight, than the evidence in opposition.

In criminal proceedings the **burden of proof**, the necessity or duty of affirmatively proving the fact or facts in dispute, rests with the prosecution.

libel   see **defamation**

life sentence   see **prison commitment**

liquor laws (offense)   UCR 22   In Uniform Crime Reports terminology, the name of the UCR category used to record and report arrests for offenses relating to regulation of the manufacture, sale, distribution, transportation, possession, or use of intoxicating liquor, except public drunkenness and driving under the influence of alcohol.

annotation

UCR provides the following list of offenses or groups of offenses as examples of the content of this category:

Manufacture, sale, transporting, furnishing, possessing, etc., intoxicating liquor.
Maintaining unlawful drinking places.
Advertising and soliciting orders for intoxicating liquor.
Bootlegging.
Operating still.
Furnishing liquor to a minor or intemperate person.
Using a vehicle for illegal transportation of liquor.
Drinking on a train or public conveyance.
All attempts to commit any of the above.

See also **driving under the influence UCR 21** and **drunkenness UCR 23.**

local law enforcement agency   see **law enforcement agency**

local law enforcement officer   see **law enforcement officer**

long-term facility   see **juvenile facility**

lottery   see **gambling**

magistrate   see **judicial officer**

majority opinion   see **opinion**

malicious mischief   see **criminal mischief**

mandatory conditional release   see **mandatory supervised release**

mandatory sentence   A statutory requirement that a certain penalty shall be set and carried out in all cases upon conviction for a specified offense or series of offenses.

annotation

The statute usually provides that an offender convicted of a specified very serious crime or specified series of crimes be confined in prison for a minimum number of years especially established for the particular offense, that the customary alternative of probation instead of imprisonment is not available, and that parole is not permitted or is possible only after unusually lengthy confinement.

See also **aggravating circumstances, maximum sentence** and **habitual offender.**

mandatory supervised release   *recommended statistical terminology* A conditional release from prison required by statute when an inmate has been confined for a time period equal to his or her full sentence minus statutory good time if any.

annotation

Persons leaving prison by mandatory supervised release are placed on conditional release status until the full sentence expires, or until some other point in time specified by law. They are usually subject to the same conditions as parolees, and can be returned by paroling authority decision to prison for technical violations of release conditions. The release itself, however, is not a paroling authority discretionary decision.

The supervision is usually performed by a state parole agency, or a state probation and parole agency.

See **parole agency caseload entries and removals** and **prison/parole population movement** for the function of this category in data structures.

manner of disposition, appellate court case   see **appellate case disposition**

manner of disposition, trial court case   see **court disposition**

MAP program   see **mutual agreement program**

maximum sentence   I. In legal usage, the maximum penalty provided by law for a given criminal offense, usually stated as a maximum term of imprisonment or a maximum fine.   II. In correctional usage in relation to a given offender, any of several quantities (expressed in days, months or years) which vary according to whether calculated at the point of sentencing or at a later point in the correctional process, and according to whether the time period referred to is the term of confinement or the total period under correctional jurisdiction.

annotation

As the above definition indicates, different time values can be established as the maximum sentence pertaining to a given offender for a given offense. The "maximum sentence" as stated by the court is usually the maximum period of confinement applicable to a specific offender for a specific offense, as selected by the court within the limits prescribed by statute, before jail time or any other irrevocable sentence credits have been subtracted.

This is, however, not necessarily the basic time value recorded in correctional data systems. For management purposes state correctional agencies need to know the maximum potential period of confinement effective at the point of admission to a state institution, which time value is ordinarily reduced from the first (court) value by jail time that has been credited and/or such other factors as statutory mandatory conditional release provisions. (In some states, the basic time value is the "maximum" set by the paroling authority after admission to prison.)

Further, there is usually a need to calculate the maximum potential period under correctional jurisdiction (confinement plus time on conditional release status). And, finally, time values generated by calculations previous to conditional release may be affected by the offender's behavior while in that status, since parole or other conditional release revocation can, in some jurisdictions, result in the loss of credits for time previously spent in confinement and/or under supervision.

The diversity of sentencing structures nationwide and different information needs make it inevitable that what is labelled "maximum sentence" in any one data system or statistical publication may be a figure of quite a different meaning from that which appears in another context. It is recommended that sentence data intended for general use be defined by explicit description of the method used to calculate the time values.

The only published current national level definitions relating to maximum sentences are those of National Prisoner Statistics (see **NPS**). In this data program a key quantity is the "maximum sentence given by court," also called "maximum prison liability" meaning the maximum sentence time value formally declared at the point of sentencing disposition and not unconditionally suspended by the court, from which no "sentence credits" for prior jail time or the like have been subtracted. This is recorded in relation to each convicted offense related to the prison commitment.

A second key quantity recorded in NPS as of prison admission or readmission date is the "time remaining on maximum sentence," also called "maximum remaining prison liability," which is the maximum sentence for each offense as of prison admission date minus such irrevocable sentence credits as presentence jail time credited, prior prison time, and other fixed credits such as irrevocable parole time, if any.

In the case of commitments to confinement on multiple sentences National Prisoner Statistics records the longest sentences up to three, and identifies each as to whether it is concurrent or consecutive, and for the latter the sequence of service. The "time remaining on total maximum sentence" is then recorded in the NPS program as the sum of all consecutive sentences or portions of sentences remaining to be served as of the date of admission, including any sentences over three that could not be displayed in the single offense-sentence format.

A **minimum sentence** is the minimum penalty provided by law for a given offense, meaning in most statistical contexts, the minimum term of confinement to be served. Like the maximum sentence, the minimum potential term of confinement applicable to a person at time of commitment can be provided by statute, or determined by a court or parole authority within statutory limits. However, in some jurisdictions there is no officially stated minimum sentence.

A formally declared minimum sentence is also a time value affected by various statutory rules and discretionary executive actions. For example, in some jurisdictions an offender is eligible for parole after a certain fraction of the minimum sentence has been served. The item reflecting the most meaningful time value for minimum period of confinement is usually, in the case of prison populations, the minimum parole eligibility date, which can be calculated, sometimes at the time of commitment, in accord with the rules operative in the particular jurisdiction. See **eligible for parole**.

See also **indeterminate sentence**.

mayhem   Intentional inflicting of injury on another which causes the removal of, or seriously disfigures, or renders useless or seriously impairs the function of, any member or organ of the body.

annotation

In UCR, mayhem is classified as **aggravated assault UCR 4a–d**. This classification is also recommended for post-arrest offense data. See **assault**.

measured capacity   see **institutional capacity**

memorandum opinion   see **opinion**

minimum eligible parole date   see **eligible for parole**

minimum sentence   see **maximum sentence**

Miranda rights   The set of rights which a person accused or suspected of having committed a specific offense has during interrogation, and of which he or she must be informed prior to questioning, as stated by the U.S. Supreme Court in deciding Miranda v. Arizona and related cases.

annotation

The act of informing a person of his Miranda rights is often called "admonition of rights," or "admonishment of rights." The information is called the

"Miranda warning." It usually includes at a minimum:

a) He or she has the right to remain silent.
b) Any statement he/she makes may be used in court against him/her.
c) He/she has the right to have an attorney present during questioning.
d) If he/she cannot afford to hire an attorney, he/she has the right to have an attorney provided free of charge.
e) If he/she waives the above rights and chooses to give information, he/she has the right to refuse further information at any point in questioning.

This information may be provided orally or in a written statement or both.

Many jurisdictions now require a statement, signed by the person to be interrogated, that he or she has heard and understood these rights. The decision of a person to waive these rights and to give information, or the signed statement recording such a decision, is often called "admonition and waiver."

The right to consult with an attorney during interrogation was first set out by the Supreme Court in its opinion in *Escobedo v. Illinois* (1964). It was later included in the full set of admonitions which were set out in the opinion in *Miranda v. Arizona* (1966). Issues relating to these rights continue to be subject to judicial review and ruling.

See **rights of defendant** for a list of the rights of an accused person at the time of arraignment, that is, appearance in court to hear the charge against him or her.

misdemeanor   An offense punishable by incarceration, usually in a local confinement facility, for a period of which the upper limit is prescribed by statute in a given jurisdiction, typically limited to a year or less.

annotation

In most jurisdictions misdemeanors are one of the two major classes of crimes, the other being felonies. See **felony** for additional information about the usage of these terms and recommendations concerning the use of this terminology in statistics.

See **infraction** for recommended usage concerning offenses for which incarceration is not a permitted penalty, or for which the period of incarceration is extremely short.

mistrial   A trial which has been terminated and declared invalid by the court because of some circumstance which creates a substantial and uncorrectable prejudice to the conduct of a fair trial, or which makes it impossible to continue the trial in accordance with prescribed procedures.

annotation

Commonly cited grounds for the declaring of a mistrial include illness of the defendant, illness of the presiding judge, and misconduct on the part of the jury, the defense, the prosecution, or the court. In some jurisdictions, a **hung jury** (see entry) can also be grounds for a mistrial.

The declaration of a mistrial can be followed by retrial on the original charges, or by a **dismissal** (see entry) of the case. The judicial decision to declare a mistrial can be appealed by either the defense or the prosecution.

mitigating circumstances   see **aggravating circumstances**

M.O.   see **modus operandi**

Model Penal Code   A generalized modern codification of that which is considered basic to criminal law, published by the American Law Institute in 1962.

annotation

The Model Penal Code differed from almost all state codes at the time of its publication, in that such matters as the general principles of **culpability** (see entry) and justification, formerly defined mainly in case law, were explicitly codified.

Many states have enacted completely revised penal codes since 1962. The formal arrangement and offense element language of these statutes is very different from earlier criminal law in many instances, although the actions that the language defines as crimes are essentially the same actions forbidden by earlier penal codes. The content and arrangement of the recently revised codes often reflect the MPC approach.

modification of probation   A change in the terms and conditions of a probation order, making them more restrictive or less restrictive, as determined by a court.

annotation

Modifications of **probation** (see entry) may be requested by the probation officer, the prosecuting attorney, the defense attorney, or the defendant or other persons.

Probation terms and conditions may be modified for a number of reasons, for example, to provide extra time for payment of fines or restitution, to shorten a jail term, to permit a change of residence to out of state or to require treatment for alcoholism or drug abuse.

modus operandi   *syn*   **method of operation**   *syn*   **M.O.**
A characteristic pattern of behavior repeated in a series of offenses that coincides with the pattern evidenced by a particular single person, or by a particular group of persons working together.

annotation

Most law enforcement agencies maintain M.O. files.

Modus operandi information can enable police to determine that the most likely perpetrator(s) of a series of crimes is a known offender, or to determine that the pattern does not fit any previously arrested or investigated person. It may also be a portion of the evidence used to establish guilt in criminal proceedings.

motion   An oral or written request made to a court at any time before, during, or after court proceedings, asking the court to make a specified finding, decision, or order.

annotation

In criminal proceedings a motion can be made by the prosecution, the defense, or the court itself. Motions are frequently oral; **petitions** (see entry) are in writing.

motive   see **intent**

motor vehicle theft   *recommended statistical terminology*   Unlawful taking, or attempted taking, of a self-propelled road vehicle owned by another, with the intent to deprive him of it permanently or temporarily.

defining features of recommended national category

unlawful taking of a self-propelled road vehicle

excluding vehicle parts

intent to permanently or temporarily deprive owner of possession

or

attempting the above act

annotation

The above category, which is used in UCR reporting, is also recommended for prosecution, courts and corrections statistics. While it is rarely an explicit, separate category in penal codes (see below), ability to capture these data is indicated by the frequent use of the category in local and state level statistical presentations of court activity and prisoner population characteristics. See Appendix B for problems in national crime classification and complete set of tentatively proposed national categories for post-arrest offense statistics.

Motor vehicle theft, as here defined, includes thefts of self-propelled motorized vehicles which run on ground surface and whose primary utilization is the transport of persons or goods. The category here and in UCR excludes such motorized vehicles as trains, farm equipment, bulldozers, construction equipment, airplanes, and motor boats. Thefts of such vehicles, as well as thefts of non-motorized vehicles, should be classified as **larceny**.

Offenses of receiving, selling, or possessing stolen motor vehicles are classified as "stolen property offenses" in the tentatively recommended categories for prosecution, courts and corrections level offense reporting. See **stolen property offenses**.

Unlawful taking of a motor vehicle with intent to permanently deprive the owner of possession is usually not codified separately from the taking of other property in penal codes. The offense can be charged under the general "theft" or "larceny" provisions. However, unlawful taking of a motor vehicle with intent to temporarily deprive the owner of possession, popularly called "joyriding," is frequently specifically codified and named "unauthorized use of a motor vehicle" or the like.

Offenses having to do with the selling of stolen vehicles are sometimes established in vehicle codes instead of penal codes. Vehicle theft itself is occasionally included there.

Transporting stolen motor vehicles across state lines is a federal offense (the Dyer Act).

For National Crime Survey **(NCS)** conventions regarding motor vehicle theft, see **household crimes**.

motor vehicle theft   UCR 7   *Uniform Crime Reports usage*   Unlawful taking, or attempted taking, of a self-propelled road vehicle owned by another, with the intent to deprive him of it permanently or temporarily.

annotation

This category is also recommended for use in post-arrest statistics. See **motor vehicle theft** for defining features and general recommendation.

Motor vehicle theft is a UCR Crime Index offense. The annual publication presents data both on the occurrence of motor vehicle theft offenses and on arrests relating to such offenses. See **Crime Index.**

In UCR data reporting, motor vehicle theft is subdivided as follows:

7.a. autos
7.b. trucks and buses
7.c. other vehicles

motor vehicle theft (NCS)   see **household crimes**

multiple sentence   see **consecutive sentence**

murder   see **criminal homicide**

murder and nonnegligent manslaughter   UCR 1a   In Uniform Crime Reports terminology, intentionally causing the death of another without legal justification or excuse, or causing the death of another while committing or attempting to commit another crime.

annotation

As the name of the UCR category indicates, murder and nonnegligent (voluntary) manslaughter are ordinarily separately codified offenses in state penal codes and are separated in many statistical descriptions of felony trial court dispositions and prisoner characteristics. See **criminal homicide** for definitions of these subtypes, defining features and general recommendation.

The two are combined as the single category UCR 1a because the discrimination between murder and voluntary manslaughter often cannot be made at the police reporting levels. This category is a UCR **Crime Index** offense.

"Murder" appears frequently in national and state level UCR publications as a cover term for both murder and nonnegligent manslaughter, that is, for all of UCR 1a, but the correct label for this class is "criminal willful homicide."

Murder and nonnegligent manslaughter UCR 1a and **negligent manslaughter UCR 1b** together make up the UCR Part I offense category **criminal homicide   UCR 1.**

In UCR, attempted murder is classified as **aggravated assault   UCR 4a–d.**

mutual agreement program   A program providing for a form of contract between a prisoner and state prison and parole officials wherein the prisoner undertakes to complete specified self-improvement programs in order to receive a definite parole date, and the agency promises to provide the necessary educational and social services.

annotation

The overall purposes of mutual agreement programs (MAP programs) are to provide prisoners with explicit choices regarding steps toward preparation for release, to objectify the mutual obligations of prisoners and officials, and to provide a framework for focus upon problems impeding successful completion of contracts.

This arrangement is also called "contract parole." See **parole**.

NCS   An abbreviation for "National Crime Survey."

annotation

NCS is a statistical program instituted in 1972. The NCS program is currently administered by the Bureau of Justice Statistics (formerly the National Criminal Justice Information and Statistics Service of LEAA) and the data are collected by the Bureau of the Census.

NCS provides information on the extent to which persons 12 years of age and older and households have been victimized by selected crimes. Data are collected on the incidence of crimes, and circumstances under which the events occurred, the effects on the victim, and whether or not incidents were reported to the police.

In addition to the ongoing national Household Survey of victimization, NCS has in the past conducted several other surveys. Through 1976, a national survey of commercial victimization was conducted. Data from this survey were published in conjunction with national household survey data.

Between 1972 and 1975 NCS conducted a series of individual city household and commercial victimization surveys. These city surveys were separate research efforts, based on population samples independent of those of the national surveys. Surveys were conducted in a total of 26 cities.

A series of attitude surveys was also conducted in connection with the city victimization surveys, utilizing a half-sample of the city survey respondents. These surveys collected information on public opinion regarding crime, crime trends, and the effectiveness of law enforcement in responding to crime.

The term "National Crime Panel" has in the past sometimes been used to designate the national survey component of NCS, in contrast to the city-level component.

For definitions of NCS crimes and other key program terms, see **criminal incident, victimization, personal crimes, household crimes** and **commercial crimes**. NCS findings have been published under various titles. For particular publications, see bibliography under "U.S. Department of Justice."

negligence   In legal usage, generally, a state of mind accompanying a person's conduct such that he or she is not aware, though a reasonable person should be aware, that there is a risk that the conduct might cause a particular harmful result.

annotation

The distinction between "criminal" and lesser negligence figures in the definition of some serious crimes, such as negligent manslaughter and different degrees of arson.

The exact states of mind and the circumstances required to establish criminal negligence cannot be simply defined. "Gross negligence" and "culpable negligence" are sometimes used as synonyms. The amount of negligence required to constitute a cause of action in a criminal matter is said to be more than the "ordinary" negligence that will justify a civil proceeding.

The **Model Penal Code** defines "negligently" as follows: "A person acts negligently with respect to a material element of an offense when he should be aware of a substantial and unjustifiable risk that the material element exists or will result from his conduct. The risk must be of such a nature and degree that the actor's failure to perceive it, considering the nature and purpose of his conduct and the circumstances known to him, involves a gross deviation from the standard of care that a reasonable person would observe in the actor's situation."

See also **culpability**.

negligent manslaughter   UCR 1b   *(called "manslaughter by negligence")*   In Uniform Crime Reports terminology, causing the death of another by recklessness or gross negligence.

annotation

See **criminal homicide UCR 1** for definition of the larger UCR class and **criminal homicide** for recommended terminology for courts and corrections offense statistics.

Vehicular negligent manslaughters are excluded from this category in reported crime data (Part I **offenses known to police**). However, in reporting and publication of UCR data on **arrests**, arrests for vehicular manslaughters are placed in this category along with other negligent manslaughter arrests.

Negligent manslaughter is a UCR **Part I offense** but not a **Crime Index** offense.

new court commitment   *recommended statistical terminology*   The entry into prison of a person who is being admitted on one or more new sentences to confinement and is not being readmitted on any previous sentence still in effect.

annotation

In this terminology this category of prison entries excludes all returns from parole or other conditional release with or without a new sentence for a new offense, all transfers in from other jurisdictions unless the inmate is beginning to serve time on a new sentence, and all returns from escape or other unauthorized departure.

In this terminology and in National Prisoner Statistics the "new court commitment" category includes persons who have violated probation and are being committed to prison for the first time in relation to a given conviction.

See **prison/parole population movement**.

new trial   In the broadest sense, any trial in which issues of fact and law are examined that have already been the subject of an earlier trial.

annotation

There are, with respect to location and sequence of events, two distinct types of new trials, one of which has a unique name:

trial de novo   A new trial conducted in a court of record as an appeal of the result of a trial in a lower court not of record.

A trial de novo takes place in a court having incidental appellate jurisdiction, usually a court of general jurisdiction (see **court**).

new trial or **retrial**   A new trial conducted in the same court in which the earlier trial took place, ordered by that same court or by a higher court having appellate jurisdiction. A new trial can be ordered because a harmful error occurred in the earlier proceeding or for other reasons, such as the discovery of new evidence that could have led to a different judgment if presented at the earlier trial.

nolle prosequi

I.   A formal entry upon the record of the court, indicating that the prosecutor declares that he or she will proceed no further in the action.   II.   *recommended statistical terminology*   The terminating of adjudication of a criminal charge by the prosecutor's decision not to pursue the case, in some jurisdictions requiring the approval of the court.

annotation

This action, also called "nolle" and "nol pross," is a type of **defendant disposition** (see entry) occurring after filing of a case in court and before judgment. In felony cases it often occurs after the initial complaint is filed in a lower court, and before an **information** or **indictment** is filed in a higher court.

In data presentations, dispositions by nolle prosequi (viewed as prosecutor's dismissals) may be combined with **dismissals** by the court in a single category "dismissed/nolle prosequi." Where general comparisons between dispositions of defendants and related court caseload activity are needed, it is recommended that defendants whose cases are terminated by dismissal or nolle prosequi prior to trial be counted separately from those where the termination occurs after a trial has begun.

In some jurisdictions felony cases can be dismissed on the prosecutor's motion in a lower court but filed anew in a higher court. This can result in inflation of nolle prosequi counts in court activity summary data, and because of variation in practice can distort comparisons between courts or court systems. It is recommended that practices relating to nolle prosequi be explicitly noted in statistical data presentations.

nolo contendere   see **plea**

nonjury trial   see **trial**

nonnegligent manslaughter   UCR   see **murder and nonnegligent manslaughter UCR 1b**

non-run time   see **time served**

not guilty by reason of insanity   *recommended statistical terminology*

The plea of a defendant or the verdict of a jury or judge in a criminal proceeding, that the defendant is not guilty of the offense(s) charged because at the time the crime(s) was committed the defendant did not have the mental capacity to be held criminally responsible for his or her actions.

annotation

A verdict of "not guilty by reason of insanity" is a possible **defendant disposition** (see entry). However, if it is followed by a **civil commitment** the latter would be considered more final.

A plea or verdict of "not guilty by reason of insanity" differs from other not guilty pleas and verdicts in that the claim or finding is not based on what the defendant is alleged or determined to have done, but rather on the issue of whether he or she possessed the mental capacity to be held responsible for a criminal act.

A verdict of "not guilty by reason of insanity" differs from a court finding that a defendant is **incompetent to stand trial** (see entry), which concerns only the defendant's mental fitness at the time of trial, and is not related to the question of guilt.

not guilty plea   see plea

not guilty verdict   see verdict

no true bill   *recommended statistical terminology*   The decision by a grand jury that it will not return an indictment against the person(s) accused of a crime(s) on the basis of the allegations and evidence presented by the prosecutor.

annotation

"No bill," "not a true bill," and "ignoramus" are synonyms for "no true bill." A case in which a grand jury has decided not to return an indictment is sometimes said to be "not found."

A grand jury finding of no true bill after a complaint has been filed in lower court may be a **defendant disposition** (see entry), terminating criminal justice jurisdiction over the defendant in those jurisdictions where the felony **trial** phase is initiated by the filing of a grand jury **indictment**.

A grand jury, after its consideration of a case, can decide:
1) To issue an **indictment** (see entry).
2) Not to issue an indictment (called "no true bill" as above).
3) To ignore felony charges, but refer the case back to the prosecutor for further prosecution on misdemeanor charges (often called "ignoramus referral").

NPS   An abbreviation for "National Prisoner Statistics."

annotation

NPS is a national data program which publishes statistical information on federal and state prisons and prisoners. The program was established in 1926, and is currently sponsored by the Bureau of Justice Statistics. The data are collected by the Bureau of Census.

There are two annual publications. *Prisoners in State and Federal Institutions* contains summary counts for each state and for the federal government, of year-end prison system populations and of additions to and subtractions from these populations. These are categorized by type of movement. *Capital Punishment* contains statistics on persons under sentence of death, persons executed, and descriptions of changes in capital punishment statutes.

NPS also collects and publishes or makes available information on state and federal prisoners additional to that covered by the annual series. The coverage of these supplementary reports and special studies includes data on the personal and social characteristics of prisoners, and their criminal histories. For publications see bibliography under "U.S. Department of Justice."

numbers game   see **gambling**

OBSCIS   An acronym for "Offender-Based State Corrections Information System."

annotation

OBSCIS is a multi-state program for the development of prisoner information systems for state correctional agencies. The OBSCIS data elements and basic OBSCIS code structure are presented in the *OBSCIS Data Dictionary*. The entries **paroling authority decisions** and **prison/parole population movement** are based on OBSCIS data elements and codes called "parole decisions" and "status and location changes." These and other data elements represent areas of standard corrections information on which a substantial consensus has been reached as to content and terminology.

obstruction of justice   A class of offenses, sometimes so named in statutes, which at its broadest consists of all unlawful acts committed with intent to prevent or hinder the administration of justice, including law enforcement, judicial, and corrections functions.

annotation

Interfering with police activities, failing to report a crime, falsely reporting a crime, harboring a fugitive, failing or refusing to obey a court order, compounding a crime, perjury, and jury tampering are examples of offenses often found under this heading.

See also **compounding a criminal offense, contempt of court, perjury,** and **resisting an officer.**

OBTS   An abbreviation for "offender-based transaction statistics."

annotation

Offender-based transaction statistics are derived from information concerning law enforcement, court and corrections proceedings recorded in such a way that the system identity of the person subject to the proceedings is preserved throughout data collection and analysis. The use of the individual offender or alleged offender as the basic unit tracked by the statistical system provides the mechanism for linking events in the different parts of the criminal justice system. The output of one agency can be linked to the input of another agency, and the flow of offenders and alleged offenders through the system can be observed over long periods of time. This capability permits study of the relationships between decisions and dispositions made at one point and decisions and dispositions made at another point in the criminal justice process.

The data elements in OBTS and computerized criminal history (CCH) systems both represent criminal history record information. However, CCH system output contains personal identifiers; OBTS system output does not.

Some states have developed OBTS programs. A national statistical program using OBTS data is currently being developed by the Bureau of Justice Statistics.

offender   *recommended statistical terminology*   An adult who has been convicted of a criminal offense.

annotation

Related terms are:

alleged offender   *recommended statistical terminology*   A person who has been charged with a specific criminal offense(s) by a law enforcement agency or court, but whose case has not reached judgment.

ex-offender   An offender who is no longer under the jurisdiction of any criminal justice agency.

This area of terminology presents problems in that there is no consensus on when each kind of offender status, once acquired, ceases to exist.

offense   see **crime**

offenses against the family and children   UCR 20   In Uniform Crime Reports terminology, the name of the UCR category used to record and report arrests for offenses relating to desertion, abandonment, non-support, neglect or abuse of spouse or child, nonpayment of alimony, or other similar acts.

annotation

If the abuse is an assault that results in serious physical injury, the offense is classified as **aggravated assault UCR 4a–d**, and the arrest is reported in that category.

See also **dependency**.

offenses known to police   In Uniform Crime Reports terminology, reported occurrences of offenses, which have been verified at the police level.

annotation

The crime data in the national UCR annual publication *Crime in the United States* are usually referred to as "reported crimes," but the correct technical term is the above. "Unfounded reported offenses" are subtracted from all reported occurrences of offenses in order to arrive at "offenses known to police," which comprise the published data. These are also called "actual offenses."

Tabulations of offenses known to the police are published for all offenses designated **Part I offenses** or **Crime Index** offenses (see entries).

An **unfounded reported offense** is the UCR name for a reported occurrence of an offense which is found by investigation not to have occurred, or not to constitute an offense, or which must be reclassified as another offense.

"Unfounding" is the general mechanism provided in UCR data reporting for making necessary adjustments to initial compilations of occurrences of offenses.

Adjustments are required for a variety of reasons. A reported incident of criminal homicide later determined to have been a justified homicide (for example, the act of a law enforcement officer acting in the line of duty and according to law), or an excusable homicide (for example, the result of accident), will be unfounded. Where an incident of aggravated assault has been reported and the victim later dies of injuries received in the incident, the offense of aggravated assault must be unfounded, and an offense of criminal homicide recorded.

Other examples of circumstances commonly causing reported offenses to be unfounded are changes in alleged victim statements, or discovery that a witness lacking full knowledge of the event incorrectly assumed that a crime was being committed.

Unfounded reported offenses are also called "unfounded complaints," "baseless offenses," or "baseless complaints."

omnibus hearing   see **pretrial conference**

open facility   see **juvenile facility**

opinion   The official announcement of a decision of a court together with the reasons for that decision.

annotation

A judge can deliver an opinion about any aspect of a case at almost any time, but the term usually appears only in connection with final decisions in **appeal proceedings**.

The various decisions comprising **appellate case dispositions** (see entry) are often accompanied by a statement of the court's reasons for arriving at the decision. These vary as to manner of presentation, content, and authorship.

An **oral opinion** is usually very brief.

A **full opinion** (or "written opinion") is in writing, and usually lengthy, presenting in detail the reasons and reasoning leading to the decision.

A **memorandum opinion** (or "memorandum decision") is also in writing, but is a very brief statement of the reasons for a decision, without detailed explanation.

A **per curiam opinion** is one issued by the court as a whole, without indication of individual authorship, while a **signed opinion** is one bearing the name of the individual judge who authored it, whether or not issued on behalf of the whole court.

Since memorandum opinions are usually issued per curiam (unsigned) and since per curiam opinions are typically brief, these two terms are sometimes used as synonyms.

A **majority opinion** is that of the majority of the judges hearing the case; a **dissenting** (or "minority") **opinion** is that of one or more judges who disagree with the decision of the majority; a **concurring opinion** states the reasons and reasoning of one or more judges who agree with the majority decision, but on different grounds.

See also **court decision**.

oral opinion   see **opinion**

organized crime   A complex pattern of activity which includes the commission of statutorily defined offenses, in particular the provision of illegal goods and services but also carefully planned and coordinated instances of offenses of the fraud, theft and extortion groups, and which is uniquely characterized by the planned use of both legitimate and criminal professional expertise, and the use for criminal purposes of organizational features of legitimate business, including availability of large capital resources, disciplined management, division of labor, and focus upon maximum profit; also, the persons engaged in such a pattern of activity.

annotation

The above definition represents the broadest range of meaning of the term.

"Organized crime" is not a statutory offense (a defined offense to which a penalty is attached). However, the term has official status when, for example, used to define kinds of crime with which special prosecutorial units are concerned ("Organized Crime Strike Force"), or used in other situations where the allocation of law enforcement and prosecutorial resources is an issue. In these situations statistical indicators such as rates of particular kinds of crime may be used in conjunction with modus operandi information to estimate the need for special programs.

The federal Omnibus Crime Control Act of 1970 defines "organized crime" for administrative purposes in section 601(b): "the unlawful activities of the members of a highly organized, disciplined association engaged in supplying illegal goods and services, including but not limited to gambling, prostitution, loansharking, narcotics, labor racketeering, and other unlawful activities of members of such organizations."

original jurisdiction   see **jurisdiction**

other assaults-simple not aggravated (UCR)   see **simple assault   UCR 9**

other nonviolent sex offenses   see **sex offenses**

other violent sex offenses   see **sex offenses**

panel of judges   A group of three or more judicial officers of a court, who jointly hear and decide a case.

annotation

Proceedings conducted by a panel of judges rather than by a single judge are most common in appellate courts. Sentencing decisions are also sometimes made by a group of judges.

A case heard jointly by all judges of a particular court is said to be heard **en banc**.

parajudge   see **judicial officer**

pardon   see **clemency**

parole   The status of an offender conditionally released from a prison by discretion of a paroling authority prior to expiration of sentence, required to observe conditions of parole, and placed under the supervision of a parole agency.

annotation

Parole is the major type of **conditional release**. See **release to parole** for recommended statistical terminology.

Parole differs from **probation** in that parole status is determined by an executive authority and follows a period of confinement, while probation status is determined by judicial authority and is usually an alternative to confinement. The behavioral conditions are similar.

Parole conditions frequently include maintaining regular employment, abstaining from drugs and alcohol, not associating with known offenders or other specified persons, regularly reporting to a parole officer or other designated person, and/or remaining within a designated geographic area. Not committing another offense is always a condition of parole.

parole agency   *recommended statistical terminology*   A correctional agency, which may or may not include a paroling authority, and of which the principal functions are pre-release investigations and parole plan preparation for prospective parolees, and the supervision of adults having parole or other conditional release status.

annotation

Supervision typically includes making sure the supervisee regularly reports to a parole officer or other designated person, engages in appropriate behavior and adheres to the other conditions of his or her release.

Parole agencies administer field services. Releases to parole and related major discretionary decisions are made by **paroling authorities**.

Agencies which supervise both parolees and probationers should be described as probation/parole agencies in data publications.

Authority and supervisory responsibility for the juvenile parole (see **aftercare**) function is variously located and organized in different jurisdictions.

parole agency caseload entries and removals   *recommended statistical terminology*   Entries to and removals from the caseload for which a given parole agency has both jurisdiction and supervisory responsibility, or for which it has supervisory responsibility only.

annotation

This classification presents parole activity from the broadest perspective of agency responsibility: all persons over whom a paroling authority or parole agency has legal control regarding confinement or release, or has supervisory responsibility, whether or not the cases were received by discretionary action, and regardless of level of supervisory responsibility.

This population can be larger than that covered by some definitions of parole caseload, because it includes persons entering conditional release status in a given state by means other than release to parole, persons transferred in by interstate compact from other states, etc. See **conditional release, parole,** and **mandatory supervised release.**

A model data structure intended to indicate data items (factual content) and terminology likely to be needed to describe parole caseload major activity for interstate comparisons and national trend data is presented below. Actions taken in response to alleged parole violations are not considered caseload movement in this model unless proceedings are completed and parole is formally revoked. See **parole violation** and **parole suspended.**

Note that many of the data items also appear in the structures for **paroling authority decisions** and **prison/parole population movement** (see entries).

Key words and phrases on this list are defined in the various "parole" entries and under **custody** and **supervision.**

parole agency caseload entries and removals
ENTRIES TO AGENCY CASELOAD
- discretionary first parole
- parole to custody—conditional release from confinement, with transfer to the physical custody of another jurisdiction for adjudication or confinement, but with assignment to parole agency caseload (also called "parole to detainer")
- transfer in from other agency, assumption of supervisory custody only
- transfer in from other agency, jurisdiction assumed
- reparole
- other conditional release (e.g., mandatory supervised release)
- furlough under parole agency supervision (full-time temporary release for work or education)

REMOVALS FROM AGENCY CASELOAD
- declared absconder (optional with agency)
- parole revoked—revocation proceedings complete
- other conditional release revoked—revocation proceedings complete
- transfer out to other agency, relinquishment of supervisory custody only
- transfer out to other agency, legal jurisdiction relinquished
- parole discharge, mandatory by expiration of sentence or other statutory provision
- parole discharge, discretionary by parole authority
- parole discharge, discretionary by other authority—executive, court, etc.
- other conditional release discharge, mandatory by expiration of sentence or other statutory provision
- other conditional release discharge, discretionary by paroling authority
- other conditional release discharge, discretionary by other authority—executive, court, etc.
- death

parole board   see **paroling authority**

parolee   *recommended statistical terminology*   A person who has been conditionally released by a paroling authority from a prison prior to the expiration of his or her sentence, and placed under the supervision of a parole agency, and who is required to observe conditions of parole.

annotation

This definition excludes (1) persons discharged from prison without conditions (usually because of expiration of sentence or **clemency**); (2) persons subject to conditional release other than parole (e.g. **mandatory supervised release**), although they may be considered part of **parole supervisory caseload** (see entry); (3) persons paroled from jails and other local confinement facilities who have not been under the jurisdiction of a state-level corrections agency.

parole officer   *recommended statistical terminology*   An employee of a parole agency whose primary duties are the supervision of parolees or pre-parole investigation or planning.

annotation

In some jurisdictions parole officers have some degree of peace officer powers. However, these persons are not **law enforcement officers** in the recommended terminology.

See also **parole agency.**

parole revocation   *recommended statistical terminology*   The administrative action of a paroling authority removing a person from parole status in response to a violation of lawfully required conditions of parole including the prohibition against commission of a new offense, and usually resulting in a return to prison.

annotation

In the recommended usage, this category excludes revocation of conditional release statuses other than parole. Further, it is limited to those cases where revocation proceedings have been completed. "Parole revoked" should not be used to describe the status of persons only alleged to have violated conditions of parole. See **parole violation** and **parole suspended** for recommended terminology.

See **paroling authority decisions, parole agency caseload entries and removals,** and **prison/parole population movement** for the function of parole revocation in data structures.

Parole conditions are the lawful requirements of behavior which the parolee must fulfill. They can include both standard requirements applied to all persons under the jurisdiction of a given agency, and special requirements pertaining to an individual parolee. Not committing a new offense is always a condition of parole.

Procedures concerning parole revocation are in many respects determined by the *Morrissey* decision of the U.S. Supreme Court, in 1972. The process occurs in two steps, and each step can end with a decision to take no further action or to continue.

The first step is a preliminary hearing (often called a "Morrissey hearing") which centers around the issue of whether there is probable cause (reasonable grounds to believe an alleged violation of conditions did occur). A finding of probable cause may result in a return to prison pending completion of proceedings. (See also **probable cause**.)

The second step, if probable cause is found, is a "parole revocation hearing" at which the issues concern whether the violation did in fact occur and whether an actual violation necessitates revocation of parole. This is the final administrative hearing on the question of whether or not a person's parole status should be revoked.

During each of these processes the legal rights of the parolee are similar though not identical to the **rights of defendants** in the initial stages of prosecution.

See *Parole Systems in the U.S.* (3rd ed., 1976, National Council on Crime and Delinquency) for an analysis of rights and legal requirements stemming from *Morrissey* and other Supreme Court decisions, and procedures in the various states. See also the Bureau of Justice Statistics publication *A National Survey of Parole-Related Legislation* for update on changes to parole.

Parole status can usually be revoked only by the authority that granted it.

Parole revocation may result in a short confinement in a local facility or return to a federal or state confinement facility.

parole supervision   *recommended statistical terminology*   Guidance, treatment or regulation of the behavior of a convicted adult who is obliged to fulfill conditions of parole or other conditional release, authorized and required by statute, performed by a parole agency, and occurring after a period of prison confinement.

annotation

The supervisory responsibilities of parole agencies normally include both persons on parole and persons with other **conditional release** statuses such as **mandatory supervised release**.

See **parole supervisory caseload** and other "parole" entries for data terminology.

See also **supervised probation.**

parole supervisory caseload   *recommended statistical terminology*
The total number of clients registered with a parole agency or officer on a given date, or during a specified time period.

annotation

The caseload of a parole agency may be larger than would result from discretionary releases to parole granted by paroling authorities, because persons subject to other **conditional release** such as **mandatory supervised release** may be placed under parole supervision although not released by paroling authority discretion.

See **parole agency caseload entries and removals.** See also **caseload (corrections).**

parole suspended   *recommended statistical terminology*   The withdrawal by a paroling authority or parole agent of a person's effective parole status, usually accompanied by a return to confinement, pending a determination of whether parole should be revoked, or pending resolution of some problem that may require a temporary return to confinement.

annotation

This term is proposed mainly to provide an overall designation for the status of parolees alleged to have violated parole conditions but not determined to have done so by completed revocation proceedings. "Revoked" should not be used to describe the status of these cases. See **parole revocation** and **parole violation**.

Parole can be effectively suspended while the parolee is awaiting the results of parole revocation procedures. It may also be in effect suspended when a parolee from one state is arrested in another state and held for prosecution or other disposition of his or her case.

Returns to prison because of parole suspension while awaiting beginning or completion of revocation proceedings are items in the **paroling authority decisions** and **prison/parole population movement** model data structures.

parole violation   *recommended statistical terminology*   An act or a failure to act by a parolee which does not conform to the conditions of parole.

annotation

This term should not be used as a synonym for **parole revocation** (see entry). Whereas a parole violation is an act committed by a parolee, a parole revocation is the formal action that may be taken by a paroling authority if occurrence of the violation is established. A parole violation will not necessarily result in a parole revocation and return to prison. Persons alleged to have committed parole violations should not be referred to as "revoked" unless revocation proceedings have been completed and have resulted in revocation. See **parole suspended** for recommended terminology.

Conditions of parole, as set forth by the paroling authority, frequently include maintaining regular employment, abstaining from drugs and alcohol, not associating with known offenders or other specified persons, regularly reporting to a parole officer or other designated person, and/or remaining within a designated geographic area. The conditions of parole also always include the requirement not to commit another crime.

A parole violation that does not consist of commission of a crime, or is not prosecuted or adjudicated as a crime, is usually called a "technical violation," to indicate that it is behavior forbidden by the conditions of parole and not statute, or treated as if not forbidden by statute.

paroling authority   *recommended statistical terminology*   A board or commission which has the authority to release on parole adults committed to prison, to revoke parole or other conditional release, and to discharge from parole or other conditional release status.

annotation

Parole board authority includes all grants of parole (except in those few states where the governor's final approval is required) and may include granting of other types of conditional release with the exception of **mandatory supervised release** (see entry).

Parole boards also perform investigative and advisory functions regarding grants of clemency, for example, pardons, which in most states are granted by the governor.

The precise extent of parole board authority varies among the states, depending upon statutory provisions concerning sentencing, eligibility for parole, authority to discharge before end of maximum sentence period and related matters.

At present, all adult paroling authorities are administratively separate from state correctional facility systems, and the majority are also separate from the parole field service agency in the state. See **parole agency.**

In most states, parole board members serve full-time. The trend is toward increasing the number of members on these boards.

Typical names for paroling authorities are "board of parole," "board of pardons and parole," "parole commission," and in jurisdictions where probation is administered by the state, "board of probation and parole." Members are also called "commissioners."

For the most recent survey description of paroling authorities see *Parole Systems in the United States* (3rd ed., 1976, National Council on Crime and Delinquency). See also the Bureau of Justice Statistics publication *A National Survey of Parole-Related Legislation* for update on changes to parole.

paroling authority decisions   *recommended statistical terminology* Outcomes of case hearings or reviews where the discretionary power of the paroling authority is exercised.

annotation

This classification represents the types of decisions made by a paroling authority at the level likely to be needed to produce significant interstate comparison and national trend data. The items listed below are a model data structure that is an expanded and reworded version of the "paroling authority decisions" data element in the **OBSCIS** (see entry) data dictionary.

Note that while each of the suggested data items represents a distinctive paroling authority decision, some of these decisions can co-occur as hearing outcomes concerning a single person. In this sense, the categories in this model are not mutually exclusive. The arrangement or inclusion of suggested items on this list depends on the purposes of the particular statistical program.

Items have been added to account for paroling authority responsibility concerning conditional releases other than parole, such as **mandatory supervised release** cases (see entry).

Note that many of the data items also appear in the structures for **parole agency caseload entries and removals** and **prison/parole population movement** (see entries).

Key words and phrases on this list are defined in the various "parole" entries.

paroling authority decisions (some decisions can co-occur with others as the outcome of a single hearing)

- determination of minimum parole eligibility date
- parole granted
- reparole
- parole to custody—conditional release from confinement for the purpose of transfer to the physical custody of another jurisdiction for adjudication or confinement (also called "parole to detainer")
- parole denied
- parole decision deferred
- parole discharge—discretionary by paroling authority
- other conditional release discharge—discretionary by paroling authority
- unconditional release from prison by clemency

  parole revoked, return to prison without new sentence:
  - violation of special conditions only (technical violation)
  - in lieu of prosecution for new offense
  - new offense conviction
  - awaiting adjudication for new offense
- parole revoked, return to prison with new sentence
- return to prison awaiting beginning or completion of parole or other conditional release revocation proceedings (parole suspended)

  other conditional release revoked, return to prison without new sentence:
  - violation of special conditions only (technical violation)
  - in lieu of prosecution for new offense
  - new offense conviction
  - awaiting adjudication for new offense
- other conditional release revoked, return to prison with new sentence
- declared absconder—warrant issued

  parole continued:
  - no new conviction
  - new conviction

  other conditional release continued:
  - no new conviction
  - new conviction
- restoration of civil rights only

Part I offenses   In Uniform Crime Reports terminology, the group of offenses, also called "major offenses," for which UCR publishes counts of reported instances, and which consist of those that meet the following five-part criterion: (1) are most likely to be reported to police, (2) police investigation can easily establish whether a crime has occurred, (3) occur in all geographical areas, (4) occur with sufficient frequency to provide an adequate basis for comparison, (5) are serious crimes by nature and/or volume.

annotation

The Part I offenses are:

1. Criminal homicide*
   a. Murder and nonnegligent (voluntary) manslaughter*
   b. Negligent (involuntary) manslaughter*
2. Forcible rape*
   a. Rape by force
   b. Attempted forcible rape
3. Robbery*
   a. Firearm
   b. Knife or cutting instrument
   c. Other dangerous weapon
   d. Strongarm
4. Aggravated assault*
   a. Firearm
   b. Knife or cutting instrument
   c. Other dangerous weapon
   d. Hands, fist, feet, etc.—aggravated injury
5. Burglary*
   a. Forcible entry
   b. Unlawful entry—no force
   c. Attempted forcible entry
6. Larceny-theft*
7. Motor vehicle theft*
   a. Autos
   b. Trucks and buses
   c. Other vehicles
8. Arson*

The national UCR annual publication *Crime in the United States* presents data both on the occurrence of Part I offenses and on arrests relating to such offenses.

In situations where two or more UCR Part I offenses (with the exception of arson) are committed as part of a single criminal episode, only the most serious of the offenses, that is, the one which has the lowest number on the preceding list, is counted and tabulated in UCR.

Arson was added to the Part I offenses as of 1979 by Congressional action. A different classification procedure is followed. When two or more UCR Part I offenses occur in the same criminal episode and one of these is arson, the arson is counted and tabulated, but the most serious of the other offenses is also counted in one of the first seven numbered offense categories. See **arson UCR 8** for more information on the special status of this category in the UCR data structure.

The UCR Index Crimes (see **Crime Index**) consist of all Part I offenses except **negligent** (involuntary) **manslaughter** (1b).

*See individual entries.

Part II offenses
In Uniform Crime Reports terminology, a set of offense categories used in UCR data concerning arrests.

annotation

The Part II offenses are: (see individual entries)

9. simple assault (other assaults—simple, not aggravated)
10. forgery and counterfeiting
11. fraud
12. embezzlement
13. stolen property; buying, receiving, possessing
14. vandalism
15. weapons; carrying, possessing, etc.
16. prostitution and commercialized vice
17. sex offenses (except forcible rape and prostitution and commercialized vice)
18. drug abuse violations
19. gambling
20. offenses against the family and children
21. driving under the influence
22. liquor laws
23. drunkenness
24. disorderly conduct
25. vagrancy
26. all other offenses (except traffic law violations)
27. suspicion
28. curfew and loitering laws—(juveniles)
29. runaway—(juveniles)

UCR publishes reported crime and arrest data for Part I offenses, but only arrest data for Part II offenses. In multiple offense situations, the published arrest data indicate only the most serious charge at time of arrest. Note that categories 27–29 do not represent criminal offenses, although they are reasons for taking persons into custody.

parties to offenses
All persons culpably concerned in the commission of a crime, whether they directly commit the act constituting the offense, or facilitate, solicit, encourage, aid or attempt to aid, or abet its commission; also, in some penal codes, persons who assist one who has committed a crime to avoid arrest, trial, conviction or punishment.

annotation

The sections dealing with criminal responsibility or accountability in contemporary criminal codes commonly divide the people culpably connected to a crime into two groups:

(1) those concerned before or during its commission, all subject to the same penalties, often called "principals," and

(2) those who have aided a criminal only after commission of a crime.

The latter are subject to lesser penalties, and are sometimes called "accessories" in statute. The offense may be called "accessory after the fact," but often has a different name, such as "concealing or aiding a fugitive from justice."

This two-part division has been adopted in most states to replace a variety of complex distinctions among parties to crime that were inconsistently named and defined among the different states. The modern rationale is that the guilt of a person who encourages or assists in the commission of a crime before or during the event is equivalent to that of a person who directly commits the criminal act (the "chief actor") and therefore requires the same penalty. Some codes explicitly state that all distinctions between "principals" (chief actors) and **accomplices** (that is, aiders, abettors, solicitors, accessories before the fact, etc.) are abolished.

The exact nature of participation in criminal activity does, however, still function in the different definitions and penalties for the **inchoate offenses** (see entry) of criminal conspiracy, solicitation, and attempt. These "incomplete" crimes are usually charged when the ultimately intended crime was not committed. Criminal facilitation, however, is an inchoate crime that can only be charged when the ultimately intended crime is completed.

Since the traditional terminology continues to function in some criminal justice usages, the traditional names for different kinds of parties to crimes are presented here, with definitions indicating the distinctions commonly made when a distinction is or was made.

principal   The chief actor in a crime, or the chief actor and all persons actually or constructively present while it was being committed. Now often the statutory name for anyone in group (1).

aider or abettor   An accomplice who solicits or knowingly assists another person to commit a crime, often only one who is actually or constructively present at the commission of the crime. Now included in group (1).

accessory before the fact   An accomplice who solicits or knowingly assists another person to commit a crime, often only one who is not present at its commission. Now included in group (1).

accessory after the fact   A person who, after a crime has been committed, knowingly assists the offender to avoid arrest, trial, conviction or punishment. Still a separate category, defined as group (2) above, also called "accessories" in some codes.

In many jurisdictions, accessories after the fact are recognized as a separate group only in relation to felonies. In some of these jurisdictions, a person who knowingly aids a misdemeanant is treated as a principal to the misdemeanor. In others, such a person does not commit any offense.

part-time temporary release   see full-time temporary release

peeping tom   A popular name for a person who trespasses for the purpose of observing persons inside a dwelling.

annotation

The NCIC Uniform Offense Classification places this item under "sex offenses," and defines it as "Use to describe an offense involving loitering, prowling or wandering upon the private property of another and peeking in the door or window of an inhabited building or structure located thereon without visible or lawful business with the owner or occupant thereof."

Some jurisdictions report "peeping tom" arrests for UCR in the category **sex offenses UCR 17.**

Some penal codes define "disorderly conduct" or "disturbing the peace" so as to include this conduct; others include it in a "criminal trespass" statute.

In the tentatively recommended classification for post-arrest offense reporting "peeping tom" offenses are assigned to the "other" category. See Appendix B.

pending caseload   see **caseload (court)**

per curiam opinion   see **opinion**

perjury   The intentional making of a false statement as part of testimony by a sworn witness in a judicial proceeding on a matter material to the inquiry.

annotation

The above definition represents the narrowest statutory meaning of the term "perjury." The broadest definition includes all false statements, oral and written, knowingly made under oath or made in any of various contexts (not the same in all states) where a penalty for false statement is provided by law.

Some jurisdictions define two or several degrees of perjury, others define a series of separately labeled offenses, for example, "perjury," "false swearing" and "unsworn falsification." Distinctions may be drawn on the basis of whether or not the statement is made under oath, whether or not the information contained is material, and whether the proceeding is judicial, administrative or legislative.

One perjury-related offense which is separately codified and named with some consistency is **subornation of perjury**: the intentional causing of another person to commit the offense of perjury.

These offenses would be assigned to the "other" category in the tentatively recommended classification for post-arrest offense reporting. See Appendix B.

perpetrator   The chief actor in the commission of a crime, that is, the person who directly commits the criminal act.

annotation

In law enforcement usage, "culprit" is a synonym for this term. See also **suspect**.

Where a crime has two or more chief actors, these persons may be called "co-perpetrators," "cohorts," or "accomplices" in law enforcement usage. See **parties to offenses** for more information.

person   In legal usage, a human being, or a group of human beings considered a legal unit, having the lawful capacity to defend rights, incur obligations, prosecute claims, or be prosecuted or adjudicated.

annotation

Examples of a legal unit constituting a legal person are a state, a territory, a government, a country, a partnership, a public or private corporation, or an unincorporated association.

In data presentations where context does not make technical distinctions clear, adults, juveniles and corporate entities should be so labelled.

personal crimes   In National Crime Survey published data, a summary offense category consisting of:

personal crimes of violence
  rape
    completed rape
    attempted rape
  personal robbery
    personal robbery with injury
      from serious assault
      from minor assault
    personal robbery without injury
  assault
    aggravated assault
      with injury
      attempted assault with weapon
    simple assault
      with injury
      attempted assault without weapon

personal crimes of theft
  personal larceny with contact
    purse snatching
      completed purse snatching
      attempted purse snatching
    pocket picking
  personal larceny without contact

annotation

Personal crimes, also called "crimes against persons" and **household crimes** are the primary groupings of NCS offense categories.

In the NCS program, criminal events are not pre-classified in data collection, either by the survey interviewer or by the respondent. Rather, the determination of whether an event is to be considered a **criminal incident** (see entry) for NCS and its proper classification is made through computerized examination of reported characteristics of the event.

Data are presented in publications with varying levels of detail. The presentation categories for personal crimes most generally employed are:

Under **personal crimes of violence:**

rape   The carnal knowledge or attempted carnal knowledge of another person of the same or opposite sex, by force or threat of force.

The complete NCS glossary entry, "rape," reads as follows: "Rape—Carnal knowledge through the use of force or the threat of force, including attempts. Statutory rape (without force) is excluded. Includes both heterosexual and homosexual rape."*

The NCS category, "rape," differs from that used in other national statistical programs, where the category is limited to forcible sexual intercourse committed by a male against a female. See **forcible rape UCR 2** and **sex offenses.**

personal robbery   The theft or attempted theft of money or property from the immediate possession of a person, by force or threat of force, with or without a weapon.

Personal robbery is subdivided according to whether or not a victim(s) suffered physical injury, and then according to whether the injury resulted from serious assault or minor assault. The complete NCS glossary entry, "robbery with injury," reads as follows: "Robbery with injury—Theft or attempted theft from a person, accompanied by an attack, either with or without a weapon, resulting in injury. An injury is classified as resulting from a serious assault irrespective of degree or extent if a weapon was used in the commission of the crime, or, if not, when the extent of the injury was either serious (e.g., broken bones, loss of teeth, internal injuries, loss of consciousness) or undetermined but requiring 2 or more days of hospitalization. An injury is classified as resulting from a minor assault when the extent of the injury was minor (e.g., bruises, black eyes, cuts, scratches, swelling) or undetermined but requiring less than 2 days of hospitalization."*

assault   An unlawful physical attack or attempted physical attack upon a person.

Assault is commonly subdivided into aggravated assault and simple assault. The complete NCS glossary entries, "aggravated assault" and "simple assault," read as follows:

"Aggravated assault—Attack with a weapon resulting in any injury and attack without a weapon resulting either in serious injury (e.g., broken bones, loss of teeth, internal injuries, loss of consciousness) or in undetermined injury requiring 2 or more days of hospitalization. Also includes attempted assault with a weapon."*

"Simple assault—Attack without a weapon resulting either in minor injury (e.g., bruises, black eyes, cuts, scratches, swelling) or in undetermined injury requiring less than 2 days of hospitalization. Also includes attempted assault without a weapon."*

Assaults for the purpose of effecting rape are classified as "rape." Assaults for the purpose of effecting robbery are classified as "personal robbery."

Under **personal crimes of theft:**

personal larceny with contact   The theft or attempted theft by stealth, of money or property from the immediate possession of a person, without the use or threat of force.

A theft from a person committed or attempted by use of force or threat of force is classified as "personal robbery."

personal larceny without contact   The theft or attempted theft by stealth, of money or property of a person, without direct contact between the victim and the offender.

Theft without contact occurring in a residence or its immediate vicinity is not classified as a personal crime. A household rather than any individual person(s) is considered to be the victim of the theft, and such incidents are classified as "household larceny." See **household crimes.**

Thefts of motor vehicles are also classified as household crimes in NCS. By NCS convention, a household rather than any individual person(s) is considered to be the victim.

*These definitions are quoted from the NCS report *Criminal Victimization in the United States, 1977.*

personal crimes of theft (NCS)   see **personal crimes**

personal crimes of violence (NCS)   see **personal crimes**

personal larceny with contact (NCS)   see **personal crimes**

personal larceny without contact (NCS)   see **personal crimes**

personal robbery (NCS)   see **personal crimes**

petition   A written request made to a court asking for the exercise of its judicial powers, or asking for permission to perform some act where the authorization of a court is required.

annotation

A petition is a formal document filed in court that initiates a case, in contrast to a **motion**, which is a request made in the course of proceedings and which is often oral. **Charging documents** (complaints, informations, indictments) are technically "petitions," but they are not called such in common usage.

In criminal cases the filing of a document called a petition is the usual method of requesting leave to make an **appeal** or of requesting a **postconviction remedy** or **sentence review**. Juvenile court cases are initiated by petitions requesting the court to make a determination as to the juvenile's status (see **juvenile petition**).

The person who files a petition in court is called a **petitioner,** and the person who answers a petition is generally called a **respondent** (see entry). Some petitions, such as a petition for a **writ,** do not require a respondent.

petition not sustained   *recommended statistical terminology*   The finding by a juvenile court in an adjudicatory hearing that there is not sufficient evidence to sustain an allegation that a juvenile is a delinquent, status offender, or dependent.

annotation

This type of **juvenile court judgment** (see entry) corresponds to a dismissal or a judgment of acquittal in criminal proceedings.

In **delinquency** cases (see entry), the allegation is that the juvenile has committed a delinquent act or a status offense. In **dependency** cases, the allegation is about the behavior of the parent or guardian, not the behavior of the juvenile.

petit jury   see **trial jury**

physical custody (corrections)   see **custody**

PINS/CHINS/JINS/MINS   Acronyms used to name a class of juveniles often consisting of status offenders but variously defined in different jurisdictions.

annotation

The juveniles so described are a service category not necessarily aligned with any traditional behavioral or statutory category. The terms should not be used in statistical publications without detailed definition.

This category, formerly used in the series *Children in Custody,* no longer functions in that program, but the definitions provided in earlier publications describe the meaning of these acronyms. "Person in need of supervision (PINS)—Detention status of a juvenile declared by a juvenile court to be in need of supervision. Encompasses those known variously as child in need of supervision (CHINS), juvenile in need of supervision (JINS), and minor in need of supervision (MINS), as well as those designated as unruly, unmanageable, or incorrigible under special statutes for status offenders. All PINS are not status offenders, and all status offenders are not PINS. Even in states with status offender statutes, juveniles with previous offenses can be adjudicated delinquent for status offenses. Conversely, a judge can declare a juvenile to be a person in need of supervision for a felony or misdemeanor." See bibliography under "U.S. Department of Justice."

See **delinquency** for preferred usages.

placement   The commitment or assignment of a person to a facility, or to any supervisory, care or treatment program, as the result of official or unofficial actions.

annotation

This term has acquired a broad meaning in current usage, ranging from the judicial action of commitment to a confinement facility, to such unofficial actions as the assignment of a runaway to a private facility or temporary foster home by a private community service agency. In juvenile justice and child welfare data it is frequently used as the name for the category of all actions assigning juveniles to facilities or programs.

Since "placement" may mean such a variety of legally different actions, statistical publications concerning placements should indicate the kind of person or agency making the placement, the legal authority under which it is done, and the judicial status(s) of the subjects.

It is recommended that in criminal justice statistics the term be used to designate assignments of adults to correctional day programs or straight probation, in contrast to **commitments** (see entry) to facilities.

plaintiff   A person who initiates a court action.

annotation

The above term is the customary name for the person who initiates a civil action. In some states the prosecution in a criminal case (that is, "the people," as represented by government) is called the "plaintiff."

"Complainant," "complaining party," and "complaining witness" are also used to mean the plaintiff.

plea   In criminal proceedings, a defendant's formal answer in court to the charge contained in a complaint, information, or indictment, that he or she is guilty or not guilty of the offense charged, or does not contest the charge.

annotation

In relation to a given charge or case, the defendant may enter different pleas at different stages of the proceedings. Court and prosecutorial management information systems often provide for recording of the nature of the plea at each stage.

With respect to sequence, the recommended terms are:

initial plea (also **first plea**)   *recommended statistical terminology*   The first plea to a given charge entered in the court record by or for the defendant.

The acceptance of an initial plea by the court unambiguously indicates that the arraignment process has been completed, and is therefore a better unit of count in reporting criminal case or defendant flow than "arraignment," which as a process is variously defined in different jurisdictions.

final plea   *recommended statistical terminology*   The last plea to a given charge entered in the court record by or for the defendant.

When distinguishing pleas by nature of response, the major types are:

not guilty plea   *recommended statistical terminology*   A defendant's formal answer in court to the charge(s) contained in a complaint, information, or indictment, claiming that he or she did not commit the offense(s) listed.

not guilty by reason of insanity   *recommended statistical terminology*   A defendant's formal answer in court to the charge(s) contained in a complaint, information, or indictment, claiming that he or she is not legally accountable for the offenses listed in the charging document because insane at the time they were committed. See entry.

guilty plea   *recommended statistical terminology*   A defendant's formal answer in court to the charge(s) contained in a complaint, information, or indictment, admitting that he or she did in fact commit the offense(s) listed.

nolo contendere   *recommended statistical terminology*   A defendant's formal answer in court to the charge(s) contained in a complaint, information, or indictment, stating that he or she will not contest the charge(s), but neither admits guilt nor claims innocence.

Guilty pleas and nolo contendere pleas are in fact usually combined into a single category in data systems and in statistical presentations, since they have the same legal effect in criminal proceedings. Both pleas can be followed by a judgment of conviction without a trial or verdict, and by a sentencing disposition. The pleas differ, however, with regard to their potential use as evidence in any related civil proceedings. A guilty plea in a criminal case can constitute evidence in a civil proceeding that relevant facts have been admitted; a nolo contendere plea cannot.

"Guilty plea" is a key disposition category in court caseload statistics. See **court disposition**.

"Guilty plea" is a major defendant "manner of disposition" subclass in the model court caseload statistical system developed by the National Court Statistics Project (see Appendix E). In this system the guilty plea category (including nolo contendere) contrasts with convictions and acquittals at trial, dismissals, and the other methods by which defendants are disposed of, classified according to impact on court caseload.

In some data systems, the term "plea" is used where only a guilty or nolo contendere plea is meant. This usage is not recommended.

police   see **law enforcement**

police department   In common usage, a municipal (city, town or village) law enforcement agency.

annotation

A police department is a local law enforcement agency. For statistical purposes, "police department" can be used with the above definition, but the term is also sometimes used as a class name for all local law enforcement agencies (municipal, regional, special district, etc.) other than **sheriff's departments.**

For classificatory recommendations see **law enforcement agency** and **level of government.**

police witness   see **witness**

population movement   In correctional usage, entries and exits of adjudicated persons, or persons subject to judicial proceedings, into or from correctional facilities or programs.

annotation

The events which are described, classified and tabulated under the general heading of population movement statistics are variously named and defined. The choice of nomenclature and referents in different jurisdictions is not consistent.

See **probation supervisory population movement, parole agency caseload entries and removals** , and **prison/parole population movement** for recommended data terminology.

post-adjudicated   see **adjudication**

postconviction remedy   *recommended statistical terminology*   The procedure or set of procedures by which a person who has been convicted of a crime can challenge in court the lawfulness of a judgment of conviction or penalty or of a correctional agency action, and thus obtain relief in situations where this cannot be done by a direct appeal.

annotation

Although "postconviction remedy" most properly refers only to relief actually granted by the court, the term is often used as above, to refer to the entire process by which such relief can be sought.

It is recommended that postconviction remedy cases be counted separately from other caseload in court activity data presentations.

Depending on the jurisdiction, application for postconviction remedy can be made either to the same court in which the original proceedings were conducted, or to a higher court. "Postconviction remedy case" is provided as a distinct caseload reporting category for both trial and appellate courts in the model court caseload statistical system developed by the National Court Statistics Project (see Appendix E).

Reasons why the appeal process may be unavailable in a given case include: the time limits within which an appeal must be made have been exceeded; the appeal process has been exhausted; or the decision or action being challenged was by an administrative agency rather than a court, and cannot be challenged by appeal.

In situations where the law in a given jurisdiction would allow a challenge to be made either through appeal or through application for postconviction remedy, there is usually a procedural requirement that the appeal process be used.

pre-adjudicated   see adjudication

pre-arraignment lockup   *recommended statistical terminology*   A confinement facility for arrested adults awaiting arraignment or consideration for pretrial release, in which the duration of stay is usually limited by statute to two days, or until the next session of the appropriate court.

annotation

This term is provided as a distinctive name for special facilities for which the sole use is very temporary detention of arrested persons awaiting first appearance in court. The pre-arraignment detention function is also performed by **jails** (see entry), which, as defined in this terminology, hold persons detained for trial and also committed persons.

See also **correctional facility (adult).**

predisposition investigation   *recommended statistical terminology*

An investigation undertaken by a probation agency or other designated authority at the request of a juvenile court, into the past behavior, family background and personality of a juvenile who has been adjudicated a delinquent, a status offender, or a dependent, in order to assist the court in determining the most appropriate disposition.

annotation

The predisposition investigation and the resulting "predisposition report" is usually made by a probation agency or special intake officer or unit attached to a juvenile court. The investigations often form a substantial part of a probation agency's or intake unit's workload.

A predisposition investigation generally corresponds to an adult **presentence investigation.**

See also **diagnostic commitment.**

preliminary hearing   *recommended statistical terminology*   The proceeding before a judicial officer in which three matters must be decided: whether a crime was committed; whether the crime occurred within the territorial jurisdiction of the court; and whether there are reasonable grounds to believe that the defendant committed the crime.

annotation

A chief purpose of the preliminary hearing is to protect the accused from inadequately based prosecution in felony cases by making a judicial test of the existence of **probable cause** (see entry) early in the proceedings.

In felony cases in states where a felony trial can be initiated by the filing of an **information** by the prosecutor, the preliminary hearing (usually in "lower court") is a key step at which it is determined whether proceedings will continue. If the court does find probable cause, bail may be set or reset, and the defendant will be bound over or "held to answer" the charge(s) in the trial court ("higher court" or "superior court").

In felony cases in states where the grand jury **indictment** is used to initiate proceedings in the trial court, defendants often waive the preliminary hearing, because the grand jury will make the probable cause determination. But some defendants request a preliminary hearing because it affords opportunity to acquire information about the basis of the prosecutor's case or move for dismissal of the case.

Whether the defendant has the right to a preliminary hearing in a misdemeanor case depends upon the jurisdiction.

Preliminary hearings are also called "preliminary examinations."

preponderance of the evidence   see **levels of proof**

presentence investigation   *recommended statistical terminology*   An investigation undertaken by a probation agency or other designated authority at the request of a court, into the past behavior, family circumstances, and personality of an adult who has been convicted of a crime, in order to assist the court in determining the most appropriate sentence.

annotation

The report resulting from such an investigation is usually called a "presentence report," but the investigations are also called "social investigations," and the reports, "social histories," "social studies," or "court reports."

The investigations often form a substantial part of an adult probation agency's workload.

Presentencing information may reach the court in various ways. For example, a confidential report may be prepared in addition to the usually public presentence report. Or, the defendant himself may submit information to the court.

A presentence investigation generally corresponds to a juvenile **predisposition investigation**.

See also **diagnostic commitment.**

presentment   Historically, written notice of an offense taken by a grand jury from their own knowledge or observation; in current usage, any of several presentations of alleged facts and charges to a court or a grand jury by a prosecutor.

presiding judge   The title of the judicial officer formally designated for some period as the chief judicial officer of a court.

annotation

The presiding judge is the individual chosen to act in the capacity of the chief officer within a given court having two or more judicial officers. The chief officer of a court is also called the "chief judge," or "chief justice."

The judicial officer who conducts a given judicial proceeding is said to "preside" over that proceeding.

pretrial conference   A meeting of the opposing parties in a case with the judicial officer prior to trial, for the purposes of stipulating those things which are agreed upon and thus narrowing the trial to the things that are in dispute, disclosing the required information about witnesses and evidence, making motions, and generally organizing the presentation of motions, witnesses and evidence.

annotation

The matters dealt with in a pretrial conference as defined above may instead be taken up in a procedure called an **omnibus hearing**. The name of the proceeding and the precise range of matters included in it depend upon the statutes, rules of court, and customs of a given jurisdiction.

In criminal proceedings, this type of pretrial activity occurs before the trial judge after an arraignment in which the defendant has pled not guilty. It may include consideration of reduction of the charges.

pretrial detention   *recommended statistical terminology*   Any period of confinement occurring between arrest or other holding to answer a charge, and the conclusion of prosecution.

annotation

Pretrial detention is usually shortened or eliminated by some form of **pretrial release**. See entry.

pretrial discovery   In criminal proceedings, disclosure by the prosecution or the defense prior to trial of evidence or other information which is intended to be used in the trial.

annotation

Pretrial discovery is the procedure by which each of the opposing parties obtains from the other those facts necessary "to promote the orderly ascertainment of the truth" during the trial. The extent and nature of the information required to be disclosed by each side before trial varies from state to state in accord with statutory provisions and/or rules of court procedure.

The information exchanged will usually include the identities of witnesses, including facts about their criminal histories if any, and relevant indisputable facts about witnesses and circumstances.

The prosecutor may be compelled to disclose such things as statements or portions of statements made by witnesses or experts or testimony from grand jury proceedings, and objects and documents belonging to the accused which the prosecution intends to use in the trial.

The defense may be compelled to disclose various facts about the defendant, which may include the taking of photographs and fingerprints, blood specimens, handwriting specimens and the like.

Information usually not subject to pretrial disclosure includes investigator's notes, opinions of counsel, and anything that would violate the constitutional prohibition of compelling the defendant to testify against himself.

pretrial release   *recommended statistical terminology*   The release of an accused person from custody, for all or part of the time before or during prosecution, upon his or her promise to appear in court when required.

annotation

Pretrial release policies and procedural requirements are sometimes spelled out in statutes or judicial rules. The release of a given arrestee is authorized by a magistrate or other judicial officer, or by another official to whom authority has been delegated.

An accused person who has been arrested ordinarily has the right to be taken before a magistrate, with more or less dispatch according to the rules of each jurisdiction, to be set free upon guarantee of his re-appearance to hear the charges against him and submit to judgment. See **initial appearance.**

The usual procedure is for the magistrate to set **bail,** which means that a sum of money or other thing of value is pledged by the accused or another person which will be forfeited if the accused fails to appear (see **bail** for the various types of guarantees). The pretrial release can be reconsidered and bail reset at later stages of adjudication.

In recent years release on own recognizance ("ROR") without financial guarantees has been used with increasing frequency, in large part because of the finding that many defendants who cannot provide a substantial money guarantee of appearance will in fact appear in court when required. This is also called a "personal recognizance" release.

Many jurisdictions have set up special programs to screen defendants for eligibility for ROR, using such criteria as stable residence and employment in the community. These are often called "pretrial release programs" but release on own recognizance is the only procedure involved. Some courts use release on "unsecured bond" (no deposit of money) to accomplish the same purpose as ROR.

Release to the custody of a third person is also used to ensure re-appearance of the defendant, sometimes in conjunction with some form of bail.

For national level statistical data, pretrial releases can be regarded as having three major subcategories relating to the above distinctions:

release on bail   *recommended statistical terminology*   A pretrial release in which re-appearance is guaranteed by a pledge that money or property will be forfeited upon nonappearance, with or without payment of a bondsman's fee or deposit of some or all of the pledge with the court.

release on own recognizance   *recommended statistical terminology*   A pretrial release in which the defendant signs a promise to appear but does not pledge anything of value to be forfeited upon nonappearance.

release to third party   *recommended statistical terminology*   A pretrial release without financial guarantee in which a person or organization other than the defendant assumes responsibility for returning the defendant to court when required.

principal   see **parties to offenses**

prison   *recommended statistical terminology*   A state or federal confinement facility having custodial authority over adults sentenced to confinement.

annotation

See **correctional facility (adult)** for classification information.

Prison facility system is a phrase often used in this dictionary in definitions of corrections population movement terms. It denotes an administrative entity that is the governmental unit that acquires **jurisdiction** and/or **physical custody** (see **custody**) of an offender committed to a prison. It distinguishes major population movement of interstate interest from "internal" movement, for example, movement from one facility to another facility administered by the same correctional agency.

prison commitment   *recommended statistical terminology*   A sentence of commitment to the jurisdiction of a state or federal confinement facility system for adults, of which the custodial authority extends to persons sentenced to more than a year of confinement, for a term expressed in years or for life, or to await execution of a death sentence.

annotation

A prison commitment is a type of **sentencing disposition** in the major class **defendant dispositions** (see entries).

In this recommended terminology, four types of prison commitment are distinguished at the point of sentencing:

(1) **definite term**   A sentence to confinement in a prison for which a single time value is specified at the time the court pronounces sentence.

(2) **minimum-maximum term**   A sentence to confinement in a prison for which a range of time is specified by the court at the time of sentencing.

(3) **life term**   A sentence to imprisonment for life specified by the court at the time of sentencing. Life terms may be subdivided as:
   —**life with possibility of parole**
   —**life without possibility of parole**

(4) **death sentence**   A sentence to the custody of a prison facility system while awaiting execution.

The object of this data structure is to provide a means of reporting actual time values and also sentences without time values at the point of sentencing. At later points in correctional processes, distinguishing between the definite term type of sentence and the minimum-maximum (or no minimum) type is likely to be invalid because statutes and other rules prescribe for both types various reductions in maximums, minimums as fixed proportions of maximums, and the like, according to jurisdiction.

prisoner   I.   A person in physical custody in a confinement facility, or in the personal physical custody of a criminal justice official while being transported to or between confinement facilities.   II.   *recommended statistical terminology*   A person in physical custody in a state or federal confinement facility.

annotation

Definition II is the usual meaning of this term in federal and state level statistics.

In current federal usage the term "inmate" has a contrasting meaning: a person in physical custody in a local jail.

Persons in confinement pending judgment or sentencing disposition are also called "detentioners" or "detainees." See **detention**.

See also **custody** for definition of "physical custody."

prison facility system   see **prison**

prison/parole population movement

prison/parole population movement *recommended statistical terminology* Entries and exits of persons committed to prison, into or from prison facility systems and postconfinement conditional release or supervisory programs.

annotation

The events which are described and tabulated under this heading, or under similar headings such as "admissions and releases" in prisoner data reporting, are variously named and classified in different jurisdictions. The scope of the data also varies, particularly with respect to the amount of parole movement information incorporated into the tabulations.

The following model data structure is a slightly revised version of the data element "status and location changes" in the **OBSCIS** (see entry) data dictionary. The revisions consist of minor rewording and data item additions.

It is intended to provide the basic data class and item terminology needed to describe all the prison and parole actions that are distinctive within a state and are also comparable at the national level.

However, this long list of data items and classes is not recommended as a universal, actual data reporting system or as a set of national output categories: the appropriate selection, definition and arrangement of units of count depends upon the procedures in a given jurisdiction and the purposes of a given data presentation. The "provisional exit" category, for example, applies to state data needs only.

The model is designed from a management perspective. It presents as subclasses types of movement that are treated as independent classes in actual statistical publications where, for example, admissions to facility systems are considered one activity area and terminations of confinement or jurisdiction a second activity area. Presentation of the terminology in the form of a complete "movement" data structure is necessary to clarify the meanings of individual items, to suggest the reasons for choices of terms and definitions, and to ensure mutually exclusive basic data items. The logical principle on which the structure and content of this model are based is that each time a prisoner or parolee significantly changes location or status, one and only one data item should represent that change. It is possible, however, that a given subject might undergo more than one significant movement during a single statistical reporting period, for example the one-year period generally employed for national level statistics.

Note that many of the data items also appear in the **paroling authority decision** and **parole agency caseload entries and removals** entries.

prison/parole population movement

1 NEW ENTRIES new state* correctional facility system entries—person is not entering the prison facility system of a given state to continue confinement on any previous sentence to that prison facility system

- New court commitment (NCC) from within state
- New court commitment following probation revocation within state
- Receiving full jurisdiction for individual from another jurisdiction excluding NCC from within state: interstate transfer of jurisdiction
- Individual received for housing for another jurisdiction: interstate transfer of physical custody

*In this data structure "state" represents state or federal correctional jurisdiction.

2 RETURNS

2a **Return to confinement in state correctional facility system**   re-entries to the prison facility system where the sentence(s) causing the most recent entry is still in effect

Parolee returned:

- Without new sentence, revocation proceedings complete, parole revoked
- With new sentence
- Without new sentence, revocation proceedings begun or pending (parole suspended)
- Medical or other reason

Returned from other conditional release:

- Without new sentence, conditional release revoked
- With new sentence
- Without new sentence, revocation proceedings begun or pending
- Medical or other reason

- Returned from probation supervision by state agency after previous imprisonment on same sentence
- Returned from out-of-state jurisdiction to which previously released for housing: interstate transfer of physical custody

Returned from provisional exit:

- Returned from exit for court appearance
- Returned from full-time release (consecutive 24-hour periods)
- Returned from hospital outside correctional system: transfer of supervisory custody only
- Returned from other provisional exit

Returned after escape from confinement (evasion of physical custody):

- Returned as violator of prison regulations only
- Returned with new sentence
- Returned without new sentence with new charges awaiting adjudication

Returned from AWOL from work furlough or other full or part-time release, excluding parole or other conditional release:

- Returned without new sentence or charges
- Returned with new sentence
- Returned without new· sentence with new charges awaiting adjudication

2b **Return to state supervision**

- Reactivation of parole, e.g., return from authorized leave out of state
- Return to state parole supervision after release to other federal or out-of-state parole agency, e.g., Interstate Compact parole
- Return from other temporary exit from state supervision

3   EXITS   departures from the prison facility system or parole caseload, authorized or unauthorized, where state correctional system jurisdiction is not relinquished

3a **Authorized facility system exits**

Conditional release:

- Parole, active supervision
- Parole, inactive supervision
- Parole to custody—conditional release to the physical custody of another jurisdiction
- Other conditional release (e.g., mandatory supervised release)
- Continued on conditional release after return for revocation hearing
- Probation supervision by state agency
- Transfer to out-of-state jurisdiction for housing without surrendering jurisdiction: interstate transfer of physical custody

Provisional exit—return expected:

- From state facility system for court appearance
- Full-time release (consecutive 24-hour periods) for work furlough, extended work furlough, etc.
- Transfer to hospital outside correctional system without surrender of jurisdiction
- Other provisional exit, including reprieves effecting release, release during appeal proceedings, etc.

3b **State supervision exit**

- Deactivation of parole, e.g., while out of state on authorized leave
- Release to out-of-state parole agency for supervision, e.g., interstate compact parole
- Other temporary exit from state supervision

3c **Unauthorized exit**

- Escape from confinement (evasion of physical custody)
- AWOL from work furlough or other full or part-time release, excluding parole or other conditional release
- Abscond from parole
- Abscond from other conditional release

4   TERMINATIONS   final separation from state correctional system: all endings of state correctional system jurisdiction over a person, including deaths and transfers to the jurisdiction of non-correctional or non-state agencies within the same state

Discharge directly from institution:

- By expiration of sentence
- By commutation
- By pardon
- By judicial action, e.g., sentence reduced by court
- To probation supervision by non-state agency

- Discharge from parole
- Discharge from other conditional release
- Discharge from probation supervision by state agency
  Termination due to death (subclassified as follows, if possible):
- Execution
- Suicide
- Accidentally killed by any means
- Intentionally killed by another person
- Natural causes
- Unknown causes
  Final release to another jurisdiction:
- To jurisdiction of mental hospital
- Transfer of jurisdiction to other prison facility or parole system

private rehabilitation agency   *recommended statistical terminology*
A private organization providing care and treatment services which may include housing, to convicted persons, juvenile offenders, or persons subject to judicial proceedings.

annotation

This general category includes residential facilities, juvenile shelters, and the like, operated by private agencies.

This term is proposed to distinguish non-governmental organizations providing rehabilitative services to offenders from the public **correctional agencies (jails, prisons, probation agencies,** and **parole agencies)** which may offer rehabilitative services, but also have officially established control and supervision responsibilities.

The major distinguishing characteristic of public vs. private agencies is that public agencies are authorized and required by law to carry out certain criminal justice functions, while private agencies are only permitted by law to perform criminal justice functions.

private security agency   *recommended statistical terminology*   An independent or proprietary commercial organization whose activities include employee clearance investigations, maintaining the security of persons or property and/or performing the functions of detection and investigation of crime and criminals and apprehension of offenders.

annotation

This term is proposed to distinguish non-governmental organizations performing security, investigative, etc., functions from public **law enforcement agencies.**

The major distinguishing characteristic of public vs. private agencies is that public agencies are authorized and required by law to carry out certain criminal justice functions, while private agencies are only permitted by law to perform criminal justice functions.

probable cause   A set of facts and circumstances which would induce a reasonably intelligent and prudent person to believe that a particular person had committed a specific crime; reasonable grounds to make or believe an accusation.

annotation

The existence of "probable cause" is required to justify arrest and the beginning of prosecution. (It is also required to initiate a **parole revocation** hearing.)

In felony cases the existence of probable cause will be established in court in a hearing usually called a **preliminary hearing** (see entry), or by a grand jury, before felony trial proceedings begin. In misdemeanor cases there is not a special hearing to determine probable cause.

See **levels of proof**.

probable cause hearing   see **preliminary hearing**

probation   The conditional freedom granted by a judicial officer to an alleged or adjudged adult or juvenile offender, as long as the person meets certain conditions of behavior.

annotation

Probation for an adjudicated person is a court ordered conditional freedom, whereas **parole** is a conditional freedom granted by a paroling authority after commitment to a period of confinement.

Conditions of adult probation, as set forth by the court which granted the probation, frequently include such admonishments as maintaining regular employment, abstaining from drugs and alcohol, not associating with known offenders or other specified persons, paying restitution or a fine, regularly reporting to a probation officer or other designated person, and/or remaining within a designated geographic area. The conditions may also include requirements that are independent sentencing dispositions, such as serving time in jail or going to prison. A brief period of incarceration followed by probation is often called "shock probation." See **split sentence**. Not committing another offense is always a condition of probation.

See **grant of probation** for recommended statistical terminology.

Juvenile probation is often designated as "informal" or "formal," depending upon the authority granting it and the nature of the conditions. See also **aftercare**. This topic is not dealt with in this dictionary because the great variety of juvenile probation-type dispositions among the various states precludes both summary description and bases for recommended usages.

probation agency   *syn*   **probation department**   *recommended statistical terminology*   A correctional agency of which the principal functions are juvenile intake, the supervision of adults and juveniles placed on probation status, and the investigation of adults or juveniles and preparation of presentence or predisposition reports to assist the court in determining the proper sentence or juvenile court disposition.

annotation

Probation agencies are classified as correctional agencies because their chief functions include the supervision of adjudicated juveniles or convicted adults. The category includes both independent probation agencies and units within other justice agencies (usually a court), if the unit primarily performs probation functions as defined above. Agencies which supervise both probationers and parolees should be described as probation/parole agencies in data publications.

State level adult and juvenile probation agencies are often separate governmental units. However, probation agencies organized at local levels of government usually operate under the authority of a court. In many states a single state agency performs both probation and parole supervision functions for adults, but juvenile probation functions are typically local and performed under the guidance of a juvenile court.

A probation agency's concern with adults is usually limited to those who have pled guilty or been convicted of an offense. Its discretionary powers regarding juveniles are much greater, in that it usually administers the **intake** (see entry) unit that can make a decision to close a case at intake, to take other actions that preclude or defer the intervention of the juvenile court, or to file a petition asking the court to assume jurisdiction over the juvenile. Some agencies administer juvenile shelter facilities. The juvenile concern is also broad in that the intake function and subsequent supervision and care authority may apply to dependent juveniles, especially those in custody pending court disposition.

For other functions see **probation workload.**

probation department   see **probation agency**

probationer   *recommended statistical terminology*   A person who is placed on probation status and required by a court or probation agency to meet certain conditions of behavior, who may or may not be placed under the supervision of a probation agency.

annotation

Adjudication need not be complete for an adult or juvenile to be placed on probation. See **adjudication withheld.**

See **probation supervisory caseload** for statistical terminology.

probation officer   *recommended statistical terminology*   An employee of a probation agency whose primary duties include one or more of the probation agency functions.

annotation

Probation officers are classified as **correctional agency** personnel in most data presentations because supervision is a major function of the agency. For other functions see **probation workload.**

The intake function of a juvenile probation agency may include the exercise of judicial authority in disposing of juvenile referrals. Probation officers who exercise judicial authority are also considered **judicial officers** in some jurisdictions and data programs.

In some jurisdictions probation officers have some degree of peace officer powers. They are not, however, **law enforcement officers** in the recommended terminology in this dictionary.

A **probation counselor** is, in the narrowest sense, a probation officer whose chief duties relate to client intake and screening, and assistance and treatment of probationers; also, a private person who assists or advises probationers; in some jurisdictions, any probation officer.

probation order   see **grant of probation**

probation revocation   *recommended statistical terminology*   A court order in response to a violation of conditions of probation, taking away a person's probationary status, and usually withdrawing the conditional freedom associated with the status.

annotation

This term should not be used as a synonym for **probation violation** (see entry). Revocation is the official action by a court in response to a probation violation, which is an act committed by the probationer.

If the grant of probation was awarded after conviction, revocation may be followed by execution of a previously set penalty, or the pronouncement and execution of a previously unpronounced penalty. If the person was placed on probation before adjudication was completed by judgment (see **adjudication withheld**) then violation of conditions may result in pronouncement of a judgment and execution of a sentence.

The person can be committed or recommitted to confinement without conviction for a new offense, but only on evidence presented during a revocation hearing that he or she has violated conditions of probation. Probation status can usually be revoked only by the authority that granted it.

Not all alleged violations result in revocation hearings or revocations. Also, a court may in some circumstances revoke probation, order the probationer to appear in court, and reinstate probationary status. However, probation revocation often results in commitment to a confinement facility to serve a previously suspended sentence.

Various legal rights pertain to the probation revocation process, such as right to counsel and advance notice of charges, but the level of proof required is not as high as that required to convict.

A probationer may be detained in jail while awaiting a court hearing concerning alleged violation of probation conditions.

See **probation supervisory population movement.**

probation supervision   see **supervised probation**

probation supervisory caseload   *recommended statistical terminology* The total number of clients registered with a probation agency on a given date, or over a given period of time, who have received grants of probation and are under active or inactive supervision.

annotation

See **supervised probation** for definitions of "active" and "inactive." Statistical reports on caseloads should count these cases separately where the distinction is applicable.

Persons or cases referred to probation agencies for intake and presentence or other investigations are also part of the work performed by a probation agency. It is recommended that activity of this type be reported as a part of **probation workload,** but excluded from caseload counts, in order to limit the latter to persons who have received **grants of probation** from the court.

See **probation supervisory population movement** for further classificatory information.

See also **caseload (corrections).**

probation supervisory population movement   *recommended statistical terminology*   Entries to and exits from the population for whom a probation agency has supervisory responsibility.

annotation

In this classificatory terminology actions are classified and described from the point of view of agency responsibility for clients.

The terminology does not cover "court probation" cases which have not been assigned to a probation agency for supervision (active or inactive) and thus are not part of the **probation supervisory caseload.** See **court probation** and **supervised probation**.

Most probation data reporting classifies movement into similar large categories, but the means of entry, the type of supervision, the confinement factor, and the point where events begin to be counted can vary, thus yielding different subsets.

The list of recommended data items in this entry is not a recommended actual data reporting structure: the appropriate selection, definition and arrangement of units of count depends upon the purposes of a given data presentation. However, the model is intended to provide the basic class and subclass terminology needed to describe probation caseload activity at a level suitable for the exchange of significant information between agencies. Presentation in the form of a complete classification structure also assists in indicating the reasons for choices of names and definitions.

Recommended reporting conventions:

1. Count probation assignments occurring before judgment (before registration of a judgment of conviction in the court record) separately from grants of probation made after judgment.

2. Specify, where applicable, whether the probation assignment is to active or inactive supervision.

Model data structure:

ENTRIES TO CASELOAD by reason

- **grant of supervised probation**   a court order, usually signed by both judicial officer and defendant or offender, granting the latter probationary status and requiring at a minimum the acceptance of supervision as a condition of probation—may be subdivided into
  - **straight probation**   probation without confinement as a condition
  - **probation with jail**   probation with a specified term of confinement in jail to be served before or during the probationary period as one of the conditions of probation
  - **probation after prison**   probation following commitment to usually brief confinement in a prison facility granted by a court (often called "split sentence" or "shock probation")

- **reinstatement of probation**   reassignment to caseload after probationary status revoked because of absconding or failure to meet other conditions
- **transfer in from other jurisdiction**   the assuming of responsibility for a probationer adjudicated in another jurisdiction—may be subdivided into
  - **transfer of jurisdiction (legal control) and supervisory custody**
  - **transfer of supervisory custodial responsibility only**

REMOVALS FROM CASELOAD by reason

- **normal termination**   *syn*   **completion of term**   expiration of probationary period as determined by court or statute
- **early termination**   court ordered discharge from probation, usually because of good behavior or other mitigating circumstance, sometimes to expedite another legal process such as a new prosecution in another jurisdiction
- **revocation**   court ordered termination of probation status because of absconding or other violation of probation conditions (often leading to commitment to jail or prison)
- **transfer out to another jurisdiction**   the relinquishing to another jurisdiction of responsibility for a probationer—may be subdivided into
  - **transfer of jurisdiction (legal control) and supervisory custody**
  - **transfer of supervisory custodial responsibility only**
- **death**

Note that "removal" can mean the ending of the jurisdiction of a given court over a probationer, or only the ending of the supervisory custody of a given probation agency, and does not necessarily indicate the end of probation status for the individual. The term is not equivalent to **probation termination** (see entry), which is only one type of removal.

See other "probation" entries for further information.

probation termination   *recommended statistical terminology*   The ending of the probation status of a given person by routine expiration of probationary period, by special early termination by court, or by revocation of probation.

annotation

This term represents endings of probation from the perspective of the probationer.

A "probation termination" is not equivalent to a removal from probation. It is only one type of removal. For example, a case that has been removed by transfer to another jurisdiction has not been terminated. See **probation supervisory population movement** for recommended terminology for caseload movement.

The probationary period can be longer than the maximum potential sentence of confinement, or series of sentences to confinement, provided by law for a given offense(s). But some jurisdictions limit the probationary period for felonies to the maximum possible period of imprisonment for the offense.

probation violation   *recommended statistical terminology*   An act or failure to act by a probationer which does not conform to the conditions of his probation.

annotation

This term should not be used as a synonym for **probation revocation** (see entry). Whereas a probation violation is an act committed by a probationer, a revocation is the action taken by a court in response to that violation. An allegation of a probation violation is not always sustained, and an actual probation violation need not necessarily result in a probation revocation.

Conditions of adult probation, as set forth by the court which granted the probation, frequently include such admonishments as maintaining regular employment, abstaining from drugs and alcohol, not associating with known offenders or other specified persons, paying restitution or a fine, regularly reporting to a probation officer or other designated person and/or remaining within a designated geographic area. Conditions of probation also always include the requirement not to commit another crime.

If a new crime is alleged, the court may revoke probation because of violation of the conditions of probation, or may initiate prosecution for the new offense, and occasionally will do both.

A probation violation that does not consist of commission of a crime or is not prosecuted as such is usually called a "technical violation," to indicate that it is behavior forbidden by the court order granting probation, and not forbidden by statute, or treated as if not forbidden by statute.

probation with jail   see **probation supervisory population movement**

probation workload   The total set of activities required in order to carry out the probation agency functions of intake screening of juvenile cases, referral of cases to other service agencies, investigation of juveniles and adults for the purpose of preparing predisposition or presentence reports, supervision or treatment of juveniles and adults granted probation, assisting in the enforcement of court orders concerning family problems such as abandonment and non-support cases, and such other functions as may be assigned by statute or court order.

annotation

The activities cited in the above definition of workload are the basic functions of almost all probation agencies. Additional responsibilities assigned by law or by a court vary greatly from one jurisdiction to another and include such duties as monitoring collection of restitution payment or fines, screening arrestees for release on own recognizance, and administering juvenile shelter or confinement facilities or adult residences. "Workload" is not a term recommended for national level statistical use.

It is recommended for correctional data presentations that the **probation supervisory caseload** be distinguishable from the total workload in order to separate the workload resulting from **grants of probation** from that resulting from the intake function, the preparation of presentence or predisposition reports and other nonsupervisory activities. Grants of probation and their impact on agency budgets are of interest in comparisons of criminal justice activity in different jurisdictions.

professional criminal   see **career criminal**

promotion of prostitution   see **prostitution**

proof beyond a reasonable doubt   see **levels of proof**

property crime   see **Crime Index**

prosecution agency   A federal, state, or local criminal justice agency or subunit of which the principal function is the prosecution of alleged offenders.

annotation

Prosecution agency is a subclass of **criminal justice agency** as defined in this dictionary.

Typical prosecution agencies are county district attorney offices, organized crime units in federal and state departments of justice, and prosecutorial subunits of regulatory agencies. The classification is based on the special, single major purpose of such agencies or subunits.

The Bureau of Justice Statistics publications *Justice Agencies in the United States* and *State and Local Prosecution and Civil Attorney Systems* have a category entitled "prosecution and civil attorney agencies." The category includes, in addition to prosecution agencies as defined above, government agencies with the primary or exclusive function of providing legal advice, assistance, and representation to the government in civil matters. This combined category is used because the criminal and civil functions are often combined in one administrative unit, and budget, manpower, and caseload data are frequently not separable according to function.

Data presentations relating to prosecution agencies should clearly indicate whether the tabulations relate to the criminal function, the civil function, or the combined functions.

prosecution withheld   see **arrestee dispositions**

prosecutor   *recommended statistical terminology*   An attorney who is the elected or appointed chief of a prosecution agency, and whose official duty is to conduct criminal proceedings on behalf of the people against persons accused of committing criminal offenses, also called "district attorney," "DA," "state's attorney," "county attorney," and "U.S. Attorney;" and any attorney deputized to assist the chief prosecutor.

annotation

Since there are different names for the official performing the prosecutorial function in different jurisdictions, it is recommended that the functional name, "prosecutor" be used to describe the class in national level data. Words indicating the level of government employing the prosecutor(s) should be added in statistical publications intended for general use.

Where it is necessary to distinguish between heads of prosecution agencies and their assistants or deputies, titles specific to the jurisdiction can be used, or in national summary data distinctive names and definitions suitable for the purpose of the presentation, such as "chief prosecutors" and "assistant prosecutors."

In many cities the city attorney prosecutes misdemeanors. But these officials, like those called "county attorney" or "county counsel" also provide legal services to units of government. ("Legal services" in Bureau of Justice Statistics terminology "denotes the legal representation of a particular government in civil matters.") These should not be counted as prosecutors in national level personnel data unless prosecution is their full time function. However, in the BJS series, *Expenditure and Employment Data for the Criminal Justice System,* it has been necessary to treat legal services activity expenditure and personnel data as criminal justice data because the criminal justice portion of such agencies' budgets and rosters cannot be consistently identified.

See also **prosecution agency.**

prosecutorial screening decision   *recommended statistical terminology*

The decision of a prosecutor to submit a charging document to a court, or to seek a grand jury indictment, or to decline to prosecute.

annotation

The prosecutorial screening process is for statistical purposes described as beginning with a complaint requested, and ending with (1) complaint granted (including complaint modified), or (2) complaint denied.

The first category is the input to prosecutorial screening:

complaint requested   *recommended statistical terminology*   A request by a law enforcement or other government agency, or a private citizen, that a prosecution agency file a complaint or information or seek an indictment alleging that a specified person(s) has committed a specified offense(s).

Law enforcement agencies are the primary source of requests for prosecution but a significant amount of prosecutorial workload may originate from the other sources.

The screening process usually consists of examination of police reports and other information about the alleged crime(s), the reaching of a conclusion about whether to charge and which charges shall be made in the charging document, and preparation of the document.

The other categories are the outputs of prosecutorial screening:

complaint granted   *recommended statistical terminology*   The decision by a prosecution agency to grant a request for a complaint by filing a complaint or an information in court, or by seeking an indictment from a grand jury, also called "complaint accepted" and "(case) papered."

complaint modified   *recommended statistical terminology*   The decision by a prosecution agency to initiate prosecution in relation to an alleged criminal event, but to alter some or all of the charges or to omit some of the charges in the document requesting the complaint.

For summary statistics, the above two categories can be combined.

The number of complaints granted and complaints modified by a prosecutor will not necessarily be equal to the number of criminal cases filed in court (see **filing**) in a given jurisdiction, since in cases where grand jury indictment is sought, the grand jury may decline to indict (see **no true bill**).

complaint denied   *recommended statistical terminology*   The decision by a prosecution agency to not file a complaint or information in court, or to not seek an indictment; also called "complaint rejected," "complaint declined," "declination," and "(case) no papered."

When a request for a complaint against an arrested person is denied, that case against that person is terminated and the action may be reported as an **arrestee disposition**. When a complaint is modified some charges are disposed of but the person is still subject to judicial proceedings.

prostitution   Offering or agreeing to engage in, or engaging in, a sex act with another in return for a fee.

annotation

Prostitution and the prostitution-related offenses described below would be classified as "commercial sex offenses" in the tentatively recommended categories for prosecution, courts and corrections level offense reporting. See **sex offenses**. See also **prostitution and commercialized vice UCR 16** for the law enforcement level statistical usage.

"Prostitution" is commonly codified as a single offense. In some jurisdictions the offense so named is more narrowly defined as offering or agreeing to engage in, or engaging in sexual intercourse by a woman in return for a fee. In some jurisdictions the offense is more broadly defined such that clients as well as prostitutes are guilty of an offense. A few jurisdictions now have a separately codified offense of "patronizing a prostitute," which is requesting or securing the performance of a sex act for a fee.

Related offenses are commonly grouped under the heading **promotion of prostitution**: The soliciting or aiding in any manner of another to engage in prostitution, or the soliciting or aiding of another to secure the services of a prostitute, or knowingly receiving any money or other thing of value which is the proceeds of prostitution.

"Promotion of prostitution" typically includes offenses of varying names and content, such as pimping, pandering, procuring for prostitution, maintaining a house of prostitution, and living off the earnings of a prostitute.

prostitution and commercialized vice   UCR 16   In Uniform Crime Reports terminology, the name of the UCR category used to record and report arrests for offenses relating to the promotion or performance of sexual acts for a fee.

annotation

The *Uniform Crime Reporting Handbook* provides, as examples of offenses included in this category, the following list of offenses or groups of offenses:

Prostitution
Keeping bawdy house, disorderly house, or house of ill fame
Pandering, procuring, transporting, or detaining women for immoral purposes, etc.
All attempts to commit any of the above

See **sex offenses** for recommendation concerning prosecution, courts and corrections offense statistics.

provisional exit   *recommended statistical terminology*   An authorized temporary exit from prison for appearance in court, work furlough, hospital treatment, appeal proceedings, or other purposes that require departure from prison but with expectation of return.

annotation

This term is proposed as the name of the class of authorized prison departures which are neither **conditional releases** nor final discharges from correctional system jurisdiction. A conditional release may also in fact be temporary, but return depends upon the released person's behavior. In a provisional exit return is officially intended and expected, unless some other official action such as a court decision supercedes correctional agency authority over the subject.

See **prison/parole population movement** for the content and function of this category in data reporting structures.

See **full-time temporary release**.

public defender   I.   An attorney employed by a government agency or subagency, or by a private organization under contract to a unit of government, for the purpose of providing defense services to indigents; also, occasionally, an attorney who has volunteered such service.   II.   *recommended statistical terminology*   The head of a government agency or subunit whose function is the representation in court of persons accused or convicted of a crime who are unable to hire private counsel, and any attorney employed by such an agency or subunit whose official duty is the performance of the indigent defense function.

annotation

Definition (II) above describes the recommended category for national level general purpose statistics. The class is limited to employees of publicly administered and financed **public defender agencies** (see entry). It excludes employees of privately administered legal aid societies.

Court decisions establishing the right to counsel for persons subject to imprisonment as a consequence of conviction have recently led to a considerable increase in the number of publicly funded defense attorneys. Some are regular full or part-time employees of government units, but in some jurisdictions defense of indigents is provided by a legal aid society.

Thus, for special purpose statistical compilations, for example those intended to reflect the overall availability of public defense services, it may be necessary to make use of a broader category, such as that described by definition (I) above. Where such a category is used, explicit definition of category content should be provided.

public defender agency   *recommended statistical terminology*   A federal, state, or local criminal justice agency or subunit of which the principal function is to represent in court persons accused or convicted of a crime(s) who are unable to hire private counsel.

annotation

For national level general data, the class includes only agencies or subunits that are publicly financed and administered, that is, **criminal justice agencies** as defined in this dictionary. Privately administered legal aid societies are excluded, even if publicly financed.

For special purpose statistical compilations, such as for budgetary purposes or to reflect the overall availability of public defense services, it may be necessary to add to the category publicly financed but privately administered organizations, and organizations which are privately financed and administered. When these broader categories are used in statistical data presentations, explicit definitions of category content should be provided.

In the Bureau of Justice Statistics series, *Expenditure and Employment Data for the Criminal Justice System*, expenditure data include all public financing for defense activities, whether the services are provided by a government agency, a private legal aid society, or by court-appointed or private counsel. However, employment data include only personnel of government agencies. In the BJS publication *Justice Agencies in the United States, Summary Report 1980*, the "public defender agency" category is limited to government agencies.

Whether or not public defense agencies as defined above are considered to be criminal justice agencies in statistical or other contexts depends upon the particular purpose for which criminal justice agencies are being identified. See **criminal justice agency** for alternative definitions and comment.

public safety department   An agency organized at the state or local level of government incorporating at a minimum various law enforcement and emergency service functions.

annotation

A local public safety agency may bring under one central administration functions otherwise assigned to separate police, sheriff's, fire, and county communications departments. The administrative scope of state level agencies of this type may include state police and highway patrol units, law enforcement support services, fire control and road safety units, and correctional agency functions.

In national level data functionally distinct subdivisions of public safety agencies, such as law enforcement units, are classified and counted separately under the applicable headings. See **criminal justice agency**.

ranch, forestry camp, and farm   see **juvenile facility**

rape   Unlawful sexual intercourse with a female, by force or without legal or factual consent.

annotation

See **sex offenses** for general statistical recommendation and defining features. See also **forcible rape UCR 2**.

Historically "rape" meant only forcible rape, but it is currently used in statutes with the broad meaning given above that includes forcible rape together with other sexual acts codified as criminal because of the victim's inability to give legal consent because underage (usually called statutory rape), or because of mental or physical defect or intoxication. Penal codes distinguish between these crime types by various names and arrangements of offense elements.

For the National Crime Survey (NCS) definition of "rape," see **personal crimes**.

rape (NCS)   see **personal crimes**

reception or diagnostic center   see juvenile facility

recidivism   The repetition of criminal behavior.

annotation

In statistical practice, a recidivism rate may be any of a number of possible counts of instances of arrest, conviction, correctional commitment, and correctional status changes, related to counts of repetitions of these events within a given period of time.

Efforts to arrive at a single standard statistical description of recidivism have been hampered by the fact that the correct referent of the term is the actual repeated criminal or delinquent behavior of a given person or group, yet the only available statistical indicators of that behavior are records of such system events as rearrests, reconvictions, and probation or parole violations or revocations. It is recognized that these data reflect agency decisions about events and may or may not closely correspond with actual criminal behavior. Different conclusions about degrees to which system decisions actually reflect actual behavior consequently produce different definitions of recidivism, that is, different judgments of which system event repetition rates best measure actual occurrences of crime among repeat offenders. This is an empirical question, and not one of definition to be resolved solely by analysis of language usage and system logic. Resolution has also been delayed by the limited capacities of most criminal justice statistical systems, which do not routinely make available the standardized offender-based transaction data (**OBTS**) which may be needed for the best measurement of recidivism.

Pending the adoption of a standard statistical description of recidivism, and the ability to implement it, it is recommended that recidivism analyses include the widest possible range of system events that can correspond with actual recidivism, and that sufficient detail on offenses charged be included to enable discrimination between degrees of gravity of offenses. The units of count should be clearly identified and the length of community exposure time of the subject population stated.

The National Advisory Commission on Criminal Justice Standards and Goals recommended a standard definition of recidivism in its volume *Corrections* (1973): "Recidivism is measured by (1) criminal acts that resulted in conviction by a court, when committed by individuals who are under correctional supervision or who have been released from correctional supervision within the previous three years, and by (2) technical violations of probation or parole in which a sentencing or paroling authority took action that resulted in an adverse change in the offender's legal status." Neither of these formulations is endorsed as adequate for all purposes. Both limit the measure and concept of recidivism to populations which are or have been under correctional supervision. Yet the maximum usefulness of data concerning the repetition of criminal behavior (rearrest rates, reconviction rates, etc.) often depends upon the comparison of the behavior of unconfined or unsupervised offenders with the behavior of those with correctional experience.

recidivist   A person who has been convicted of one or more crimes, and who is alleged or found to have subsequently committed another crime or series of crimes.

annotation

In corrections usage, the term "recidivist" generally refers to an offender who has been released on **probation, parole** or other **conditional release** and who is alleged or found to have committed one or more additional crimes while in that status, usually within a specified period of time after release.

In this usage, the term contrasts with **habitual offender** and **career criminal** (see entries). The term "repeat offender" is sometimes used to refer to recidivists as defined above, but is also used more broadly to designate any person who has repeatedly been convicted of crimes.

The exact criteria used in identifying recidivists may vary between jurisdictions, between agencies, and according to the purpose of particular statistical presentations. See **recidivism**.

reduced charge   see **included offense**

reduced sentence   see **clemency**

referral received   see **intake**

referral to intake   see **intake**

release on bail   see **pretrial release**

release on own recognizance   see **pretrial release**

release to parole   *syn*   **grant of parole**   *syn*   **entry to parole**
recommended statistical terminology   ,A release from prison by discretionary action of a paroling authority, conditional upon the parolee's fulfillment of specified conditions of behavior.

annotation

See **paroling authority decisions, parole agency caseload entries and removals,** and **prison/parole population movement** for the function of release to parole in data structures.

Release to parole and **mandatory supervised release** are the two major classes of **conditional releases** from prison. A release to parole is a discretionary act on the part of a state paroling authority provided by statute with such discretion (see **parole**). However, the aggregate of persons "on parole" in a given jurisdiction at a given time may include persons not released to parole by a paroling authority. In some jurisdictions, persons released from prison pursuant to a mandatory supervised release statute will become part of the group for which a parole agency has supervisory responsibility.

The length of time of parole is usually determined by the length of the sentence less the length of time served in a confinement facility. The original sentence can, of course, be reduced by executive **clemency, good time** deductions for good behavior in prison or on parole, or other means.

See **mutual agreement program** for requirements that may have to be met before release to parole is granted.

Violation of the conditions of parole (a **parole violation**) can result in **parole revocation**.

Some jurisdictions provide parole for persons serving **jail** sentences. This terminology does not apply to such local procedures, nor to juvenile parole (see **aftercare**).

release to third party   see **pretrial release**

remand   see **bind over**

reparole   *recommended statistical terminology*   A release to parole occurring after a return to prison from an earlier release to parole, on the same sentence to confinement.

annotation

If the return to prison from the first release to parole is accompanied by a new conviction and a new sentence to prison that increased the prisoner's total prison liability, some jurisdictions will not consider the second release a reparole. ("Liability" increases when the new sentence is for a term of confinement longer than the total time remaining to be served on the current sentences, or because the new sentence is to be served consecutively to those already in effect.) Data presentations should indicate their reporting conventions.

See **paroling authority decisions** and **parole agency caseload entries and removals** for the use of this item in data structures.

reprieve   see **clemency**

request to appeal case   *recommended statistical terminology*   A case filed in an appellate court by submission of a petition asking that the court review a judgment or decision of a trial court, administrative agency, or intermediate appellate court.

annotation

This and other recommended terminology for appellate court caseload statistical terminology reflect the usages of the model court caseload statistical system developed by the National Court Statistics Project. A term list outline of the complete model classification scheme for general caseload inventory and for case and defendant manner of disposition is presented in Appendix E of this volume.

The filing of a petition making a request to appeal is the first action taken where the subject matter of an appeal falls within the discretionary jurisdiction of the appellate court, that is, where the court at its choosing may consent or refuse to hear the appeal. Possible appellate court decisions regarding request to appeal cases are request **granted** or request **denied**. If the request is granted, the matter then becomes the subject of an **appeal case** (see entry).

resident   A person required by official action or his own acceptance of placement to reside in a public or private facility established for purposes of confinement, supervision or care.

annotation

Inmates of confinement facilities are now sometimes referred to as "residents." See also **prisoner**.

In recommended data terminology, "to reside" means to occupy at night as opposed to full time confinement. See **residential commitment.**

residential commitment   *recommended statistical terminology*   A sentence of commitment to a correctional facility for adults, in which the offender is required to reside at night, but from which he or she is regularly permitted to depart during the day, unaccompanied by any official.

annotation

A residential commitment is usually a type of sentencing disposition, occasionally a disposition made when adjudication is withheld in order that the defendant receive, for example, treatment for drug addiction. The disposition is usually combined with probation status. See **defendant dispositions** and **grant of probation.**

"Residential commitments" in this terminology include commitments to facilities called by such names as "residential treatment centers," "community facilities," "community-based facilities," "halfway houses," and "group homes." See **residential facility** and **correctional facility (adult).**

The contrasting types of commitments are **jail commitment** and **prison commitment.**

residential facility   *recommended statistical terminology*   A correctional facility from which residents are regularly permitted to depart, unaccompanied by any official, for the purpose of daily use of community resources such as schools or treatment programs, and seeking or holding employment.

annotation

This term and category is proposed as a necessary contrast to confinement facilities, that is, jails and prisons where all or the great majority of inmates are physically restricted to the premises at all times. See **correctional facility (adult)** for classification information.

resisting an officer   Resisting or obstructing a law enforcement officer in the performance of an official duty.

annotation

This type of offense is variously named and defined in state statutes. Its elements often include the use of force in resistance, or behavior that requires the use of force by the officer to overcome it. The "resistance" need not be only on the part of one whose arrest is being attempted; anyone who interferes with the law enforcement officer's purpose can be charged. Sometimes resistance of arrest is an offense only if the arrest is lawful.

Resistance to a law enforcement officer is not considered an assault unless it goes to the point where the officer's safety is endangered. See **assault on a law enforcement officer.**

respondent   Generally, the person who formally answers the allegations stated in a petition which has been filed in a court; in criminal proceedings, the one who contends against an appeal.

annotation

In criminal proceedings, the respondent to an **appeal** is usually the prosecution. See also **appellant**.

restitution   *recommended statistical terminology*   A court requirement that an alleged or convicted offender pay money or provide services to the victim of the crime or provide services to the community.

annotation

Restitution is a type of **defendant disposition** (see entry).

Although restitution is rarely the only consequence of prosecution or conviction, it is listed in this dictionary as a type of defendant disposition because it occurs in combination with various major types of **sentencing dispositions** as a separable and significant element. Besides being a condition of probation, it can be a requirement combined with a commitment to prison or jail, or with confinement followed by probation status.

When restitution is a condition of probation, failure to comply can lead to reappearance in court and revocation of probation.

Although restitution can be viewed as a means of compensating a victim for loss, the term "victim compensation" in current criminal justice terminology has a strategically different meaning. Victim compensation usually occurs through a governmentally administered program intended to provide at least a partial "reimbursement" of a victim's losses, and does not depend on the offender being identified or prosecuted.

retained counsel   see **attorney**

retrial   see **new trial**

reversed   see **appellate case disposition**

rights of defendant   Those powers and privileges which are constitutionally guaranteed to every defendant.

annotation

At the time of **arraignment** a defendant is typically informed of at least the following: the right to remain silent, the right to a court-appointed attorney if the defendant does not have the financial means to privately retain an attorney; the right to release on reasonable bail; the right to a speedy public trial before a jury or a judge; the right to the process of the court to subpoena and produce witnesses in the defendant's own behalf and to see, hear and question the witnesses appearing before the defendant; the right not to incriminate himself or herself.

Some or all of these rights are also read to a suspect when he or she is questioned or arrested, and at other steps in proceedings. See **Miranda rights**.

riot   The coming together of a group of persons who engage in violent and tumultuous conduct, thereby causing or creating a serious, imminent risk of causing injury to persons or property, or public alarm.

annotation

The offense names "riot," "disorderly conduct," and "unlawful assembly" have various and overlapping meanings in the penal codes of different states. There is no clear statistical classification for this area of criminal behavior. See **disturbing the peace** for general recommendation.

Examples of "riot" definitions from two states' penal codes are:

"A riot is a public disturbance involving an assemblage of three or more persons acting together or in concert which by tumultuous and violent conduct, or the imminent threat of tumultuous and violent conduct, results in injury or damage to persons or property or creates a clear and present danger of injury or damage to persons or property."

"A person commits riot if, with two or more other persons acting together, such person recklessly uses force or violence or threatens to use force or violence, if such threat is accompanied by immediate power of execution, which disturbs the public peace."

The basic purpose of such statutory language is to authorize law enforcement discretion in assessing and reacting to potentially dangerous situations involving mob actions. The minimum number of persons who must be acting together in order to constitute a riot is usually specified in the statutes. It varies from as few as two to as many as ten.

An offense which is generally codified separately is **inciting to riot**: The attempt by any person to cause other persons to engage in conduct which would constitute a riot.

robbery   *recommended statistical terminology*   The unlawful taking or attempted taking of property that is in the immediate possession of another, by force or the threat of force.

defining features *of recommended national category and tentatively recommended subcategories*

robbery

unlawful taking of property in the immediate possession of another

by use or threatened use of force

or

attempting the above act

armed robbery

unlawful taking of property in the immediate possession of another

by use or threatened use of a deadly or dangerous weapon

or

attempting the above act

unarmed robbery

unlawful taking of property in the immediate possession of another

by use or threatened use of force

without a deadly or dangerous weapon

or

attempting the above act

annotation

This crime type, which is used in UCR reporting, is also recommended for prosecution, courts and corrections statistics. See Appendix B for problems in national crime classification and complete set of tentatively proposed national categories for post-arrest offense statistics.

Armed and unarmed robbery are ordinarily distinguished in law by separate penalties.

In popular speech the term, "mugging," is often used to mean a type of strongarm robbery in which the offender suddenly approaches the victim from behind. In some areas of the country, the term has a broader meaning, including any assault by a stranger in a public place.

For the National Crime Survey (NCS) classification of robberies see **personal crimes** and **commercial crimes**.

robbery   UCR 3   *Uniform Crime Reports usage*   The unlawful taking or attempted taking of property that is in the immediate possession of another by force or threat of force.

annotation

This category is also recommended for use in post-arrest statistics. See **robbery** for defining features and general recommendation.

Robbery is a UCR Crime Index offense. The annual publication *Crime in the United States* presents data both on the occurrence of robbery offenses and on arrests relating to such offenses. See **Crime Index**.

In UCR data reporting, robbery is subdivided as follows:

3.a. firearm
3.b. knife or cutting instrument
3.c. other dangerous weapon
3.d. strongarm

In UCR "purse snatching" is classified in **larceny-theft UCR 6**.

ROR   see **pretrial release**

runaway   *recommended statistical terminology*   A juvenile who has been adjudicated by a judicial officer of a juvenile court, as having committed the status offense of leaving the custody and home of his or her parents, guardians or custodians without permission and failing to return within a reasonable length of time.

annotation

A runaway is a type of **status offender**. See **delinquency**.

Statutes defining the status offense usually specify either a length of time that the juvenile must be away, or declare habitual running away a status offense. The codification of this offense varies greatly among different states.

This term should not be used in statistical reporting to describe juveniles who have left a correctional facility without authorization. These are called **AWOLS** in the national *Children in Custody* series and are defined as those who have left without authorization and have been formally removed from the facility resident rolls.

runaway—(juveniles) UCR 29   In Uniform Crime Reports terminology, the name of the UCR offense category used to record and report apprehensions of juvenile runaways for protective custody, as defined by local statute.

annotation

The *UCR Handbook* states: "For purposes of the Uniform Crime Reporting program, report in this category apprehensions for protective custody as defined by your local statute. Count arrests made by other jurisdictions of runaways from your jurisdiction. Do not include protective custody actions with respect to runaways you take for other jurisdictions."

See also **delinquency.**

search   see **illegal search and seizure**

search warrant   *recommended statistical terminology*   A document issued by a judicial officer which directs a law enforcement officer to conduct a search at a specific location, for specified property or persons relating to a crime(s), to seize the property or persons if found, and to account for the results of the search to the issuing judicial officer.

annotation

A search warrant can be issued only if a judicial officer is satisfied that there is **probable cause** (see entry) to believe that the person(s) or object(s) being sought will be found at the location indicated. See also **illegal search and seizure.**

security   The restriction of inmate movement within a correctional facility, usually divided into maximum, medium and minimum levels.

annotation

Security level is not solely a physical characteristic of correctional facilities but a type of physical custodial status of inmates, relating both to restrictive architectural features of buildings or areas and to human regulation of inmate movement within the facility.

No standard definition of security levels is offered in this terminology because the defining physical and behavioral restrictive features vary greatly among jurisdictions. The proposed correctional facility terminology distinguishes between confinement facilities and residential facilities, according to the inmates' daily access, or lack of daily access, to external community activities and resources, and not according to internal restrictiveness. See **correctional facility (adult).**

Data publications concerning security classifications should provide the definitions of security and security levels used in the reporting jurisdiction.

seizure   see **illegal search and seizure**

self-defense   The protection of oneself or one's property from unlawful injury or the immediate risk of unlawful injury; the justification for an act which would otherwise constitute an offense, that the person who committed it reasonably believed that the act was necessary to protect self or property from immediate danger.

sentence I. The penalty imposed by a court upon a person convicted of a crime. II. The court judgment specifying the penalty imposed upon a person convicted of a crime. III. Any disposition of a defendant resulting from a conviction, including the court decision to suspend execution of a sentence.

annotation

Historically, "sentence" has meant an opinion, or a judgment, conclusion, or decision reached after deliberation on any issue.

Modern criminal justice usage reflects this potentially broad range of meaning. In some uses, "sentence" is restricted in meaning to being exactly equivalent to a penalty, that is, an actual fine or commitment to confinement. In other situations, particularly in language used to collect or present statistical data on court dispositions of defendants, any decision made at the point where a sentence can be announced is listed under the heading or cover term, "sentence." Thus the meaning of this term can be broadened to explicitly include actual penalties of fines and incarceration plus all alternatives to such penalties, such as probation.

In order to avoid conflicts between proposed standard data terminology and special legal or statistical usages, the term **sentencing disposition** (see entry) is recommended as the data terminology name for the class of all court dispositions of defendants after conviction, consisting of penalties such as fines and confinement, and all post-conviction alternatives to such penalties. See **defendant dispositions** for subclasses.

When "sentence" is used in the sense of a penalty of confinement, it can be characterized in different dimensions: mandatoriness, time duration, time sequence, authority determining time duration, place of confinement, and severity. See **mandatory sentence, maximum sentence, indeterminate sentence, consecutive sentence**, and other "sentence" terms.

sentence credit time *recommended statistical terminology* Time already spent in confinement in relation to a given offense(s), deducted at the point of admission on a sentence to jail or prison from the maximum jail or prison liability of the sentence for the offense(s).

annotation

Sentence credit time can be deducted by the court or in accord with a statute, from the jail or prison time to be served on a given sentence. The time may have been spent in jail awaiting trial or sentencing, or under **diagnostic commitment** (see entry). Credit time is not the same as **good time** (see entry), which is calculated with respect to time spent in prison, and can vary according to the particular statutory penalty, and is often dependent upon good behavior.

See also **time served**.

sentenced to time served see **balance of sentence suspended**

sentence effective date *recommended statistical terminology* With respect to a term of confinement, the date from which time served is calculated, not necessarily coincident with the date sentence was pronounced or the date of entry to confinement after sentencing.

annotation

Sentence credit time for time spent in detention awaiting and during trial is usually deducted from a sentence to a term of confinement, and the sentence effective date can therefore predate conviction. Events such as appeal proceedings can delay entry to any confinement so that the sentence effective date can postdate conviction by months or years.

See also **sentence credit time, time served,** and **good time.**

sentence review   *recommended statistical terminology*   The reconsideration of a sentence imposed on a person convicted of a crime, either by the same court which imposed the sentence or by a higher court.

annotation

Sentence review is usually requested on the grounds that the penalty is harsh or excessive, either in relation to circumstances of the specific case or in relation to sentences imposed in similar cases.

An application for sentence review can be part of an **appeal** or application for **postconviction remedy** which raises other issues as well, or it can be a separate action. See entries.

It is recommended that cases which concern only requests for sentence review be counted separately from other cases in court activity data presentations. "Sentence review only case" is provided as a distinct caseload reporting category for both trial and appellate courts in the model court caseload statistical system developed by the National Court Statistics Project (see Appendix E).

sentencing continued   see **sentencing postponed**

sentencing dispositions   *recommended statistical terminology*   Court dispositions of defendants after a judgment of conviction, expressed as penalties, such as imprisonment or payment of fines; or any of a number of alternatives to actually executed penalties, such as suspended sentences, grants of probation, or orders to perform restitution; or various combinations of the above.

annotation

This term replaces the first edition term, "sentence," as the recommended name for the category of court dispositions of defendants after conviction. "Sentence" is not a suitable name for this large class of units of count because in some usages it means an actual penalty only.

See **defendant dispositions** for recommended data structure and terminology for sentencing dispositions.

sentencing hearing   *recommended statistical terminology*   In criminal proceedings, a hearing during which the court or jury considers relevant information, such as evidence concerning aggravating or mitigating circumstances, for the purpose of determining a sentencing disposition for a person convicted of an offense(s).

annotation

A sentencing hearing is held after a judgment of conviction has been entered, the **presentence investigation** (if any) conducted and the presentence report (if any) submitted to the court.

Sentencing hearings can include arguments made by the defense in favor of a lesser sentence than that recommended in the presentence report; arguments made by the prosecution for or against the recommendations in the presentence report; the court's consideration of the mitigating or aggravating circumstances brought out by the defense and prosecution; and announcement of the court's decision.

sentencing postponed   *recommended statistical terminology*   The delay for an unspecified period of time, or to a remote date, of the court's pronouncement of any other sentencing disposition for a person convicted of an offense, in order to place the defendant in some status contingent on good behavior in the expectation that a penalty need never be pronounced or executed.

annotation

This is a type of **defendant disposition** (see entry). The term is proposed for data publications to represent those instances where the court chooses as a matter of policy to delay pronouncing any other sentencing disposition. It is a substitute for the term recommended in the first edition of this book, "sentence-imposition suspended." See **suspended sentence**.

It is recommended that delays for practical reasons be designated as **sentencing continued** in order to distinguish them from postponements granted as an alternative to pronouncing a sentence. Typical reasons for sentencing continuations include: the court has not received the presentence report; the defendant cannot be present in the courtroom for the hearing (e.g., the defendant is testifying in another trial, is in another geographical jurisdiction); illness on the part of any of the major participants in the case (e.g., the judicial officer, the prosecutor, the defense attorney, the defendant). These usually very temporary delays are important in agency management data but are not a category of defendant dispositions.

The scheduling of a sentencing hearing itself can be delayed, or once the hearing has begun, the conclusion can be delayed. However, many jurisdictions require that sentencing be completed within a specified period of time after judgment.

serious misdemeanor   A class of misdemeanors having more severe penalties than other misdemeanors, or procedurally distinct; sometimes a statutory name for a type of misdemeanor having a maximum penalty much greater than the customary maximum one year incarceration for misdemeanors.

annotation

In some jurisdictions this term is the official penal code name of a class of offenses. In others, it is the unofficial name for higher penalty range misdemeanors, or for offenses that can be charged as either misdemeanors or as felonies. The term can also be officially or unofficially used to designate misdemeanors which are prosecuted only in a particular court or by a particular agency.

Other terms with similar meaning and also with variable usage are "high misdemeanor,'' ''indictable misdemeanor,'' ''penitentiary misdemeanor,'' and ''aggravated misdemeanor.''

When any of these terms is used in statistical publications to characterize offense or offender data, the class content should be explicitly defined.

See **misdemeanor** and **felony**.

severance   In criminal proceedings the separation, for purposes of pleading and/or trial, of multiple defendants named in a single charging document, or of multiple charges against a particular defendant listed in a single charging document.

annotation

A motion requesting severance of defendants or charges can be made at any time before or during trial. The most common reason for requesting severance is to prevent prejudice to a defendant. For example, a defendant who has no prior record can request that his or her case be severed from that of a co-defendant who does have a prior record.

sex offenses   I.   In current statistical usage, the name of a broad category of varying content, usually consisting of all offenses having a sexual element except forcible rape and commercial sex offenses.   II.   *tentatively recommended major national category for prosecution, courts and corrections statistics*   All unlawful sexual intercourse, unlawful sexual contact, and other unlawful behavior intended to result in sexual gratification or profit from sexual activity.

defining features *of tentatively recommended national category (II) and of subcategories*

sex offenses

unlawful sexual intercourse or sexual contact, or

other unlawful behavior intended to result in sexual gratification or profit from sexual activity

or

attempting the above act(s)

   violent sex offenses

   forcible rape

   unlawful vaginal penetration of a female of any age

   against the will of the victim

   with use or threatened use of force

   or

   attempting such an act

   other violent sex offenses

   unlawful sexual penetration or physical contact other than forcible rape

   between members of the same sex or different sexes

   against the will of the victim

   with use or threatened use of force

   or

   attempting such act(s)

nonviolent sex offenses

statutory rape

sexual intercourse with a female

without force or threat of force

when female has consented in fact, but is below age of consent specified in state law

commercial sex offenses

unlawfully performing, or causing or assisting another person to perform, a sex act for a fee, or

causing or assisting another person to obtain performance of a sex act by paying a fee, or

receiving money known to have been paid for performance of a sex act

or

attempting such act(s)

other nonviolent sex offenses

unlawful behavior, other than statutory rape and commercial sex offenses, intended to result in sexual gratification

without use or threatened use of force

annotation

The above classification structure, which departs in several respects from current statistical terminology, is tentatively recommended for national post-arrest offense statistics. Neither the Uniform Crime Reports (UCR) classification nor the NCIC Uniform Offense Classifications (UOC) provides an optimum total structure for post-arrest sex offense data (see below), although the contents of the "forcible rape" and "commercial sex offenses" categories in the above structure are identical to corresponding crime types in UCR. See Appendix B for problems in national crime classification and complete set of tentatively proposed national categories for post-arrest offense statistics.

The above proposal provides the correct generic name for the entire offense area and subdivides it in accord with distinctions that are intrinsically significant and reasonably reportable. No age of victim distinction is reflected here, except for "statutory rape," because of the complexities resulting when the age feature is added to the critical violence/nonviolence distinction.

In the Uniform Crime Reports system forcible rape (see **forcible rape UCR 2**) is a Part I offense category and all other sex offenses except **prostitution and commercialized vice UCR 16** are classified as **sex offenses UCR 17**.

NCIC-UOC has three groups: "sexual assault" (all sexual intercourse and contact offenses involving force, plus statutory rape), "sex offenses," and "commercialized sexual offenses." See Appendix D.

For individual entries relating to the sex offense group, see **rape, indecent exposure, sodomy, prostitution, incest** and **adultery**.

sex offenses   UCR 17   In Uniform Crime Reports terminology, the name of the UCR category used to record and report arrests made for "offenses against chastity, common decency, morals, and the like," except forcible rape, prostitution and commercialized vice.

annotation

See **sex offenses** for recommendation on the classification of all sex offenses for prosecution, courts and corrections offense statistics.

The *Uniform Crime Reporting Handbook* gives the following as examples of offenses and offense groups, arrests for which are placed in the UCR 17 category:

> Adultery and fornication
> Buggery
> Incest
> Indecent exposure
> Indecent liberties
> Intercourse with an insane, epileptic, or venereally diseased person
> Seduction
> Sodomy or crime against nature
> Statutory rape
> All attempts to commit any of the above

For definitions of the other UCR categories for offenses of a sexual nature, see **forcible rape UCR 2** and **prostitution and commercialized vice UCR 16.**

sexual assault   see **sex offenses**

shelter   see **juvenile facility**

sheriff   *recommended statistical terminology*   The elected chief officer of a county law enforcement agency, usually responsible for law enforcement in unincorporated areas and for the operation of the county jail.

annotation

For national level general data, sheriffs whose responsibilities are limited to civil processes should be excluded from this class.

See also **law enforcement officer** and **law enforcement agency.**

sheriff's department   *recommended statistical terminology*   A local law enforcement agency organized at the county level, directed by a sheriff, which exercises its law enforcement functions at the county level, usually within unincorporated areas, and operates the county jail in most jurisdictions.

annotation

Although a given sheriff's department may devote less than half of its budget to law enforcement activities, all sheriff's departments that perform any criminal law enforcement activities should be counted as **law enforcement agencies** (see entry) in order to account for the location of police authority at the county or equivalent level. (A parish, for example, is equivalent in level to a county.)

Some sheriff's departments have contractual arrangements with cities or districts such that they perform law enforcement duties within incorporated areas, municipalities, or special districts. Such city and district contractual service units should not be counted as separate law enforcement agencies in national data.

If the department operates a jail it should be counted also as a **correctional agency** (see entry) where appropriate.

shock probation   *see* **split sentence**

short-term facility   *see* **juvenile facility**

simple assault   *see* **assault**

simple assault   UCR 9   *Uniform Crime Reports usage (called "other assaults—simple, not aggravated")*   Unlawful threatening, attempted inflicting, or inflicting of less than serious bodily injury, in the absence of a deadly weapon.

annotation

This category is also recommended for use in post-arrest statistics. See **assault** for defining features and general recommendation.

Non-aggravated assault is classified by UCR as Part II UCR 9, labeled "other assaults," for collecting and publishing data on **arrests,** and also as Part I 4e, labeled "other assaults—simple, not aggravated," for collection, though not publication of data on **offenses known to police.**The data on simple assaults are collected as 4e along with data on aggravated assaults "as a quality control matter and also for the purpose of looking at total assault violence."

UCR provides the following list of offenses as examples of the content of this category: "simple assault, minor assault, assault and battery, injury by culpable negligence, resisting or obstructing an officer, intimidation, coercion, and hazing."

slander   *see* **defamation**

smuggling   Unlawful movement of goods across a national frontier or state boundary, or into or out of a correctional facility.

annotation

Smuggling offenses are of two general types. In one, the offense consists of movement of ordinary goods without observing special conditions, such as payment of import duties. In the other, the movement of particular goods across particular boundaries, and/or by particular persons, is prohibited.

Examples of smuggling offenses include goods moved across a boundary with intent to avoid payment of import duties or excise taxes, or with intent to avoid special restrictions, such as bringing plants or animals into this country without observing quarantine requirements. Movement may also be prohibited because of the nature of the material (for example, pornographic photographs), or because of the source, such as the import into the U.S. of foreign goods in violation of a trade embargo.

Smuggling offenses would be assigned to the "other" category in the tentatively recommended classification for post-arrest offense reporting. See Appendix B.

sodomy   Unlawful physical contact between the genitals of one person and the mouth or anus of another person, or with the mouth, anus or genitals of an animal.

annotation

This offense would be classified as "other violent sex offenses" or as "other nonviolent sex offenses" in the tentatively recommended categories for prosecution, courts and corrections level offense reporting, depending upon whether or not force was used or threatened in the commission of the offense. See **sex offenses** for detailed classification.

There is great variation in statutory usage of the term "sodomy." In one state, for example, the crime of "sodomy" is anal intercourse between males. In another state, it is anal intercourse between persons of the same or opposite sex, performed without the consent of one of the participants. In still another state, it is any of the sex acts defined above, performed by persons of the same or opposite sex.

In many states, "sodomy" is not used in statutes, and other terms, such as "crime against nature," "unnatural intercourse," "deviate sexual conduct" or "sexual abuse" appear instead.

In UCR, sodomy is included in **sex offenses UCR 17.**

solicitation   see **inchoate offense**

special judge   A judge who is appointed to hear, and exercise all judicial functions for, a specific case.

annotation

Special judges are appointed in addition to, not in lieu of, regularly appointed or elected judges. They conduct all criminal proceedings pertaining to a specific case only.

In calculating caseload data with respect to individual judicial officers, or with respect to a given court, cases heard by special judges are usually counted separately from the cases heard by the regular judicial officers.

speedy trial   The right of the defendant to have a prompt trial, as guaranteed by the Sixth Amendment of the U.S. Constitution: "In all criminal prosecutions, the accused shall enjoy the right to a speedy and public trial. . ."

annotation

Although the U.S. Constitution and the constitutions of almost all the states provide that the accused shall enjoy the right to a speedy trial, the requirements vary among jurisdictions. Most states and the federal government (Speedy Trial Act of 1974) have enacted statutes setting forth the time within which the defendant must be tried following the date of his arrest, his detention, his first appearance, or the filing of charges in court. If the accused is not brought to trial within the specified period, the case is dismissed. Jurisdictions differ, however, on whether dismissal on these grounds constitutes a bar to subsequent prosecution for the same offense(s).

Most speedy trial statutes provide a method for computing "excludable delay," delay not included in calculations of elapsed time for speedy trial purposes. Examples of "excludable delay" are periods of time spent on other proceedings concerning the defendant, such as a hearing on mental competency to stand trial, trial on other charges, or probation or parole revocation hearings. Other examples are delays due to continuances granted at the request of the defendant or because of the absconding of the defendant, and the execution of procedures necessary to obtain the presence of a confined prisoner.

split sentence   A sentence explicitly requiring the convicted person to serve a period of confinement in a local, state or federal facility followed by a period of probation.

annotation

"Shock probation" is frequently used as another name for a split sentence. Neither term is recommended. Since one agency may mean by these words prison plus probation, and another, jail plus probation, it is recommended that specific terms be used in data reporting: **probation with jail** or **prison and probation**. See **defendant dispositions**.

See also **probation supervisory population movement**.

state highway patrol   *recommended statistical terminology*   A state law enforcement agency of which the principal functions consist of prevention, detection, and investigation of motor vehicle offenses, and the apprehension of traffic offenders.

annotation

In some states, state police functions include highway patrol; in others the **state police** and the state highway patrol are separate organizational units with identifiably separate functions. It is recommended that state highway patrols be counted separately from other state level law enforcement agencies where organized as distinct units.

See **law enforcement agency**.

state highway patrol officer   *recommended statistical terminology*   An employee of a state highway patrol who is an officer sworn to carry out law enforcement duties, primarily traffic code enforcement.

annotation

See **law enforcement officer**.

state law enforcement agency   see **law enforcement agency**

state law enforcement officer   see **law enforcement officer**

state police   *recommended statistical terminology*   A state law enforcement agency whose principal functions usually include maintaining statewide police communications, aiding local police in criminal investigation, police training, and guarding state property, and may include highway patrol.

annotation

In some states the duties of traffic code enforcement are performed by the state police, in others there is a separate **state highway patrol** (see entry). It is recommended that state highway patrols be counted separately from other state law enforcement agencies where organized as distinct units.

State police also perform local law enforcement functions in some instances, in unincorporated areas or in support of local police.

See **law enforcement agency**.

state police officer   *recommended statistical terminology*   An employee of a state police agency who is an officer sworn to carry out law enforcement duties, sometimes including traffic enforcement duties.

annotation

For national level general data this class should include personnel who guard state property, if sworn officers. Employees of separate state highway patrol agencies should be described as **state highway patrol officers** (see entry).

See **law enforcement officer.**

state's attorney   see **prosecutor**

status offender   see **delinquency**

status offense   see **delinquency**

statutory rape   see **sex offenses**

stay of execution   The stopping by a court of the carrying out or implementation of a judgment, that is, of a court order previously issued.

annotation

Popular usage associates this term with temporary suspension of a death sentence. See "reprieve" under **clemency.**

A "stay" is a halting of judicial proceedings by court order.

stolen property; buying, receiving, possessing   UCR 13   In Uniform Crime Reports terminology, the name of the UCR category used to record and report arrests for offenses of knowingly buying, receiving, possessing, or attempting to buy, receive, or possess, stolen property.

annotation

See **stolen property offenses** for defining features and general recommendation.

stolen property offenses   *tentatively recommended national category for prosecution, courts and corrections statistics*   The unlawful receiving, buying, distributing, selling, transporting, concealing, or possessing of the property of another by a person who knows that the property has been unlawfully obtained from the owner or other lawful possessor.

defining features *of tentatively recommended national category*

unlawfully and knowingly

receiving, buying, distributing, selling, transporting, possessing or concealing the unlawfully obtained property of another

or

attempting the above act(s)

annotation

The category is tentatively recommended for national post-arrest offense data. It is used in UCR reporting (see **stolen property; buying, receiving,** possessing UCR 13). See Appendix B for problems in national crime classification and complete set of tentatively proposed national categories for post-arrest offense statistics.

The crime type defined above may be codified as one statutory offense or several. In some penal codes all stolen property offenses are defined as part of the "theft" group. "Stolen property," however, frequently occurs as a major category in statistical presentations characterizing courts and corrections populations by offense.

stop and frisk   The detaining of a person by a law enforcement officer for the purpose of investigation, accompanied by a superficial examination by the officer of the person's body surface or clothing to discover weapons, contraband, or other objects relating to criminal activity.

annotation

"Stop and frisk" is a police activity that is less than the thorough examination of a person or premises that would constitute a "search." A "stop and frisk" is intended to stop short of any activity that could be considered a violation of a citizen's constitutional rights.

See **illegal search and seizure.**

street crime   A class of offenses, sometimes defined with some degree of formality as those which occur in public locations, are visible and assaultive, and thus constitute a group of crimes which are a special risk to the public and a special target of law enforcement preventive efforts and prosecutorial attention.

annotation

Crimes typically included in "street crime" are **robbery**, purse snatching, and any kind of **assault** outside a residence.

street time   see **time served**

strongarm robbery   see **robbery**

subpoena   *recommended statistical terminology*   A written order issued by a judicial officer, prosecutor, defense attorney or grand jury, requiring a specified person to appear in a designated court at a specified time in order to testify in a case under the jurisdiction of that court, or to bring material to be used as evidence to that court.

annotation

Subpoenas can be served in various ways. They may be served in person by a law enforcement officer, or by another person authorized to do so. In some jurisdictions some types of subpoenas may be served by mail or by telephone. Failure to obey a subpoena is **contempt of court.**

A subpoena issued for the appearance of a hostile witness or person who has failed to appear in answer to a previous subpoena, and which authorizes a law enforcement officer to bring that person to the court, is often called an "instanter."

A subpoena to serve as a witness is called a "subpoena testificatum." A subpoena to bring material is called a "subpoena duces tecum."

See **citation (appear)**, **summons**, and **warrant** for other orders requiring court appearance.

summons　*recommended statistical terminology*　In criminal proceedings, a written order issued by a judicial officer requiring a person accused of a criminal offense to appear in a designated court at a specified time to answer the charge(s).

annotation

A document issued by a **law enforcement officer** requiring court appearance of an accused person is, in this terminology, classified as a **citation (appear)** (see entry). For the purposes of interstate or national information exchange, it is recommended that "summons" be used to mean the order signed by a judicial officer. This is the traditional sense of summons, which should be preserved in order to distinguish between issuing authorities.

See also **subpoena** and **warrant**.

supervised probation　*recommended statistical terminology*　Guidance, treatment or regulation by a probation agency of the behavior of a person who is subject to adjudication or who has been convicted of an offense, resulting from a formal court order or a probation agency decision.

annotation

Supervision of adults may be in lieu of prosecution, or in lieu of judgment, or after a judgment of conviction. Supervised probation may be a substitute for confinement or may occur after a period of confinement in jail or prison. See also **parole supervision**.

Probation supervision differs according to the degree of intensity of supervision and amount of services provided to subjects. A common broad distinction (known by a variety of names) is between **active supervision**: contact between the agency and the client occurs on a regular basis, and **inactive supervision**: contact occurs only when initiated by the client or other interested party outside the probation agency, and is not on a regular basis. Inactive cases are sometimes called "banked" cases. More detailed level of service distinctions are made by some probation agencies.

Probation supervision is not a necessary feature of probationary status. A court may place an offender on probation without assignment to a **probation supervisory caseload** (see **court probation**), or may request a private citizen to assume specified responsibilities in connection with the probationer.

For the data items representing placements on probation see **grant of probation** and **defendant dispositions**.

supervision　Authorized and required guidance, treatment, and/or regulation of the behavior of a person who is subject to adjudication or who has been adjudicated to be an offender, performed by a correctional agency.

annotation

"Supervision" may be accompanied by treatment or other supportive effort on the part of the agency, but does not necessarily include this feature.

See **supervised probation** and **parole supervision**.

See also **custody** for differences between supervisory responsibility and legal or physical control of a subject.

supervisory custody (corrections)   see **custody**

suppression hearing   A hearing to determine whether or not the court will prohibit specified statements, documents, or objects from being introduced into evidence in a trial.

annotation

The kinds of issues considered in a suppression hearing include the legality of' the manner in which evidence was obtained (see **illegal search and seizure**); the legality of a defendant identification procedure; the admissability of a confession; and prior arrests of the defendant.

Suppression hearings are commonly initiated before trial on a motion by the defendant, occasionally by the court.

suspect   An adult or juvenile considered by a criminal justice agency to be one who may have committed a specific criminal offense, but who has not been arrested or charged.

annotation

Defendant and **alleged offender**, which are, in data reporting, units of count describing persons who have been formally accused of a crime, should not be used as synonyms for this term.

See also **perpetrator**.

suspended sentence   I.   The court decision to delay imposing or executing a penalty for a specified or unspecified period, also called "sentence withheld."   II.   *recommended statistical terminology*   A court disposition of a convicted person pronouncing a penalty of a fine or commitment to confinement, but unconditionally discharging the defendant or holding execution of the penalty in abeyance upon good behavior.

annotation

Suspended sentences (II) are a type of **sentencing disposition** within the major class **defendant dispositions** (see entry for classification structure).

The recommended definition (II) limits the use of the term to those instances where a sentence is pronounced but execution (carrying out) held in abeyance. **Sentencing postponed** (see entry) should be used where pronouncement of sentence is deferred contingent on defendant behavior.

These recommended terms replace the terms "sentence-imposition suspended" and "sentence-execution suspended" which were recommended in the first edition of this book to represent the distinction. "Impose" and "execute" have the same meaning in many legal contexts, and their usage in statistical contexts can thus be a source of confusion.

Since sentences can be suspended conditionally or unconditionally, and the latter is a final termination of court jurisdiction, the following terminology is recommended:

conditionally suspended sentence   *recommended statistical terminology*
A court disposition of a convicted person specifying a penalty of a fine or commitment to confinement but holding execution of the penalty in abeyance upon good behavior. (Whether this disposition is considered equivalent or complementary to a **grant of probation**, or is considered an entirely distinct legal action depends upon the jurisdiction.)

unconditionally suspended sentence   *recommended statistical terminology*   A court disposition of a convicted person pronouncing a penalty of a fine or commitment to confinement but unconditionally discharging the defendant of all obligations and restraints.

When a sentence is suspended for a limited amount of time that is known in advance, that disposition should not be treated as a suspended sentence in national or interstate data reporting.

suspicion   see **levels of proof**

suspicion   UCR 27   In Uniform Crime Reports terminology, the name of the UCR offense category used to record and report arrests made on grounds of suspicion, in jurisdictions where the law permits, where the arrestee is later released without being charged with an offense.

annotation

The edition of the *Uniform Crime Reporting Handbook* for use in 1980 states that "While 'suspicion' is not an offense, it is the ground for many arrests in those jurisdictions where the law permits. After examination by the police, the prisoner is either formally charged or released. Those formally charged are entered in one of the Part I or II offense classes. This class is limited to 'suspicion' arrests where persons arrested are released by the police."

swindle   see **confidence game**

technical violation   see **parole violation** and **probation violation**

theft   Generally, any taking of the property of another with intent to permanently deprive the rightful owner of possession; in the broadest legal usage the name of the group of offenses having this feature: larceny, fraud, embezzlement, false pretenses, robbery and extortion.

annotation

See **larceny** for general statistical recommendation.

"Theft" should not be used as the name of an offense or offense class in crime statistics without explicit definition. Even in jurisdictions where statutory consolidation of theft offenses has occurred, "theft" is the statutory name for only one class of theft offenses, typically the theft by stealth (larceny) and by deceit (fraud) group. Offenses such as **robbery** and **extortion**, which have in addition the element of force, are separately named, defined and penalized. In statistical reporting motor vehicle thefts and fraud type offenses are usually tabulated separately from other theft type offenses. See **motor vehicle theft** and **fraud offenses** for general statistical recommendations.

threat   The declaration by words or actions of an unlawful intent to do some injury to another, together with an apparent ability to do so.

annotation

In some jurisdictions, the making of a threat, or of a certain kind of threat, constitutes the statutory offense of "menacing." Threat is an element in such offenses as **extortion**, coercion, and intimidation.

A threat is implied in an attempt to commit a crime, but a threat is "less" than an attempt because it does not require that an overt act directed toward immediate accomplishment of a crime take place. See also **attempt** under the entry **inchoate offense**.

In UCR, threats to cause bodily injury to another are classified as **assaults**.

time served   Generally, time spent in confinement in relation to conviction and sentencing for a given offense(s), calculated in accord with the rules and conventions specific to a given jurisdiction; also, total time served under correctional agency jurisdiction.

annotation

Statistical presentations intended for general distribution should describe the method of calculating time served.

Time served is calculated for individuals in order to determine, for example, when a particular prisoner will be **eligible for parole** or have served his or her **maximum sentence**. For a person committed to prison all or some portion of the time spent in confinement pending conviction or sentencing may be credited as confinement time served on the sentence, depending upon statute or judge's decision. All time spent in the legal status of prisoner may be counted towards time served in confinement, although the person may be on work furlough, in hospital, or otherwise not in the physical custody of the prison.

Time on parole or other conditional release counts as total time served under correctional agency jurisdiction, but this can be discounted if conditional release status is revoked and thus will delay the date of expiration of sentence.

Statistical presentations of averages, medians or ranges of time served are often focused upon prison facility system population flow and may, for example, disregard presentence jail time that nevertheless counts toward individual prisoner release dates.

In National Prisoner Statistics (**NPS**) data for periods prior to 1978, "time served" means time between first admission to the **physical custody** of a given state prison facility system and first release from that system (whether conditional or unconditional), including any time spent on temporary release for work furlough, court proceedings, or the like. In 1978 and later data, "time served" is calculated as time between first assignment to correctional agency **jurisdiction** in the legal status of prisoner and termination of prisoner status, without respect to where the prisoner is in confinement or whether he or she is temporarily released for work furlough, etc.

Other phrases used with special meanings that are precise in a given jurisdiction are:

dead time or **nonrun time**   Time that does not count as prison time served towards a required term in confinement, or as time served on parole towards total time under correctional jurisdiction. Time elapsed after escape and before apprehension is dead time for counting time in confinement. Time spent out of confinement pending an appeal decision may also be declared "dead time" in counting prison time, depending upon the rules of a jurisdiction, or decisions made in individual cases.

street time   Time spent on conditional release. If parole or other conditional release is revoked, and the person reconfined, all or part of this time may become "dead time" in calculations of time served under correctional jurisdiction, according to administrative or court decision.

See also **sentence credit time** and **good time**.

traffic offenses   I. A group of offenses usually informally categorized as such, and usually consisting of those infractions and very minor misdemeanors relating to the operation of self-propelled surface motor vehicles which are excluded from most information systems relating to criminal and correctional proceedings.   II. *tentatively recommended national category for prosecution, courts and corrections statistics*   Motor vehicle violations requiring appearance in court, other than "hit and run" and "driving under the influence."

defining features of tentatively recommended national category (II)

violations of statutes relating to the operation, maintenance, use, ownership, licensing and registration of self-propelled road vehicles

excluding driving under the influence, hit and run, and violations of law not requiring appearance in court

annotation

Definition (II) is tentatively recommended as a national crime classification because of the possibility that counts of this offense type may be significant in assessing court workload for various purposes. See Appendix B for problems in national crime classification and complete set of tentatively proposed national categories for post-arrest offense statistics.

In common usage most "traffic offenses" (I) are **infractions** (see entry), that is, offenses not punishable by incarceration or by minimal incarceration: parking violations, violations of equipment standards, and the like. "Moving violations," such as speeding or improper turns, are also frequently included in this group. All these offenses have in common the feature that they are not likely to be contested and in many or most jurisdictions are handled by administrative or quasi-judicial bodies or procedures quite separate from the major business of the courts. The majority of instances in this group, such as parking violations, are dealt with by citations permitting forfeit of money as an alternative to appearance in court. Failure to respond to such citations, however, may result in issuing of a court order for appearance.

training school   see **juvenile facility**

transfer (corrections)   The movement of a person from one correctional facility or caseload to another.

annotation

The term "transfers" should not be used in population movement statistics intended for general use without complete definition of the category. A given transfer can involve one to three kinds of changes, changes in: **jurisdiction, supervisory custody** and **physical custody** (see **custody** for definitions). The definition should indicate which of these kinds of changes are occurring in relation to the kind of transfer counted, and whether the movement is from one state to another, from one agency to another or within a given agency.

See **prison/parole population movement** for examples of "transfer" usages in data reporting.

transfer hearing   *recommended statistical terminology*   A preadjudicatory hearing in juvenile court for the purpose of determining whether juvenile court jurisdiction should be retained over a juvenile alleged to have committed a delinquent act, or whether it should be waived and the juvenile transferred to criminal court for prosecution as an adult.

annotation

A transfer hearing is not an **adjudicatory hearing**. See entry.

A transfer hearing determines whether a juvenile is amenable to rehabilitation or treatment within the juvenile justice system. If the juvenile court certifies that neither the facilities nor the programs are appropriate for that juvenile, then he or she is transferred to criminal court for prosecution as an adult. See **transfer to adult court**.

In some jurisdictions a transfer hearing is called a "certification hearing," "waiver hearing," or "fitness hearing."

transfer to adult court   *recommended statistical terminology*   The decision by a juvenile court, resulting from a transfer hearing, that jurisdiction over an alleged delinquent will be waived, and that he or she should be prosecuted as an adult in a criminal court.

annotation

"Transfer to adult court" is not a **juvenile court judgment** nor a **juvenile disposition** but is a juvenile court case disposition.

Juvenile courts usually waive jurisdiction over alleged delinquents only when a serious felony has been alleged, and when the juvenile is near the statutory age boundary between juvenile and adult.

At a **transfer hearing** (see entry), probable cause to believe that the juvenile committed the offense must be shown. After a transfer to adult court, the prosecutor decides whether prosecution will take place and what offense will be charged.

This action is sometimes called "waiver" or "certification." A juvenile whose case has been transferred to a criminal court is sometimes called a "certified juvenile."

Recent revisions of criminal and juvenile law have, in some instances, reduced juvenile court original jurisdiction over cases resulting from certain serious crimes, or allowed for waiver in more kinds of cases.

Defendant charging and disposition data should indicate which cases began in juvenile court.

transfer to juvenile court   *recommended statistical terminology*   The decision by a criminal court, at any point after filing of a criminal complaint but before judgment, that jurisdiction over an alleged juvenile offender will be waived, and that he or she should be adjudicated in a juvenile court.

annotation

Transfer to juvenile court is a type of **defendant disposition** (see entry), since such a transfer terminates criminal court jurisdiction over the defendant.

Recent revisions of criminal and juvenile law have, in some instances, expanded criminal court original jurisdiction over cases resulting from certain serious crimes committed by juveniles. These statutes provide for the possibility of transfer of such cases to a juvenile court for adjudication.

trial   I.   The examination in a court of the issues of fact and law in a case, for the purpose of reaching a judgment.   II.   *recommended statistical terminology*   In criminal proceedings, the examination in a court of the issues of fact and law in a case, for the purpose of reaching a judgment of conviction or acquittal of the defendant(s).

annotation

jury trial   *recommended statistical terminology*   In criminal proceedings, a trial in which a jury is empaneled to determine the issues of fact in a case and to render a verdict of guilty or not guilty.

A defendant is guaranteed the right to a jury trial when a serious crime is charged. Practice varies among jurisdictions in cases where a minor offense is charged. The right to a jury trial may be waived by the defense.

nonjury trial   *recommended statistical terminology*   In criminal proceedings, a trial in which there is no jury, and in which a judicial officer determines all issues of fact and law in a case. (This type of trial is also called a "judge trial," "bench trial," or "court trial.")

A **trial on transcript** (also "trial by the record") is a nonjury trial in which the judicial officer makes a decision on the basis of the record of pretrial proceedings in a lower court.

Usually, a trial will deal with all and only the charges specified and defendants named in a single charging document filed in court. Sometimes, however, a single trial will deal with matters set out in two or more charging documents, or a single charging document will be the basis for two or more trials. See **joinder** and **severance**.

A **consolidated trial** is one in which two or more defendants named in separate charging documents are tried together, or where a given defendant is tried on charges contained in two or more charging documents.

Determinations of the beginning and end points of trials in criminal proceedings are essential for preparation of elapsed time data concerning the criminal justice process, to ensure compliance with legal mandates concerning the treatment of persons subject to criminal proceedings. See **rights of defendant** and **speedy trial**.

There is currently some variation among the states regarding the identification of the beginning and end points of trials for these purposes. Beginning points frequently used are: the start of jury selection or the completion of jury selection (for jury trials), or the swearing of the first witness or introduction of the first evidence or testimony (for jury and nonjury trials). The sets of end points most frequently used are:

> dismissal of case during trial
> entering of judgment of acquittal
> entering of judgment of conviction

and,

> dismissal of case during trial
> rendering of not guilty verdict
> rendering of guilty verdict

A few states use the set of endpoints:

> dismissal of case during trial
> entering of judgment of acquittal
> pronouncement of sentence following judgment of conviction

Determination of the beginning point of trials is also a key factor in the preparation of statistical data concerning court caseload. In court caseload statistical presentations, counts of disposed cases are typically displayed in categories according to the manner of disposition of the case. A primary distinction is between cases disposed of by jury trial, cases disposed of by nonjury trial, and cases disposed of without trial, reflecting the different management impacts of these methods of disposing of cases. The criterion for assignment of a case to one of the "trial" categories is whether a trial was begun.

In the model court caseload statistical system developed by the National Court Statistics Project, "jury trial" and "nonjury trial" are recommended manner of disposition categories for disposed cases. The recommended process points for identification of trial commencements are:

- jury sworn and first evidence introduced (jury trials)
- first evidence introduced (nonjury trials)

A term list outline of the complete model classification scheme for general caseload inventory and for case and defendant manner of disposition is presented in Appendix E of this volume.

trial court   see **court**

trial court case   *recommended statistical terminology*   A case which has been filed in a court of general jurisdiction or a court of limited jurisdiction.

annotation

This and other recommended terminology for court caseload statistics reflect the usages of the model court caseload statistical system developed by the National Court Statistics Project under Bureau of Justice Statistics sponsorship. In that model, "trial court case" is the major classification category for trial court caseload. It includes four major subcategories:

> civil case
> criminal case
> traffic case
> juvenile case

A term list outline of the completed model classification scheme for general caseload inventory and for case and defendant manner of disposition is presented in Appendix E of this book.

trial de novo   see **new trial**

trial judge   A judicial officer who is authorized to conduct jury and nonjury trials, and who may or may not be authorized to hear appellate cases; or the judicial officer who conducts a particular trial.

annotation

See **judicial officer.**

trial jury   *syn*   **petit jury**   *recommended statistical terminology*   A statutorily defined number of persons selected according to law and sworn to determine, in accordance with the law as instructed by the court, certain matters of fact based on evidence presented in a trial, and to render a verdict.

annotation

A trial jury's powers and duties ordinarily are to determine matters of fact only. It is the power and duty of the presiding judicial officer to interpret the law of the case. In certain circumstances, however, in accordance with the law as instructed by the court, a trial jury may also advise the court regarding sentencing or recommend a specific sentence (which the court may or may not be required to act upon, depending upon the jurisdiction). See **jury sentencing.**

The size of a trial jury is set by statute and, depending upon jurisdiction, is 12 or a number less than 12. Some jurisdictions specify a minimum of 6 jurors, but allow for less if a juror falls ill.

See also **grand jury.**

trial on transcript   see **trial**

truant   *recommended statistical terminology*   A juvenile who has been adjudicated by a judicial officer of a juvenile court, as having committed the status offense of violating a compulsory school attendance law.

annotation

A truant is a type of **status offender.** See **delinquency.**

Compulsory attendance statutes may specify the number of days of continuous absence which constitute a violation or provide a more general definition of truancy, such as habitual absence. The codification of this offense varies greatly among different states.

"Truancy" is the name of the status offense.

trusty   An inmate of a jail or prison who has been entrusted with some custodial responsibilities, or who performs other services assisting in the operation of the facility.

annotation

Trusties have special privileges and freedoms, including more physical mobility than other inmates.

Trusty status is usually given as a reward for good behavior. Satisfactory performance of trusty duties can, in some jurisdictions, result in a shortening of time to be served.

A trusty in most cases performs duties which would otherwise be performed by a correctional officer or other facility staff. Thus, by providing extra manpower the use of trusties can reduce the workload of regular employees, and consequently reduce facility budgetary needs.

A trusty can in effect have quasi-correctional officer status, when he or she performs duties which would otherwise be the responsibility of a correctional officer.

UCR   An abbreviation for the Federal Bureau of Investigation's "Uniform Crime Reporting" program.

annotation

The Uniform Crime Reporting program began as a voluntary program initiated in 1930 by the Committee on Uniform Crime Records of the International Association of Chiefs of Police (IACP). In that same year Congress authorized the FBI to serve as the national clearinghouse for crime statistics. The IACP's committee and other national and state level law enforcement association committees currently serve as advisors to the UCR program, and participate in the continuing effort to improve data scope and quality.

The national UCR program produces a major annual report called *Crime in the United States*. The bulk of the information in these reports relates to reported instances (offenses known to police) of the FBI's Crime Index offenses, reported arrests for all crimes, and law enforcement agency employee data. The detail includes information concerning crimes cleared by arrest, arrests and dispositions of arrested persons, and dispositions of juveniles taken into custody. The reported crime and reported arrest data are categorized by geographical area and related to various factors.

UCR also produces three other annual publications, *Law Enforcement Officers Killed, Assaults on Federal Officers,* and *Bomb Summary*.

For a listing of UCR crime categories and definitions of key program terms, see **Part I offenses, Part II offenses, Crime Index, offenses known to police, clearance,** and **arrests (UCR)**.

It is important to note that the UCR program does not publish any data on reported crimes outside the Part I categories. The other crime types were developed to categorize arrests only. The major crime types are defined at length in a manner specifically designed to establish clearcut category boundaries. The crime categories for arrests are defined variously, sometimes by formal but very brief definition, sometimes by listing examples. Some of the Part II categories consist of single crimes, some of groups of crimes. The groups often contain instances of statutory crime types for which mutually exclusive statistical definitions cannot be developed. Consequently, only the major crime types are consistently treated as classificatory terminology in this dictionary.

The UCR Part I offense classification is rank ordered, with lower number indicating higher severity. For any criminal event involving more than one type of offense, only the most serious offense is counted.

UCR crime counts are arrived at by police agency matching of the UCR definitions to information in crime and arrest reports. The resulting data are delivered in pre-aggregated form to the FBI, either from the originating agency or from a central state agency responsible for data processing.

There are now state level UCR programs operational in 45 states. These programs collect the data necessary for the national program and are responsible for reporting data to the national level. Many collect and publish additional data as well.

A few state UCR programs are "incident based," that is, initial and follow-up information is collected and maintained on an incident-by-incident basis. Each reported crime is uniquely identified in the system, so that a variety of pertinent facts relating to the crime can be systematically added when the crime is first reported or at later times, and systematically retrieved. The additional information may include exactly where and when it happened, recovery of property lost by the crime, and law enforcement actions subsequent to the crime.

unarmed robbery   see **robbery**

unconditionally suspended sentence   see **suspended sentence**

unconditional release   The final release of an offender from the jurisdiction of a correctional agency; also, a final release from the jurisdiction of a court.

annotation

In corrections statistics this term has been used as the name of a category with varying subclasses, sometimes limited to legally authorized exits from prison facility systems without parole or other **conditional release** status to follow. In other instances, discharges from parole and deaths while in prison or on parole have been included in the category. Use of this term is not recommended. Usage has been discrepant in practice and the phrase is inherently somewhat ambiguous.

In the model **prison/parole population movement** (see entry) data structure the kinds of population movements often designated "unconditional releases" have been placed in the major category "terminations," meaning final separations from state correctional systems. This category contains all the individual items necessary to construct any "unconditional release" set plus other kinds of final separations, arranged and named at greater length for the sake of clarity.

Recommended terminology for the various court actions in relation to release of offenders from court jurisdiction is presented in the model data structures listed in the entries **defendant dispositions** and **probation supervisory population movement**.

unfounded   see **offenses known to police**

UOC   The Uniform Offense Classifications used by the FBI's National Crime Information Center to represent offense types in automated individual criminal history record systems.

annotation

The complete list of the Uniform Offense Classifications is presented in Appendix D. This system was not devised for statistical use, but some statistical programs have employed UOC coded data as initial input. See Appendix B for discussion of problems in national crime classification.

UPR   An abbreviation for "Uniform Parole Reports."

annotation

UPR is a statistical program sponsored by the Bureau of Justice Statistics and administered by the National Council on Crime and Delinquency. It was established in 1964 by the National Institutes of Health. It has published statistical information on parolees, parole authority decisions, and parole agency workloads.

For publications, see bibliography under "U.S. Department of Justice."

usury   The charging of interest greater than that permitted by law in return for the loan of money.

annotation

Usury is also called "loan sharking." This offense is assigned to the "other" category in the tentatively recommended classification for post-arrest offense reporting. See Appendix B.

vacated sentence   A sentence which has been declared nullified by action of a court.

vagrancy   UCR 25   In Uniform Crime Reports terminology, the name of the UCR category used to record and report arrests made for offenses relating to being a suspicious character or person, including vagrancy, begging, loitering, and vagabondage.

annotation

At common law "vagrancy" was the offense committed by a person who lived without a proper means of support, one who lived off charity although able to work. Statutory definitions vary and some have been declared unconstitutional because vague.

See also **suspicion UCR 27.**

See **disturbing the peace** for general recommendation for prosecution, courts and corrections statistics.

vandalism   UCR 14   In Uniform Crime Reports terminology, the name of the UCR category used to record and report arrests made for offenses of destroying or damaging, or attempting to destroy or damage, the property of another without his consent, or public property, except by burning.

annotation

Arrests of persons charged with damaging or destroying property by burning are counted as **arson UCR 8.**

See also **criminal mischief.**

vehicular manslaughter   see **criminal homicide**

venue   see **jurisdiction**

verdict   *recommended statistical terminology*   In criminal proceedings, the decision of the jury in a jury trial or of a judicial officer in a nonjury trial, that the defendant is guilty or not guilty of the offense for which he or she has been tried.

annotation

For purposes of data collection and display, a verdict, which is a finding of guilt or nonguilt by a jury or a judicial officer, should be distinguished from a judgment, which is the final determination of the court. The items "guilty" and "not guilty" occasionally appear in court caseload data presentations under the heading "dispositions" to indicate judgments in criminal cases. These terms properly characterize verdicts rather than judgments and their usage as final disposition categories is not recommended. See **court disposition** for recommendations.

guilty verdict   *recommended statistical terminology*   In criminal proceedings, the decision by jury or judicial officer on the basis of the evidence presented at trial, that the defendant is guilty of the offense(s) for which he or she has been tried.

A guilty verdict indicates that it was concluded that the evidence offered of the defendant's guilt was sufficient to prove guilt beyond a reasonable doubt. A guilty verdict does not necessarily lead to a judgment of conviction; the judicial officer can enter a judgment of acquittal if the requirements of law have not been satisfied.

not guilty verdict   *recommended statistical terminology*   In criminal proceedings, the decision by jury or judicial officer on the basis of the evidence presented at trial, that the defendant is not guilty of the offense(s) for which he or she has been tried.

A not guilty verdict indicates that the evidence left at least a reasonable doubt as to the defendant's guilt. A not guilty verdict must lead to a judgment of acquittal; the court cannot enter a judgment of conviction unless the defendant has been found guilty or he or she has pled guilty.

A **directed verdict** is a not guilty verdict (1) returned by the jury at the direction of the court, or (2) entered on the record by the court after dismissal of the jury, when the judicial officer decides that the case presented against the defendant obviously falls short of that required to establish guilt.

In statistics describing defendant flow in detail, verdicts of **not guilty by reason of insanity** are often distinguished from other not guilty verdicts because the verdict is not based on what the defendant is believed to have done, but rather on the evidence as to whether he or she possessed the mental capacity to be responsible for the criminal act. See **not guilty by reason of insanity**.

victim   A person who has suffered death, physical or mental anguish, or loss of property as the result of an actual or attempted criminal offense committed by another person.

annotation

In law a victim can be a single human being, or a group of human beings considered as a unit.

victimization   In National Crime Survey terminology, the harming of any single victim in a criminal incident.

annotation

"Harm" in the above definition means at minimum physical injury, economic loss, or psychological distress. The NCS offenses cover attempts as well as completed acts, thus including instances where no physical or economic harm has resulted.

In NCS terminology a critical distinction is made between a victimization and a **criminal incident** (see entry). The procedures by which data are compiled relating to these two units of count differ significantly. Only one criminal incident is recorded for any continuous sequence of criminal behavior, even though it may contain acts which constitute two or more NCS offenses or involve two or more separate victims. One victimization is recorded for each separate victim (meaning person or household) harmed as a result of a given criminal incident.

The number of household victimizations will be equal to the number of incidents of **household crimes,** since each incident is treated as having a single, unique household as victim. However, the number of recorded victimizations of persons can be greater than the number of recorded incidents of personal crimes, because more than one person can be victimized in what is identified as a single incident of a **personal crime.** For example, where two persons have been robbed in the same event, two victimizations of persons are recorded, and one criminal incident.

violation   I.   The performance of an act forbidden by a statute, or the failure to perform an act commanded by a statute.   II.   An act contrary to a local government ordinance.   III.   An offense punishable by a fine or other penalty but not by incarceration.   IV.   An act prohibited by the terms and conditions of probation or parole.

annotation

Since the meaning of "violation" extends from acts contrary to penal statutes to behavior not in accord with special rules (sometimes requirements relating to only one person), the term should not be used in data reporting without explicit definition.

See **crime, infraction, probation violation,** and **parole violation** for preferred usages. For acts contrary to prison administrative regulations see **infraction (corrections).**

violent crime   see **Crime Index**

violent sex offenses   see **sex offenses**

voluntary commitment   In corrections usage, admission to a correctional, residential, or medical facility or program for care or treatment without a court commitment and by personal choice.

annotation

This term and "voluntary placement" or "voluntary admission" are used to describe those instances where a person elects to enter a treatment facility or program, as opposed to being ordered there by a court. (See **commitment** and **new court commitment.**)

Voluntary placement in a treatment program is often made an alternative to prosecution or conviction and sentencing, or may be a condition of probation. In some jurisdictions this alternative is available for adults only for medical problems.

In the national series *Children in Custody*, the *1977 Advance Report* considers as "voluntary admissions" those "juveniles who admitted themselves to a facility or were referred by a parent, court, or school, without being adjudged for an offense . . ."

voluntary manslaughter   see **criminal homicide**

wanted person   A person sought by law enforcement authorities because an arrest warrant has been issued or because he has escaped from custody.

annotation

Wanted persons may be crime **suspects**, escapees, absconders from **supervised probation** or **parole supervision**, or persons avoiding prosecution, confinement or giving testimony in criminal proceedings. See "abscond" entries.

In FBI usage **fugitive** includes both escapees and persons avoiding prosecution or custody: "fugitives from justice."

No warrant is necessary to arrest persons who have escaped from lawful confinement or failed to return after authorized leave. The message requesting apprehension transmitted to law enforcement officials is sometimes called a "pickup order." It need not be in writing.

Arrest (or bench) warrants will be issued by a judicial officer or in some cases a court clerk when a person has failed to obey a court order, and can be issued by a prosecutor when a complaint has been filed in court.

See also **contempt of court** and **escape**.

warden   The official in charge of operation of a prison; the chief administrator of a prison; the prison superintendent.

warrant   In criminal proceedings, any of a number of writs issued by a judicial officer, which direct a law enforcement officer to perform a specified act and afford him protection from damage if he performs it.

annotation

See also **arrest warrant, bench warrant, search warrant,** and **writ.**

weapons; carrying, possessing, etc.   UCR 15   In Uniform Crime Reports terminology, the name of the UCR category used to record and report arrests for offenses relating to the regulation of the manufacture, sale, distribution, possession, use, or transportation of deadly weapons and accessories.

annotation

See **weapons offenses** for defining features and general recommendation.

weapons offenses   *tentatively recommended national category for prosecution, courts and corrections statistics*   Unlawful sale, distribution, manufacture, alteration, transportation, possession, or use, or attempted sale, distribution, manufacture, alteration, transportation, possession, or use of a deadly or dangerous weapon or accessory.

defining features of tentatively recommended national category

unlawful distribution, sale, manufacture, alteration, transport, possession, or use of a deadly or dangerous weapon or accessory

use other than in the commission or attempted commission of another crime

or

attempting the above act(s)

annotation

This category is tentatively recommended for post-arrest offense data. It is used in UCR reporting (see **weapons; carrying, possessing, etc. UCR 15**). See Appendix B for problems in national crime classification and complete set of tentatively proposed national categories for post-arrest offense statistics.

weekend sentence   see **intermittent sentence**

white-collar crime   Nonviolent crime for financial gain committed by means of deception by persons whose occupational status is entrepreneurial, professional or semi-professional and utilizing their special occupational skills and opportunities; also, nonviolent crime for financial gain utilizing deception and committed by anyone having special technical and professional knowledge of business and government, irrespective of the person's occupation.

annotation

Actual instances of white-collar crime are prosecuted as the offenses defined in statutes under such headings as **theft, fraud** and **embezzlement.**

The term reflects a traditional classification of occupations into white-collar: those utilizing technical knowledge and skills in the manipulation of numbers and concepts, and blue-collar: those utilizing skill in the manipulation of objects. It originally referred to nonviolent crime committed by persons in the upper socio-economic class in their occupational roles, and defined a social class of interest to social scientists.

In current criminal justice usage of the term, the focus of the meaning has shifted to the nature of the crime instead of the persons or occupations. The categorization of "white-collar" crime as crime having a particular modus operandi (committed in a manner that utilizes deception and special knowledge of business practices and committed in a particular kind of economic environment) is of use in coordinating the resources of the appropriate agencies for purposes of investigation and prosecution.

The kinds of crime designated as business crime, **consumer fraud, confidence games,** tax violations, bankruptcy fraud, insurance fraud and the like are often regarded as equivalent to or included within the general range of white-collar crime. Some of these types of activity also fall within categories of **organized crime** operations.

willful homicide   see **criminal homicide**

witness   In criminal justice usage, generally, a person who has knowledge of the circumstances of a case; in court usage, one who testifies as to what he has seen, heard, otherwise observed, or has expert knowledge of.

annotation

Related terms are:

police witness   A police officer who is a witness. He may be the arresting officer, an officer who assisted in the arrest, or an investigating officer.

complaining witness, complaining party, prosecuting witness   In criminal proceedings, the person who originally causes the case to be prosecuted, or who initiates the complaint against the defendant, usually the victim.

eyewitness   A person who directly perceives an event or thing related to a criminal case, via sight, hearing, touch, or smell, usually a person other than the victim.

expert witness   A person who, on the basis of his training, work or experience as an expert in the field, is qualified to testify on the standard and scientific facts in a particular science, trade or art.

writ   A document issued by a judicial officer ordering or forbidding the performance of a specified act.

annotation

The kinds of writs which are normally issued in connection with criminal trial proceedings are **arrest warrants, bench warrants, search warrants, subpoenas** and **summonses** (see entries).

The majority of writs are primarily or exclusively civil in application, although a few kinds of writs are used in connection with post-trial proceedings related to criminal cases. The **writ of habeas corpus** (see entry) is a fundamental means of seeking postconviction relief when **appeal** (see entry) is not possible.

In some jurisdictions and in some circumstances two other kinds of writs are used in post-trial criminal matters:

writ of certiorari   A writ issued from an appellate court for the purpose of obtaining from a lower court the record of its proceedings in a particular case. In some states this writ is the mechanism for **discretionary reviews** (see **appeal case**). A request for review is made by petitioning for a writ of certiorari, and granting of review is indicated by issuance of the writ.

writ of error coram nobis   *syn*   **coram nobis**   A writ issued by a court for the purpose of correcting a judgment entered in the same court, on the ground of error of fact. This writ is sought where the error which is alleged to have occurred does not appear on the record of court proceedings. The petitioner asks the court to go beyond the official record to examine the relevant facts. If the petitioner's allegations are sustained, the writ is issued to correct the judgment.

writ of habeas corpus   *syn*   **habeas corpus**   In criminal proceedings, the writ which directs the person detaining a prisoner to bring him or her before a judicial officer to determine the lawfulness of the imprisonment.

annotation

"Habeas corpus" is also used to mean the action resulting from the issuing of the writ.

The full name of the type of writ described above is "habeas corpus ad subjiciendum." This writ is one of the oldest protections of personal liberty and is considered fundamental to due process of law.

Other types of writs of habeas corpus are used to move persons in custody in one jurisdiction to another for trial, or to bring them to court to testify.

youthful offender   *recommended statistical terminology*   A person, adjudicated in criminal court, who may be above the statutory age limit for juveniles but is below a specified upper age limit, for whom special correctional commitments and special record sealing procedures are made available by statute.

annotation

The special correctional commitment may be to a juvenile facility, to a special section of an adult facility, or to a separate facility for the confinement of persons between the age limits specified in the particular statute. Such provisions exist in federal law and in the laws of several states.

Many jurisdictions permit arrest and court information concerning young adults to be sealed according to the record sealing procedures that apply to juveniles.

The term "youthful offender" should not be used in interstate and national information exchange without explicit definition.

Classificatory terminology

This Appendix lists all terms for which a recommended and/or established statistical usage is presented in this dictionary, except for the offense terms listed in Appendices B (outline of recommended post-arrest offense categories) and C (outline of Uniform Crime Reports offense categories).

The lists contain all **main entry** and **subentry terms** (terms defined within the annotation for a main entry term) for which a recommended or established statistical usage is presented.

Subentry terms are indented below the appropriate main entry term in order to indicate the place in the text where the term and definition are to be found. Indentation does not necessarily indicate a class-subclass relationship. Where hierarchical relationships exist, they are described in the entries.

Several main entry terms have been placed in brackets [ ]. These are nonstatistical terms which head entries where statistical terminology is presented in the annotation.

The terms are grouped according to subject in nine sections:

General offense terms

Law enforcement, prosecution, and court process terms

Corrections process terms

Government units

Nongovernment units

Government personnel

Other persons

Juvenile justice terms

National Crime Survey terms

Terms on the process lists are presented roughly in order of process sequence, and government unit and personnel terms are listed in class order where possible, but these lists should not be read as representing suggested data classification structures. Model data classification structures, where offered, are presented in the entries in the main body of the text.

General offense terms

crime
felony
misdemeanor
infraction

offenses known to police
Crime Index
    crime rate

Law enforcement, prosecution, and court process terms

clearance
    clearance by arrest
    clearance by exceptional means
    clearance rate
citation (appear)
    citation (forfeit)
summons
subpoena
arrest warrant
bench warrant
arrest
arrests (UCR)
search warrant
initial appearance
pretrial detention
pretrial release
    release on bail
    release on own recognizance
    release to a third party
bail revocation
    bail forfeiture
prosecutorial screening decision
    complaint requested
    complaint granted
    complaint modified
    complaint denied
arrestee dispositions (see entry
        for subclass terminology)
filing
charging document
trial court case
criminal case
preliminary hearing
dismissal
bind over
[plea]
    initial plea
    final plea
    not guilty plea
    not guilty by reason of insanity
    guilty plea
    nolo contendere
trial
    jury trial
    non-jury trial
verdict
    not guilty verdict
    guilty verdict
defendant dispositions (see entry
        for complete subclass terminology)
[court disposition]
    manner of disposition, trial court case
[caseload, court]
    court caseload inventory
no true bill

nolle prosequi
transfer to juvenile court
adjudication withheld (see entry
        for subclass terminology)
incompetent to stand trial
civil commitment
not guilty by reason of insanity
diagnostic commitment
judgment
acquittal
conviction
presentence investigation
sentencing hearing
sentencing dispositions (see
        "defendant dispositions" for subclass
        terminology)
sentencing postponed
    sentencing continued
suspended sentence
    unconditionally suspended sentence
    conditionally suspended sentence
balance of sentence suspended
    sentenced to time served
grant of probation
    probation order
court probation
supervised probation
[split sentence]
    probation with jail
    prison and probation
restitution
fine
    forfeit
placement
commitment
residential commitment
jail commitment
prison commitment
    definite term
    minimum-maximum term
    life term
    death sentence
consecutive sentence
    concurrent sentence
intermittent sentence
sentence effective date
sentence credit time
appellate court case
appeal case
request to appeal case
postconviction remedy
sentence review
appellate case disposition
    manner of disposition, appellate
court case

Corrections process terms

custody
 jurisdiction (corrections)
 physical custody (corrections)
 supervisory custody (corrections)
probation supervisory caseload
probation supervisory population
  movement (see entry for subclass
  terminology)
probation violation
probation revocation
probation termination
prison/parole population movement
  (see entry for complete subclass
  terminology)
new court commitment
provisional exit
full-time temporary release
  part-time temporary release
escape
 AWOL
abscond (corrections)
conditional release
mandatory supervised release
unconditional release
court ordered release from prison
expiration of sentence
parole agency caseload entries and removals (see
  entry for subclass terminology)
paroling authority decisions (see
  entry for subclass terminology)
parole supervision
parole supervisory caseload
release to parole
parole violation
parole revocation
parole suspended
reparole

Government units

criminal justice agency
law enforcement agency
 federal law enforcement agency
 state law enforcement agency
 local law enforcement agency
state police
state highway patrol
sheriff's department
prosecution agency
public defender agency
court
 trial court
 court of general jurisdiction
 court of limited (special)
  jurisdiction
 appellate court
 court of last resort
 intermediate appellate court
grand jury
trial jury
juvenile court
correctional agency
parole agency
paroling authority
probation agency
correctional facility (adult)
prison
 prison facility system
jail
pre-arraignment lockup
residential facility
diagnosis or classification center
correctional day program
juvenile facility
 correctional facility (juvenile)

Nongovernment units

private rehabilitation agency
private security agency

Government personnel

law enforcement officer
    federal law enforcement officer
    state law enforcement officer
    local law enforcement officer
state police officer
state highway patrol officer
sheriff
deputy sheriff
chief of police
prosecutor
public defender
judicial officer
probation officer
parole officer

Other persons

adult
defendant
offender
    alleged offender
prisoner
parolee
probationer
youthful offender

Juvenile justice terms

[*delinquency*]
    delinquent act
    delinquent
    alleged delinquent
    status offense
    status offender
    alleged status offender
[*dependency*]
    dependent
truant
runaway
juvenile petition
detention hearing
transfer hearing
transfer to adult court
adjudicatory hearing
juvenile court judgment
petition not sustained
predisposition investigation
disposition hearing
juvenile disposition

National Crime Survey terms

criminal incident
victimization
personal crimes (NCS)
    personal crimes of violence
    rape
    personal robbery
    assault
    personal crimes of theft
    personal larceny with contact
    personal larceny without contact
household crimes (NCS)
    household burglary
    household larceny
    motor vehicle theft
commercial crimes (NCS)
    commercial robbery
    commercial burglary

National crime classification

I. Recommendations

This section presents an outline of a possible national terminology and classification framework for description of the offense characteristics of prosecution, courts, and corrections cases and populations. It brings together for convenient reference selected crime categories defined and discussed in the alphabetical text of the dictionary.

Although some of the categories in this classification are identical to those in established systems, and others are very similar, it was not possible to use the whole of any existing crime classification system as a starting point for post-arrest crime data. The reasons why are discussed in Section II of this Appendix. However, as indicated by the summary list of proposed categories that follows, the proposed post-arrest classification corresponds with the FBI's Uniform Crime Reporting categories at many points.

The purpose of presenting this post-arrest crime type terminology is to provide statisticians with a prototype that can serve as a focus of discussion and begin to illustrate some of the different kinds of problems that will be encountered if a significant degree of standardization of post-arrest level offense data reporting is to be accomplished.

Definite recommendations were made when the crime category fits the criteria for national-level use for the generation of offense data comparable between jurisdictions and agency levels. These are:

(1) Frequency and/or seriousness of offense type such that it is of interest at the national level.

(2) Coverage by positive definition of the large majority of the cases to be statistically described; that is, minimization of the "all other" category.

(3) Maximum feasible correspondence with desired distinctions among crime types for national level data, as evidenced by classification schemes in current programs.

(4) Correspondence with the inherent categorization within input material (including concurrence with penal code distinctions) such that data collection and reporting is practicable from different jurisdictions and agency levels.

A given term and definition was assumed to meet these criteria when the category is used with a clear and reasonably workable definition in an existing national program, when the category also appears in state and local data, and when the category boundaries coincide with basic distinctions made in penal codes. Penal code structure correspondence is highly significant because the penal code description of an offense is customarily the only input datum available to statistical clerks at post-arrest levels of crime data collection.

In short, definite recommendations for standard categories were made when there was substantial evidence that there is basic agreement on the significance and practical reportability of a crime type.

Tentative recommendations of categories for national use were made when a crime category met only some of the criteria or met some of them to a less than satisfactory extent. In most of these cases it is the practical problems in classification of actual offense instances which interfere with standardization, not inability to agree on a theoretically preferred crime category.

The list of recommended and tentatively recommended categories is presented below, then repeated with defining features for convenient reference. (Each of the 21 major types listed following is further defined and discussed in an individual entry in the alphabetical text, except for primary categories (1) and (2). Categories (1) and (2) are discussed together in the entry **criminal homicide**.) The order of offense groups has some relation to traditional seriousness rankings but is controlled by the need to present structure clearly. It is specifically not a proposed severity scale.

List of recommended and tentatively recommended national post-arrest offense categories

Proposed category	Status*	Corresponding UCR category**
1. criminal willful homicide	R	UCR 1a
1a. murder	T	
1b. voluntary manslaughter	T	
2. involuntary manslaughter	R	
3. kidnapping	T	
4. sex offenses	T	
4a. violent sex offenses	T	
4a1. forcible rape	T	UCR 2
4a2. other violent sex offenses	T	
4b. nonviolent sex offenses	T	
4b1. statutory rape	T	
4b2. commercial sex offenses	T	UCR 16
4b3. other nonviolent sex offenses	T	
5. robbery	R	UCR 3
5a. armed robbery	T	UCR 3a through c
5b. unarmed robbery	T	UCR 3d
6. assault	R	UCR 4
6a. aggravated assault	R	UCR 4a through d
6b. simple assault	R	UCR 4e = UCR 9
7. burglary	R	UCR 5
8. larceny	R	UCR 6
9. motor vehicle theft	R	UCR 7
10. arson	T	
11. drug law violations	R	UCR 18
12. escape	T	
13. fraud offenses	T	UCR 10, 11, 12
14. stolen property offenses	T	UCR 13
15. weapons offenses	T	UCR 15
16. gambling	T	UCR 19
17. driving under the influence	T	UCR 21
18. intoxication	T	UCR 23
19. disturbing the peace	T	
20. hit and run	T	
21. traffic offenses	T	

*R = Recommended.   T = Tentatively recommended.

** UCR categories with corresponding explicit definitions or with examples indicating correspondence. See Appendix C for UCR category names.

Definitions of recommended and tentatively recommended national post-arrest offense categories (see Appendix C for corresponding UCR category names)

1. **criminal willful homicide**   *recommended*   UCR 1a
   intentionally causing the death of another person
   without legal justification
   or
   causing the death of another
   while committing or attempting to commit another crime

   1a.   **murder**   *tentatively recommended*
          intentionally causing the death of another person
          without extreme provocation or legal justification
          or
          causing the death of another
          while committing or attempting to commit another crime

   1b.   **voluntary manslaughter**   *tentatively recommended*
          intentionally causing the death of another
          with provocation that a reasonable person would find extreme
          without legal justification

2. **involuntary manslaughter**   *recommended*
   causing the death of another person
   without intent to cause death
   with recklessness or gross negligence, including by reckless or grossly negligent operation of a motor vehicle

3. **kidnapping**   *tentatively recommended*
   unlawful transport or confinement of a person without his or her consent, or
   if a minor, without the consent of his or her guardian
   including hijack of vehicle containing persons
   or
   attempting the above act

4. **sex offenses**   *tentatively recommended*
   unlawful sexual intercourse or sexual contact, or
   other unlawful behavior intended to result in sexual gratification or profit from sexual activity
   or
   attempting the above act(s)

4a. **violent sex offenses**

    4a1. **forcible rape**   UCR 2

        unlawful vaginal penetration of a female of any age

        against the will of the victim

        with use or threatened use of force

        or

        attempting such an act

    4a2. **other violent sex offenses**

        unlawful sexual penetration or physical contact other than forcible rape

        between members of the same sex or different sexes

        against the will of the victim

        with use or threatened use of force

        or

        attempting such act(s)

4b. **nonviolent sex offenses**

    4b1. **statutory rape**

        sexual intercourse with a female

        without force or threat of force

        when female has consented in fact, but is below age of consent specified in state law

    4b2. **commercial sex offenses**   UCR 16

        unlawfully performing, or causing or assisting another person to perform, a sex act for a fee, or

        causing or assisting another person to obtain performance of a sex act by paying a fee, or

        receiving money known to have been paid for performance of a sex act

        or

        attempting such act(s)

    4b3. **other nonviolent sex offenses**

        unlawful behavior, other than statutory rape and commercial sex offenses, intended to result in sexual gratification

        without use or threatened use of force

5. **robbery**   *recommended*   UCR 3

unlawful taking of property in the immediate possession of another
by use or threatened use of force

or

attempting the above act

　5a.   **armed robbery**   *tentatively recommended*   UCR 3a–c

unlawful taking of property in the immediate possession of another
by use or threatened use of a deadly or dangerous weapon

or

attempting the above act

　5b.   **unarmed robbery**   *tentatively recommended*   UCR 3d

unlawful taking of property in the immediate possession of another
by use or threatened use of force
without a deadly or dangerous weapon

or

attempting the above act

6. **assault**   *recommended*   UCR 4

unlawful intentional inflicting of bodily injury

or

attempting or threatening the above act

　6a.   **aggravated assault**   *recommended*   UCR 4a–d

unlawful intentional inflicting of serious bodily injury

or

unlawful threat or attempt to inflict bodily injury or death
by means of a deadly or dangerous weapon
with or without actual infliction of any injury

　6b.   **simple assault**   *recommended*   UCR 4e = 9

unlawful intentional inflicting of less than serious bodily injury
without a deadly or dangerous weapon

or

attempt or threat to inflict bodily injury
without a deadly or dangerous weapon

7. **burglary**   *recommended*   UCR 5

unlawful entry of a fixed structure, or a vehicle or vessel used for regular
residence, or a vehicle or vessel in a fixed location regularly used for industry
or business

with or without force

with intent to commit a felony or larceny

or

attempting the above act

8. **larceny (theft by taking)**   *recommended*   UCR 6

taking away property (excluding self-propelled motorized road vehicles, but including vehicle parts) which the possessor is entitled to retain

property is in the immediate or constructive possession of another (including in his vehicle, or in his premises if open to the public)

excluding taking that requires unlawful entry or force or is accomplished by deception

or

attempting the above act

9. **motor vehicle theft**   *recommended*   UCR 7

unlawful taking of a self-propelled road vehicle

excluding vehicle parts

intent to permanently or temporarily deprive owner of possession

or

attempting the above act

10. **arson**   *tentatively recommended*

intentional damaging or destruction by means of fire or explosion

of the property of another without his or her consent, or of any property with intent to defraud

or

attempting the above act(s)

11. **drug law violations**   *recommended*   UCR 18

unlawful purchase, distribution, sale, manufacture, cultivation, transport, possession or use of a controlled substance or drug

or

attempting the above act(s)

12. **escape**   *tentatively recommended*

unlawful departure of a lawfully confined person from a place of confinement or from custody while being transported

person confined because arrested, charged or convicted of a crime

13. **fraud offenses**   *tentatively recommended*   UCR 10, 11, 12

unlawfully depriving a person of his property or legal rights

by means of deceit or intentional misrepresentation

without damage to property or injury or threatened injury to persons

or

attempting or preparing to attempt the above offense

14. **stolen property offenses**   *tentatively recommended*   UCR 13

    unlawfully and knowingly

    receiving, buying, distributing, selling, transporting, possessing or concealing the unlawfully obtained property of another

    or

    attempting the above act(s)

15. **weapons offenses**   *tentatively recommended*   UCR 15

    unlawful distribution, sale, manufacture, alteration, transport, possession, or use of a deadly or dangerous weapon or accessory

    use other than in the commission or attempted commission of another crime

    or

    attempting the above act(s)

16. **gambling**   *tentatively recommended*   UCR 19

    unlawful making or receiving of wagers on a game of chance or uncertain event, or

    operating, or promoting or permitting the operation of, an unlawful game of chance or wagering establishment

17. **driving under the influence**   *recommended*   UCR 21

    unlawful operation of a motor vehicle while under the influence of alcohol or a controlled substance or drug

18. **intoxication**   *tentatively recommended*   UCR 23

    being in a public place while intoxicated through consumption of alcohol or intake of a controlled substance or drug

19. **disturbing the peace**   *tentatively recommended*

    unlawful interruption of the peace, quiet or order of a community

20. **hit and run**   *tentatively recommended*

    unlawful departure by vehicle operator from the scene of an accident that has resulted in damage to property or injury to a person

21. **traffic offenses**   *tentatively recommended*

    violations of statutes relating to the operation, maintenance, use, ownership, licensing and registration of self-propelled road vehicles

    excluding driving under the influence, hit and run, and violations of law not requiring appearance in court

II. Problems

The first section of this appendix proposes selection criteria and a tentative set of categories for statistics describing the offense characteristics of prosecution, courts, and corrections cases and populations. Although some of the individual categories in this classification are identical to those in established classification systems, and some are similar, it was not possible to use the whole of any existing system as a starting point for development of a classification for post-arrest data. While there are single categories in every system which are valid, practicable, and nearly universally used, there is no system offering a classification structure (coherent set of categories and full definitions) that can be consistently applied to available input data to yield nationally comparable statistics.

The FBI's Uniform Crime Reports (UCR) classification and the FBI's National Crime Information Center Uniform Offense Classifications (UOC) are the only national-level crime classification systems. Elements of one or the other of these sets of crime categories, definitions, and reporting procedures are found in almost every crime data program.

UCR and UOC establish many basic categorical distinctions generally agreed as necessary for any kind of offense typology. However, UCR was designed as a system for law enforcement crime data reporting. UOC was designed for the coding of offense types in individual criminal histories, not for any statistical purpose. As a set of categories neither of these systems meets the requirements for national defendant and convicted offender offense statistics.

UCR lacks such preferred and feasible categories for post-arrest statistics as murder, attempted murder, voluntary manslaughter, kidnapping, and escape.

UOC provides definitional language that is in accord with much common usage in law and data programs, and considerable detail (45 major-level categories and 450 minor-level, plus special code options for offenses of general applicability). This has encouraged some statistical programs to attempt to use UOC-coded material as initial input for crime statistics. But UOC's detail functions overall as a severe disadvantage in any statistical system. To require that the reporting process eventually yielding counts of offense instances in a maximum of, probably, 25 national categories should begin with a classification of crime instances into 450 categories is certain to increase costs and unreliability. Further, UOC's coding structure does not establish categories of mutually exclusive content. For example, there is no category for aggravated assault, as such. Rather, there are subcategories according to exact type of weapon used. When this is not known, the offense item must be placed in the general "assault" category, thus making simple and aggravated assault indistinguishable in the instances where weapon type is not known. This general pattern is repeated through the UOC framework, resulting in inability to aggregate reliably from UOC-coded material into such important traditional categories as criminal willful homicide, forcible rape, burglary, and motor vehicle theft.

In theory, UCR and UOC categories could be revised, or new categories created, and more complete definitions written to meet the needs for defendant and offender crime statistics, it being relatively easy to agree upon major national categories. But in fact, each national post-arrest offense data classification has been different from the others, and none has been able to guarantee accurate or consistent classification of occurrences. When these problems are investigated, it is found that the core problem is inability to classify individual crime instances correctly, rather than inability to agree on preferred categories.

This apparently merely practical problem prevents the resolution of terminological problems. In criminal justice statistical terminology, adequate definitions are usually much more than conventional definitions of terms. Technically adequate definitions are descriptions of the exact content of each category in the classification system. Sometimes a set of basic distinctions derived from the traditional justice vocabulary is sufficient to clearly indicate category content. More often, the exact nature of the input material must be recognized, and complex rules for assigning actual instances to categories must be stated. This is particularly important in crime classification, where the discrepancy between the language and classificatory concepts of traditional penal law and that of contemporary penal codes is great. These differences are, with respect to many types of crime, so great that even basic categorical distinctions cannot be established on a nationwide basis with any confidence that classification of actual instances from original input material will in fact be practicable.

A standard terminology and workable classification methods have evolved over decades in UCR reporting, where national-level crime type definitions are applied to particular instances of crimes and arrests by law enforcement agency personnel having access to crime and arrest reports. This system is supported by a half-century of experience, a detailed reporting handbook, and coordinated resources of technical expertise and guidance at both local and national levels. These conditions have enabled the total set of crime categories to be tailored to fit both preferred crime typology and the actual capacities of agencies to classify and report crime occurrences and arrest charges correctly. Both UCR classification and UOC codification have imperfections, but the long-term institutionalization of their methods enables agencies to maintain levels of consistency that make the data useful.

The situation regarding the classification of the offense characteristics of prosecution, courts, and corrections cases and populations is entirely different. The experience and practices of UCR and UOC crime data reporting are not useful precedents because the nature of the original input material at post-arrest levels requires different methods for classifying each offense instance. There are technical problems in developing crime classifications for which there are also no precedents in criminal case or defendant disposition classification.

At post-arrest levels of the criminal justice process there is usually no offense description available to the statistical clerk other than the penal code designation of the offense: letters and numbers indicating the state penal code section, or a word or short phrase traditionally naming that offense in that jurisdiction. This is the original input material for both state and national post-arrest offense statistics and it is, for nationwide reporting purposes, highly ambiguous. The same crimes are known by different names in different states, and the same name may refer to different crimes. The different state penal codes place the sets of offense elements that are the actual definitions of crimes into different structural arrangements. A given section label may identify one crime or several, and the subgroups are created by different classification criteria in different states.

To eliminate ambiguity in national-level reporting of post-arrest offense data it is necessary to go beyond the penal code section labels and state-specific names of crimes to the offense element sets that unambiguously define crimes in each jurisdiction. Such analysis has been performed for some crimes, but never for the full range of crimes of national statistical relevance. Each national post-arrest crime classification has been based on estimates of the extent to which a given national crime type category definition will correspond with the inherent categorization of the original input material in the 50 states. The result has been that some offense types, such as robbery, which are reliably distinguishable from other types at any level of original description, are correctly classifiable, but many other types are not. At some point in each existing post-arrest crime classification and reporting procedure, individual discretion has had to be exercised; there is always a large number of instances where the basic categorization or the category definition does not match the characteristics of the input material, with consequent unreliability of data.

In the course of the dictionary effort to develop definitions setting forth the basic categorical distinctions among crime types, material from 28 state penal codes was analyzed. It was found that for many crimes (see **fraud offenses**, for example) the relatively clearcut traditional groupings found in law dictionaries are not reflected in the offense element set arrangements in contemporary penal codes. The problems presented by such non-matches can be overcome at law enforcement levels of reporting, where narrative descriptions of criminal events are available to data reporters, and where national level classification systems have been institutionalized over a long period of time, but not at other levels.

Therefore, while the traditional definitions of major crime types are provided in entries in this dictionary, the tentatively recommended national statistical classification for post-arrest offense data reflects a judgment of what is statistically feasible nationwide. This estimate is largely based on analysis of the original input material: the penal code offense designations available to statisticians from the case and offender documentation maintained in prosecution, courts, and corrections agencies.

Uniform Crime Reports crime categories

Part I offenses *reported crime data and*
arrest data

1. Criminal homicide
   a. Murder and nonnegligent (volun-
      tary) manslaughter
   b. Negligent (involuntary)
      manslaughter

2. Forcible rape
   a. Rape by force
   b. Attempted forcible rape

3. Robbery
   a. Firearm
   b. Knife or cutting instrument
   c. Other dangerous weapon
   d. Strongarm

4. Aggravated assault
   a. Firearm
   b. Knife or cutting instrument
   c. Other dangerous weapon
   d. Hands, fists, feet, etc.—aggravated
      injury

5. Burglary
   a. Forcible entry
   b. Unlawful entry—no force
   c. Attempted forcible entry

6. Larceny-theft

7. Motor vehicle theft
   a. Autos
   b. Trucks and buses
   c. Other vehicles

8. Arson (see note below)

Note: Arson was added to the Part I offenses as
of 1979 by Congressional action. A special classification procedure is followed for incidents
involving arsons, different from the simple hier-
archization used to classify non-arson incidents.
When two or more UCR Part I offenses occur in
the same criminal episode and one of these is arson, the arson is counted and tabulated, but the
most serious of the other offenses is also counted
as one of the first seven numbered offenses. See
arson UCR 8 for more information on the
special status of this category in the UCR data
structure.

Part II offenses *arrest data only*

9. Simple assault (other assaults—simple,
   not aggravated)

10. Forgery and counterfeiting

11. Fraud

12. Embezzlement

13. Stolen property; buying, receiving,
    possessing

14. Vandalism

15. Weapons; carrying, possessing, etc.

16. Prostitution and commercialized vice

17. Sex offenses (except forcible rape and
    prostitution and commercialized vice)

18. Drug abuse violations
    Sale/manufacturing
    a. Opium or cocaine and their deriv-
       atives (morphine, heroin, codeine)
    b. Marijuana
    c. Synthetic narcotics—manufactured
       narcotics which can cause true
       drug addiction (Demerol, metha-
       dones)
    d. Dangerous nonnarcotic drugs (bar-
       biturates, Benzedrine)
    Possession
    e. Opium or cocaine and their deriv-
       atives (morphine, heroin, codeine)
    f. Marijuana
    g. Synthetic narcotics—manufactured
       narcotics which can cause true
       drug addiction (Demerol, metha-
       dones)
    h. Dangerous nonnarcotic drugs (bar-
       biturates, Benzedrine)

19. Gambling
    a. Bookmaking (horse and sport
       book)
    b. Numbers and lottery
    c. All other

20. Offenses against the family and
    children

21. Driving under the influence

22. Liquor laws

23. Drunkenness

24. Disorderly conduct

25. Vagrancy

26. All other offenses (except traffic law
    violations)

27. Suspicion

28. Curfew and loitering laws—(juveniles)

29. Runaway—(juveniles)

NCIC Uniform Offense Classifications[1]

Uniform Offense Classifications
Offenses of General Applicability

The following offenses of general applicability are to be integrated into the related substantive literal and numerical uniform offense classification by adding the general offense alpha abbreviation, below, or more nearly complete word(s) or complete word(s) when space allows, to the substantive literal uniform offense classification when translated and printed. The appropriate alpha General Offense Character (GOC), below, will be used to supplement the substantive numerical uniform offense classification.

General offense	General Offense Character (GOC)	General offense alpha abbreviation
Accessory after the fact	Z	ACAF
Accessory before the fact	Y	ACBF
Aid/abet	X	ABET
Assault to commit	B	ASLT
Attempt to commit	A	ATPT
Conspiracy to commit	C	CNSP
Facilitation of	F	FACL
Solicitation to commit	S	SOLC
Threat to commit	T	THRT

The offense definitions provided within your jurisdiction will apply for these terms. However, in no case will these terms stand alone as an offense (e.g. conspiracy or solicitation will not alone), but will in all instances be used with the substantive offense involved.

For example, literal offenses (as indicated at the left below) would be printed by translating the data included in the General Offense Character (GOC) and numeric offense codes (AON or CON) (as indicated at the right below).

Literal offense (as translated and printed)	General Offense Character (GOC)	Numeric offense code (AON or CON)
ATPT Robbery—business—gun—	A	1201
CNSP Heroin—smuggling—	C	3511
ASLT Rape—stgarm—	B	1103

(Words and characters underscored indicate use of above general offenses.)

---

[1]This entire appendix is reprinted from the source document: *Computerized Criminal History Files: Policies, Formats, Procedures (Arrest, Judicial and Custody-Supervision Segments, and Uniform Offense Classification Definitions)*, U.S. Department of Justice, Federal Bureau of Investigation, National Crime Information Center.

Uniform Offense Classifications
Substantive offenses and numerical codes

Stated charge not clear—	0001
Arrest data not received—	0002

Sovereignty

Treason—	0101
Treason misprision—	0102
Espionage—	0103
Sabotage—	0104
Sedition—	0105
Selective Service—	0106
(free text)	0199

Military

Desertion—	0201
(free text)	0299

Immigration

Illegal entry—	0301
False citizenship—	0302
Smuggling aliens—	0303
(free text)	0399

Homicide

Homicide—(free text)	0900
Homicide—wilful kill—family—gun—	0901
Homicide—wilful kill—family—(identify weapon)	0902
Homicide—wilful kill—nonfamily—gun—	0903
Homicide—wilful kill—nonfamily—(identify weapon)	0904
Homicide—wilful kill—pub off—gun—	0905
Homicide—wilful kill—pub off—(identify weapon)	0906
Homicide—wilful kill—pol off—gun—	0907
Homicide—wilful kill—pol off—(identify weapon)	0908
Homicide—neglig mansl—veh—	0909
Homicide—neglig mansl—(identify weapon)	0910
Homicide—wilful kill—gun—	0911
Homicide—wilful kill—(identify weapon)	0912
Homicide—(free text)	0999

Kidnapping

Kidnap—(free text)	1000
Kidnap minor for ransom—	1001
Kidnap adult for ransom—	1002
Kidnap minor to sexually asslt—	1003
Kidnap adult to sexually asslt—	1004
Kidnap minor—	1005
Kidnap adult—	1006
Kidnap hostage for escape—	1007
Abduct—no ransom or asslt—	1008
Kidnap—hijack aircraft—	1009
Kidnap—(free text)	1099

Sexual Assault

Sex asslt—(free text)	1100
Rape—gun—	1101
Rape with—(identify weapon)	1102

Rape—strongarm—	1103
Sex asslt—sodomy—boy—gun—	1104
Sex asslt—sodomy—man—gun—	1105
Sex asslt—sodomy—girl—gun—	1106
Sex asslt—sodomy—woman—gun—	1107
Sex asslt—sodomy—boy—(identify weapon)	1108
Sex asslt—sodomy—man—(identify weapon)	1109
Sex asslt—sodomy—girl—(identify weapon)	1110
Sex asslt—sodomy—woman—(identify weapon)	1111
Sex asslt—sodomy—boy—stgarm—	1112
Sex asslt—sodomy—man—stgarm—	1113
Sex asslt—sodomy—girl—stgarm—	1114
Sex asslt—sodomy—woman—stgarm—	1115
Stat rape—no force—	1116
Sex asslt—carnal abuse—	1117
Sex asslt—(free text)	1199

Robbery

Robbery—(free text)	1200
Robbery—business—gun—	1201
Robbery—business—(identify weapon)	1202
Robbery—business—stgarm—	1203
Robbery—street—gun—	1204
Robbery—street—(identify weapon)	1205
Robbery—street—stgarm—	1206
Robbery—resid—gun—	1207
Robbery—resid—(identify weapon)	1208
Robbery—resid—stgarm—	1209
Forcible purse snatching—	1210
Robbery—banking-type inst—	1211
Robbery—(free text)	1299

Assault

Asslt—(free text)	1300
Aggrav asslt—family—gun—	1301
Aggrav asslt—family—(identify weapon)	1302
Aggrav asslt—family—stgarm—	1303
Aggrav asslt—nonfamily—gun—	1304
Aggrav asslt—nonfamily—(identify weapon)	1305
Aggrav asslt—nonfamily—stgarm—	1306
Aggrav asslt—pub off—gun—	1307
Aggrav asslt—pub off—(identify weapon)	1308
Aggrav asslt—pub off—stgarm—	1309
Aggrav asslt—pol off—gun—	1310
Aggrav asslt—pol off—(identify weapon)	1311
Aggrav asslt—pol off—stgarm—	1312
Simple asslt—	1313
Aggrav asslt—gun—	1314
Aggrav asslt—(identify weapon)	1315
Intimidation—	1316
Asslt—(free text)	1399

The free text areas in which the last two characters of the offense numeric are 99 are those intended for use by police agencies in reporting current crimes. Those ending in 00 are for the conversion of historical data only.

Abortion

Abortion—(free text) 1400
Abortional act on other— 1401
Abortional act on self— 1402
Submission to abortional act— 1403
Abortifacient—
  (selling, mfg., delivering, etc.) 1404
Abortion—(free text) 1499

Arson

Arson—(free text) 2000
Arson—business—endangered life— 2001
Arson—resid—endangered life— 2002
Arson—business—defraud insurer— 2003
Arson—resid—defraud insurer— 2004
Arson—business— 2005
Arson—resid— 2006
Burning of— 2007
Arson—pub bldg—endangered life— 2008
Arson—pub bldg— 2009
Arson—(free text) 2099

Extortion

Extort—(free text) 2100
Extort—threat injure person— 2101
Extort—threat damage prop— 2102
Extort—threat injure reputation— 2103
Extort—threat accuse person of crime— .. 2104
Extort—threat of informing of vio— 2105
Extort—(free text) 2199

Burglary

Burgl—(free text) 2200
Burgl—safe—vault— 2201
Burgl—forced entry—resid— 2202
Burgl—forced burgl—forced entry—
  nonresid— 2203
Burgl—no forced entry—resid— 2204
Burgl—no forced entry—nonresid— 2205
Burgl tools—possess— 2206
Burgl—banking-type inst— 2207
Burgl—(free text) 2299

Larceny

Larc—(free text) 2300
Pocketpicking— 2301
Purse snatching—no force— 2302
Shoplifting— 2303
Larc—parts from veh— 2304
Larc—from auto— 2305
Larc—from shipment— 2306
Larc—from coin machine— 2307
Larc—from bldg— 2308
Larc—from yards— 2309
Larc—from mails— 2310
Larc—from banking-type inst— 2311
Larc—from interstate shipment— 2312
Obstruct correspondence—
  (postal violation) 2313
Theft of US Govt prop— 2314
Larc on US Govt reserv— 2315
Larc—postal— 2316

Larc—(free text) 2399

Stolen vehicle (theft, sale, receipt, etc.)

Stolen vehicle—(free text) 2400
Theft and sale veh— 2401
Theft and strip veh— 2402
Theft and use veh other crime— 2403
Veh theft— 2404
Theft veh by bailee— 2405
Receiv stolen veh— 2406
Strip stolen veh— 2407
Possess stolen veh— 2408
Interstate transp stolen veh— 2409
Aircraft theft— 2410
Unauth use of veh—
  (includes joy-riding) 2411
Stolen vehicle—(free text) 2499

Forgery (counterfeiting)

Forgery—(free text) 2500
Forgery of checks— 2501
Forgery of—(identify object) 2502
Counterfeiting of—(identify object) 2503
Pass forged—(use "pass" for "utter"
  and/or "distribute")—
  (identify object) 2504
Pass counterfeited—(use "pass" for
  "utter" and/or "distribute")—
  (identify object) 2505
Possess forged—(identify object) 2506
Possess counterfeited—(identify object) .. 2507
Possess tools for—
  ("forgery" or "counterfeiting") 2508
Transport forged—(identify object) 2509
Transport counterfeited—
  (identify object) 2510
Transport tools for—
  ("forgery" or "counterfeiting") 2511
Forgery—(free text) 2589
Counterfeiting—(free text) 2599

Fraudulent activities

Fraud—(free text) 2600
Fraud—confidence game— 2601
Fraud—swindle— 2602
Mail fraud— 2603
Fraud—imperson— 2604
Fraud—illeg use credit cards— 2605
Fraud—insuff funds check— 2606
Fraud—false statement— 2607
Fraud by wire— 2608
Fraud—(free text) 2699

Embezzlement

Embezzle—(free text) 2700
Embezzle—business prop— 2701
Embezzle—interstate shipment— 2702
Embezzle—banking-type inst— 2703
Embezzle—public prop—
  (U.S., state, city prop.) 2704
Embezzle—postal— 2705
Embezzle—(free text) 2799

Stolen property

Stolen prop—(free text) 2800
Sale of stolen prop— 2801
Transport interstate stolen prop— 2802
Receiv stolen prop— 2803
Possess stolen prop— 2804
Conceal stolen prop— 2805
Stolen prop—(free text) 2899

Damage property

Damage prop—(free text) 2900
Damage prop—business— 2901
Damage prop—private— 2902
Damage prop—public— 2903
Damage prop—business—with
  explosive— 2904
Damage prop—private—with explosive— . 2905
Damage prop—public—with explosive— . 2906
Damage prop—(free text) 2999

Dangerous drugs

Dangerous drugs—(free text) 3500
*Hallucinogen—mfr— 3501
*Hallucinogen—distrib— 3502
*Hallucinogen—sell— 3503
*Hallucinogen—possess— 3504
*Hallucinogen—(free text) 3505
Heroin—sell— 3510
Heroin—smuggl— 3511
Heroin—possess— 3512
Heroin—(free text) 3513
Opium or deriv—sell— 3520
Opium or deriv—smuggl— 3521
Opium or deriv—possess— 3522
Opium or deriv—(free text) 3523
Cocaine—sell— 3530
Cocaine—smuggl— 3531
Cocaine—possess— 3532
Cocaine—(free text) 3533
Synth narcotic—sell— 3540
Synth narcotic—smuggl— 3541
Synth narcotic—possess— 3542
Synth narcotic—(free text) 3543
Narcotic equip—possess— 3550
Marijuana—sell— 3560
Marijuana—smuggl— 3561
Marijuana—possess— 3562
Marijuana—producing— 3563
Marijuana—(free text) 3564
Amphetamine—mfr— 3570
Amphetamine—sell— 3571
Amphetamine—possess— 3572
Amphetamine—(free text) 3573
Barbiturate—mfr— 3580
Barbiturate—sell— 3581
Barbiturate—possess— 3582
Barbiturate—(free text) 3583
Dangerous drugs—(free text) 3599

Sex offenses (not involving sexual assault or commercialized sex)

Sex offense—(free text) 3600

Sex offense—against child—fondling— ... 3601
Homosexual act with girl— 3602
Homosexual act with boy— 3603
Incest with minor— 3604
Indecent exposure— 3605
Bestiality— 3606
Incest with adult— 3607
Seduction of adult— 3608
Homosexual act with woman— 3609
Homosexual act with man— 3610
Peeping tom— 3611
Sex offense—(free text) 3699

Obscenity

Obscene material—(free text) 3700
Obscene material—mfr— 3701
Obscene material—sell— 3702
Obscene material—mailing— 3703
Obscene material—possess— 3704
Obscene material—distrib— 3705
Obscene material—transport— 3706
Obscene communication— 3707
Obscenity—(free text) 3799

Family offenses

Family offense—(free text) 3800
Neglect family— 3801
Cruelty toward child— 3802
Cruelty toward wife— 3803
Bigamy— 3804
Contrib delinq minor— 3805
Neglect child— 3806
Nonpayment of alimony— 3807
Nonsupport of parent— 3808
Family offense—(free text) 3899

Gambling

Gambling—(free text) 3900
Bookmaking— 3901
Card game—operating— 3902
**Card game—playing— 3903
Card game— 3904
Dice game—operating— 3905
**Dice game—playing— 3906
Dice game— 3907
Gambling device—possess— 3908
Gambling device—transport— 3909
Gambling device—not registered— 3910
Gambling device— 3911
Gambling goods—possess— 3912
Gambling goods—transport— 3913
Gambling goods— 3914
Lottery—operating— 3915
Lottery—runner— 3916
**Lottery—playing— 3917
Lottery— 3918
Sports tampering— 3919
Transmit wager information— 3920
Establish gambling place— 3921
Gambling—(free text) 3999

**Offense not to be entered in National Index

Commercialized sexual offenses

Commercial sex—(free text)	4000
Keeping house ill fame—	4001
Procure for prostitute—(pimping)	4002
Commercial sex—homosexual prostitution—	4003
Prostitution—	4004
Frequent house ill fame—	4005
Transp female interstate for immoral purp—	4006
Commercial sex—(free text)	4099

Liquor (not to include tax and revenue matters or driving under the influence of liquor)

Liquor—(free text)	4100
Liquor—mfr—	4101
Liquor—sell—	4102
Liquor—transport—	4103
Liquor—possess—	4104
**Misrepresenting age—minor—	4105
Liquor—(free text)	4199

Drunkenness

**Drunkenness—(free text)	4200
**Drunkenness—(free text)	4299

Obstructing the police

Obstruct police—(free text)	4800
Resisting officer—	4801
Obstruct criminal invest—	4802
Making false report—	4803
Evidence—destroying—	4804
Witness—dissuading—	4805
Witness—deceiving—	4806
Refusing to aid officer—	4807
Compounding crime—	4808
Unauth communication with prisoner—	4809
Illegal arrest—	4810
Crossing police lines—	4811
Failure report crime—	4812
Failing to move on—	4813
Obstruct police—(free text)	4899

Flight—escape

Escape—(identify institution)	4901
Flight to avoid—(prosecution, confinement, etc.)	4902
Aiding prisoner escape—(identify type institution)	4903
Harboring—(escapee or fugitive)	4904
Flight—escape—(free text)	4999

Obstructing judiciary, Congress, legislature, or a commission

Obstruct—(specify judic, Congr, legis, commsn)—(free text)	5000
Bail—secured bond—	5001
Bail—personal recog—	5002
Perjury—	5003
Perjury—subornation of—	5004
Contempt of court—	5005
Obstructing justice—	5006
Obstructing court order—	5007
Misconduct—judic officer—	5008
Contempt of Congress—	5009
Contempt of legislature—	5010

Parole violation—	5011
Prob violation—	5012
Condit release violation—	5013
Mandatory release violation—	5014
Failure to appear—	5015
Obstruct—(specify judic, Congr, legis, commsn)—(free text)	5099

Bribery

Bribery—(free text)	5100
Bribe—giving—	5101
Bribe—offering—	5102
Bribe—receiving—	5103
Bribe—(free text)	5104
Conflict of interest—	5105
Gratuity—giving—	5106
Gratuity—offering—	5107
Gratuity—receiving—	5108
Gratuity—(free text)	5109
Kickback—giving—	5110
Kickback—offering—	5111
Kickback—receiving—	5112
Kickback—(free text)	5113
Bribery—(free text)	5199

Weapon offenses

Weapon offense—(free text)	5200
Altering identification on—(specify weapon)	5201
Carrying concealed—(specify weapon)	5202
Carrying prohibited—(specify weapon)	5203
Explosives—teaching use—(specify)	5204
Explosives—transporting—(specify)	5205
Explosives—using—(specify)	5206
Incendiary device—possess—(specify)	5207
Incendiary device—using—(specify)	5208
Incendiary device—teaching use—(specify)	5209
(Do not use if ARSON)	
Licensing—registration—(specify weapon)	5210
Explosives—possessing—(specify)	5211
Possession of—(specify)	5212
Firing—(specify weapon)	5213
Selling—(specify weapon)	5214
Threat to bomb—(specify)	5215
Threat to burn—(specify)	5216
Weapon offense—(free text)	5299

Public peace

Public peace—(free text)	5300
Anarchism—	5301
Riot—inciting—	5302
Riot—engaging in—	5303
Riot—interfere fireman—	5304
Riot—interfere officer—	5305
Riot—(free text)	5306
Assembly—unlawful—	5307
**False fire alarm—	5308
Harassing communication—	5309
Desecrating flag—	5310
Disord conduct—(specify conduct)	5311
**Disturb peace—(specify conduct)	5312
**Curfew—	5313
**Loitering—	5314
Public peace—(free text)	5399

**Offense not to be entered in National Index

Traffic offense

Traffic offense—(free text)	5400
Hit and run—	5401
Transp dangerous material—	5402
Driving under influence drugs—	5403
Driving under influence liquor—	5404
**Moving traffic viol—	5405
**Nonmoving traffic viol—	5406
Traffic offense—(free text)	5499

Health-safety

Health—safety—(free text)	5500
Drugs—adulterated—	5501
Drugs—misbranded—	5502
Drugs—(free text)	5503
Food—adulterated—	5504
Food—misbranded—	5511
Food—(free text)	5512
Cosmetics—adulterated—	5520
Cosmetics—misbranded—	5521
Cosmetics—(free text)	5522
Health—safety—(free text)	5599

Civil rights

Civil rights—(free text)	5600
Civil rights—(free text)	5699

Invasion of privacy

Invade privacy—(free text)	5700
Divulge eavesdrop info—	5701
Divulge eavesdrop order—	5702
Divulge message contents—	5703
Eavesdropping—(free text)	5704
Eavesdrop equip—(free text)	5705
Opening sealed communication—	5706
Trespassing—(free text)	5707
Wiretap—failure to report—	5708
Invade privacy—(free text)	5799

Smuggling

Smuggling—(free text)	5800
Smuggle contraband—(specify type)	5801
Smuggle contraband into prison—(specify type)	5802
Smuggle to avoid paying duty—(specify type)	5803
Smuggling—(free text to further describe)	5899

Election laws

Election laws—(free text)	5900
Election laws—(free text to further describe)	5999

Antitrust

Antitrust—(free text)	6000
Antitrust—(free text to further describe)	6099

Tax revenue

Tax revenue—(free text)	6100
Income tax—(further describe)	6101
Sales tax—(further describe)	6102
Liquor tax—(further describe)	6103
Tax revenue—(free text to further describe)	6199

Conservation

Conservation—(free text)	6200
Conservation—animals—(describe offense further)	6201
Conservation—fish—(describe offense further)	6202
Conservation—birds—(describe offense further)	6203
Conservation—license—stamp—(describe offense)	6204
Conservation—environment—(describe offense)	6205
Conservation—(free text)	6299

Vagrancy

**Vagrancy—(free text)	6300
**Vagrancy—(free text to describe further)	6399

Crimes against person

(free text)	7099

Property crimes

(free text)	7199

Morals-decency crimes

(free text)	7299

Public order crimes

(free text)	7399

**Offense not to be entered in National Index

State court model caseload reporting terminology

The term lists presented in this Appendix represent the essential data categorization schemes of the model court caseload statistical system developed by the National Court Statistics Project (a joint effort of the Conference of State Court Administrators and the National Center for State Courts) under Bureau of Justice Statistics sponsorship. The model was developed as part of the State Court Caseload Statistics program, to encourage development of fully comparable cross-jurisdictional caseload data. The full model, including recommended tabulation procedures, is presented in the publications *State Court Model Annual Report* (published by the National Center for State Courts) and *State Court Model Statistical Dictionary* (published by the Bureau of Justice Statistics).

The *State Court Model Statistical Dictionary* is not a parallel to this criminal justice data terminology dictionary, either in content or in purpose. The model court statistical dictionary is an integral part of the model system for court caseload statistics developed by NCSP. It presents a fully developed classification structure and associated terminology. The terms provide a complete set of labels for presentation of court caseload statistics in accord with the model. The definitions provide rules for each step in the generation of the final data. This dictionary, by contrast, concentrates on basic categorical distinctions which underlie a variety of statistical descriptions of criminal justice matters. The terminology in this dictionary as a whole neither presents nor reflects any single, fully developed, statistics system.

The NCSP model system presents recommended classification structures for statistical presentation of court caseload data in two primary areas: general **court caseload inventory,** the four classic counts of cases pending at the beginning of the reporting period, cases filed and disposed during the period, and cases pending at the end of the period; and case and defendant **manner of disposition,** characterizing the means by which completed cases and defendants were disposed.

The lists which follow present the model categories for appellate court and trial court case type and for appellate court case and trial court case manner of disposition.

Appellate court case
>   **Request to appeal**
>> **Civil case** request to appeal (by subject matter of case, as under civil case following)
>> **Criminal case** request to appeal (by subject matter of case, as under criminal case following)
>> **Post conviction remedy case** request to appeal
>> Request to **appeal of administrative agency case**
>> **Juvenile case** request to appeal (by subject matter of case, as under juvenile case following)
>   **Sentence review only case**
>   **Appeal case**
>> **Civil case appeal** (by subject matter of case)
>> **Criminal case appeal** (by subject matter of case)
>> **Postconviction remedy case**
>> **Appeal of administrative agency case**
>> **Juvenile case appeal** (by subject matter of case)
>   **Original proceeding case**
>> **Original jurisdiction case**
>> **Disciplinary matter**
>> **Advisory opinion case**

Trial court case
  Civil case
    Tort case
      Auto tort case
      Professional tort case
      Product liability tort case
      Other tort case
    Contract case
    Real property rights case
    Small claims case
    Domestic relations case
      Marriage dissolution case
      Support/custody case
      Adoption case
      Other domestic relations case
    Mental health case
    Estate case
      Probate/wills/intestate case
      Guardianship/conservatorship/trusteeship case
      Other estate case
    Appeal case
      Appeal of administrative agency case
      Appeal of trial court case
    Extraordinary writ case
    Postconviction remedy case
    Other civil case
  Criminal case
    Felony case
    Misdemeanor case
    Preliminary hearing (limited jurisdiction court only)
    Ordinance (non-traffic) violation case
    Appeal case
      Appeal of trial court case
    Extraordinary writ case
    Postconviction remedy case
    Sentence review only case
    Other criminal case

Traffic case
    DWI/DUI case
    Other traffic violation case
    Parking violation case
Juvenile case
    Criminal-type offender case
    Status offender case
    Non-offender case
    Other juvenile matters

Manner of disposition, appellate court cases
  Opinion
      Affirmed
      Modified
      Reversed
      Reversed and remanded
      Remanded
      Granted/denied
  Memorandum decision
      Affirmed
      Modified
      Reversed
      Reversed and remanded
      Remanded
      Granted/denied
  Order (decision without opinion)
      Affirmed
      Modified
      Reversed
      Reversed and remanded
      Remanded
      Granted/denied
  Dismissed/withdrawn/settled
  Transferred
  Other manner of disposition

Manner of disposition, trial court cases
    Civil case manner of disposition
        Jury trial
        Non-jury trial
        Uncontested/default
        Dismissed/withdrawn/settled (before trial)
        Transferred (before/during trial)
        Arbitration
        Other manner of disposition
    Criminal case manner of disposition
        Jury trial
            Conviction (defendants)
                Guilty plea (defendants)
            Acquittal (defendants)
                Dismissed (defendants)
        Non-jury trial
            Conviction (defendants)
                Guilty plea (defendants)
            Acquittal (defendants)
                Dismissed (defendants)
        Dismissed/nolle prosequi (before trial, defendants)
        Bound over (defendants)
        Transferred (before/during trial, defendants)
        Guilty plea (before trial, defendants)
        Bail forfeiture (defendants)
        Other manner of disposition (defendants)
    Traffic case manner of disposition
        Jury trial
            Conviction
            Acquittal
        Non-jury trial
            Conviction
            Acquittal
        Transferred (before/during trial)
        Guilty plea (before trial)
        Bail forfeiture
        Dismissed/nolle prosequi (before trial)
        Parking fine
        Other manner of disposition